Finding Dorothy Sc

Woodbourne Library
Washington-Centerville Public Library
Centerville, Ohio

DISCARD

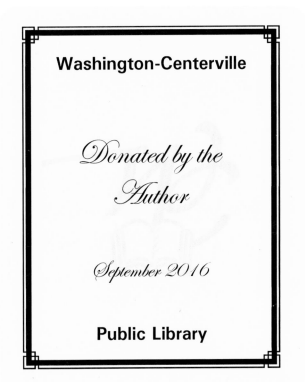

Washington-Centerville

Donated by the
Author

September 2016

Public Library

D1291826

Dorothy Faeth Scott, the twenty-fifth woman to join Nancy Love's Women's Auxiliary Ferrying Squadron (WAFS), November 21, 1942. *Courtesy: The Scott Family Collection.*

Air Transport Command wings worn by the original twenty-eight WAFS (Women's Auxiliary Ferrying Squadron). *Photo by Joe Weingarten, from the author's personal collection.*

Finding Dorothy Scott

Letters of a WASP Pilot

Sarah Byrn Rickman

Texas Tech University Press

Copyright © 2016 by Sarah Byrn Rickman

All rights reserved. No portion of this book may be reproduced in any form or by any means, including electronic storage and retrieval systems, except by explicit prior written permission of the publisher. Brief passages excerpted for review and critical purposes are excepted.

This book is typeset in Minion Pro. The paper used in this book meets the minimum requirements of ANSI/NISO Z39.48-1992 (R1997). ∞

Designed by Kasey McBeath

Cover: Dorothy Scott on the wing of an AT-6, Love Field, Dallas.
Courtesy: The Scott Family Collection.

Library of Congress Cataloging-in-Publication Data

Names: Rickman, Sarah Byrn, author.

Title: Finding Dorothy Scott : letters of a WASP pilot / Sarah Byrn Rickman.

Description: Lubbock, Texas : Texas Tech University Press, 2016. | Includes bibliographical references and index.

Identifiers: LCCN 2016014519 (print) | LCCN 2016021036 (ebook) | ISBN 9780896729728 (hard cover : alk. paper) | ISBN 9780896729735 (e-book)

Subjects: LCSH: Scott, Dorothy Faeth, 1920-1943—Correspondence. | Women Airforce Service Pilots (U.S.)—Biography. | United States. Army Air Forces. Air Transport Command. Ferrying Division—Biography. | World War, 1939-1945—Aerial operations, American. | World War, 1939-1945—Participation, Female. | Women air pilots—United States—Correspondence. | Air pilots, Military—United-ed States—Correspondence.

Classification: LCC D790.5 .R5297 2016 (print) | LCC D790.5 (ebook) | DDC 940.54/4973092 [B] —dc23

LC record available at https://lccn.loc.gov/2016014519

16 17 18 19 20 21 22 23 24 / 9 8 7 6 5 4 3 2 1

Texas Tech University Press
Box 41037 | Lubbock, Texas 79409-1037 USA
800.832.4042 | ttup@ttu.edu | www.ttupress.org

To Dawn and to Kimberly and her staff
at the TWU library WASP Archives

Contents

Illustrations

Acknowledgments

This book is based on Dorothy Scott's letters written to her family while she was serving with the WAFS/WASP from November 21, 1942, to December 3, 1943. The Dorothy Scott Collection, donated by her twin brother, Edward A. Scott, now deceased, is part of the WASP Archives, the Woman's Collection, Texas Woman's University, Denton. The letters are quoted, and information from them used, throughout this narrative.

∿

Texas Woman's University—its renowned Woman's Collection at the university's Blagg-Huey Library and the WASP Archive that has been a part of that collection since 1992—is the reason you hold this book in your hands today.

I first visited TWU in March 2000 when I began work on my first WASP book, *The Originals: The Women's Auxiliary Ferrying Squadron of World War II*, published in 2001 by Disc-Us Books. *Finding Dorothy Scott: Letters of a WASP Pilot* is my seventh WASP book. All were written with the help of resources found at the ever-growing WASP Archive available to researchers at TWU.

I began by working with Dawn Letson, who, in 2008, asked me to edit the archive's acquisition of Dorothy Scott's "letters home" written during World War II. I told her I would like to use Dorothy's letters to write her biography—a book I felt would be a welcome addition to the growing body of WASP literature. Three of the original WAFS died in service. Biographies of two of them, Cornelia Fort and Evelyn Sharp, were written in the late 1990s. Dorothy Scott was the third WAFS fatality. This completes the trilogy.

When Dawn retired, her successor Kimberly Johnson, current director of special collections, followed through with me on the project and has now helped me see two books—my sixth, *WASP of the Ferry Command: Women Pilots, Uncommon Deeds*, and my seventh, *Finding Dorothy Scott*—through to publication.

To Dawn and to Kimberly and her staff at the TWU library WASP Archives, a heartfelt thank-you for ALL your help with Dorothy's story. This book is dedicated to you!

Sarah Byrn Rickman
Spring 2016

Preface

No stone angels, no blocks of marble with massive shoulders point the way to her grave. But three small American flags fluttering in the breeze were hard to miss in the vast grassy expanse dotted with flat stones. A rectangular slab identified her: Dorothy Faeth Scott, Oroville, Washington, February 16, 1920–December 3, 1943, plus the letters W.A.S.P., a winged star within a circle, and a pair of pilot's wings. The bronze flag holder bears the inscription, "Dorothy Scott WAFS Pilot–US."

Women pilots—1,102 of them—flew military aircraft for the US Army Air Forces (USAAF) in World War II. They were known originally as WAFS (Women's Auxiliary Ferrying Squadron) and later as WASP—Women Airforce Service Pilots. Thirty-eight died serving their country.

Dorothy Scott was one of the thirty-eight.

Dorothy is buried in Valhalla Memorial Gardens in Burbank, California. Her mother, Katherine Faeth Scott (1882–1946), is buried next to her. In 1954, Dorothy's father, G. M. Scott, joined his wife, his father, and his daughter in the family plot.

On September 10, 2009, I stood looking down at Dorothy's final resting place. What did I really know of this young woman—of her unselfish patriotism? Does that simple flat stone do justice to what she gave for her country—her life, at age twenty-three? What can do justice to such a sacrifice?

The guttural whine of jet engines in takeoff mode interrupted my thoughts. A giant red and blue bird—a Southwest Airlines jetliner—rose from behind a line of trees off the cemetery's perimeter. With the inherent grace of the breed, the aircraft climbed out at what Dorothy would have considered a stall-inducing angle of attack—something far steeper than the rate of ascent she knew to be safe in the airplanes of her era.

The jet crossed above and disappeared into the opposite distance—a fleeting moment in time, a metaphor for Dorothy's life.

The roar repeats every few minutes. Runway 15/33 at Burbank's Bob Hope Airport lies beyond that tree line. How fitting. Daily, airplanes soar over this young woman—who would be ninety-six had she lived to see this written. But Dorothy fell in love with flight and gave her life doing what she loved—flying.

Dorothy's story was almost lost to us.

If not for her twin brother's love and devotion, we would know next to nothing about the twenty-fifth woman to join that first elite squadron of World War II women fliers. But Edward Scott saved his beloved sister's wartime letters home and donated them to the WASP Archive in 2000, not long before his own death.

I am a WASP author and historian. Because of those letters, in September 2009, I visited Dorothy's grave and met Tracy Scott, Edward Scott's elder son. Tracy never knew his Aunt Dorothy. She died three months before he was born. But he is the keeper of the family history. And Tracy told me something that struck a chord. "Somehow, my father realized that his sister was different. I think he regarded her as the smartest woman who ever lived."

Gary Devon, the editor of the *Okanogan Valley Gazette-Tribune*, told me when I visited Oroville, Washington, in 2005 searching for Dorothy, that Ed Scott often came by the newspaper office just to talk to him about Dorothy—to tell him stories about her. Ed did not want her to be forgotten.

In the end, by leaving her letters to posterity in the care of the official WASP Archive at Texas Woman's University in Denton, Edward Scott ensured that his twin sister, Dorothy, would not be forgotten.

What remains now is to tell her story.

A retired journalist and aspiring fiction writer, I wrote a novel in the late 1990s about the WASP who trained at Avenger Field, Sweetwater, Texas. By then I had met Nancy Batson Crews, one of the original twenty-eight WAFS, and we had forged a friendship. I asked her to read my manuscript, entitled *Flight from Fear*, for comment. She obliged. But Nancy, no fan of fiction, had other ideas about what I might be capable of writing.

"Sayruh," said the Alabama native in her signature Southern accent, "why are you writing made-up stories when there is a perfectly good true story that needs telling?"

She challenged me to write the story of the original twenty-eight WAFS and their leader, visionary pilot Nancy Harkness Love, who had the clout of the Ferrying Division, Air Transport Command, USAAF, behind her. The twenty-eight were, almost to a woman, professional pilots—flight instructors, owners of commercial air services, utility pilots, former barnstormers—all paid for their know-how in things related to flight. All possessed no fewer than five hundred flight hours—most had considerably more—plus they held 200-horsepower ratings.[1]

Crews and others believed the WAFS story had been overlooked, ignored at the expense of a larger story—the story of the women pilots, originally known as the Women's Flying Training Detachment (WFTD), who graduated from the USAAF first flight-training facility for women. Notable racing pilot Jacqueline Cochran had lobbied for the WFTD program and been given the go-ahead by USAAF Commanding General H. H. "Hap" Arnold. The earliest graduates, like the WAFS before them, were assigned to the Ferrying Division. Later graduates were sent to other USAAF duties and commands as Cochran sought to expand the use of the women and broaden her influence. In August 1943, all the Army's women pilots—the original WAFS, the women currently in training at the flight school, and those who had already graduated and were on active duty—became known as the Women Airforce Service Pilots (WASP) under Cochran. Love retained the direct leadership of the women ferry pilots. The WASP would ultimately number 1,102—the 28 original WAFS plus 1,074 graduates of the training facility.

To help me get started on the project, Nancy Crews organized a reunion in June 1999 and invited the surviving WAFS. There were nine of them then. Five of the other eight accepted Nancy's invitation. Those three-and-a-half days we spent in Birmingham were an unforgettable experience. I met and got acquainted with the five and videotaped interviews with each of them: Barbara Erickson London, Florene Miller Watson, Teresa James Martin, Gertrude Meserve Tubbs LeValley, and Barbara Poole Shoemaker. Unable to attend were Phyllis Burchfield Fulton, Barbara Donahue Ross, and Bernice Batten. I later met and interviewed Barbara, corresponded with and interviewed Phyllis by phone, and established snail-mail contact with Bernice.

Though inspired by the reunion and armed with stories from the six I had spent time with, I realized that I needed to do further research. Texas Woman's University (TWU), the home of the WASP Archive, was the place to begin.

TWU's Woman's Collection is the largest depository of research material about women in the southern half of the United States. That led WASP President Pat Pateman and Historian Marty Wyall to TWU when, in 1991, they started the search for a home for the WASP Archive. In the July 1992 issue of the *WASP News*, Wyall said:

After numerous contacts with University/College libraries and Air Museums, including visits to Wellesley, Radcliffe, Ninety-Nines Headquarters, the International Women's Air and Space Museum, and NASM, we concluded that the best place would be Texas Woman's University. During the [WASP] National Board Meeting in Dallas, 8 April 1992, the Board members visited TWU to consider our recommendation, and unanimously agreed TWU was the "right place." It met more than our requirements.

Placing the archive in Texas was most fitting for two other reasons. First Houston and then Sweetwater were the training sites for all the WASP, other than the original twenty-eight. Second, Dallas Love Field was the home of one of the largest contingents of WASP during World War II, the women's squadron of the 5th Ferrying Group of the Ferrying Division, Air Transport Command (ATC). Among the one hundred twenty-eight WASP who would serve there was Dorothy Scott.

Since 1992, the WASP Archive has assisted more than fifteen thousand researchers. Users—students, historians, authors, filmmakers, journalists, documentarians, scholars, and aviation enthusiasts—come from around the world. The collection includes more than one million documents, fifty thousand photographs, seven hundred oral histories, six hundred personal WASP collections, uniforms, and artifacts representing the largest collection of WASP materials under one roof.

In February 2000, I made my first visit to TWU. I looked at everything in the collection relating to the original twenty-eight. Information was plentiful on some, sparse on others. One on whom there was almost nothing was Dorothy Scott, who died in service at age twenty-three. Considerable material was available on the other two original WAFS who perished during WWII—Cornelia Fort and Evelyn Sharp—including full-length, well-researched, published biographies on both. Why not Dorothy? Why was there so little in the files about her?

But the mystery of Dorothy would have to wait. I already had my assignment, and that was to tell the story of the original twenty-eight.

In March 2000, I went to Florida to do extensive interviewing with WAFS Teresa James, whom I had met at Nancy Crews's reunion. In June 2000, I traveled to Virginia to meet and interview Nancy Love's younger two daughters, Allie and Marky Love, the keepers of their mother's legacy. From there, I went back to Alabama for the first of four extensive interview and working sessions with Nancy Crews.

The bad news was that Nancy was ill. It was lung cancer, and it turned out to be terminal. Thus began a race with time. I returned for visits in August and November, by which time we had secured a publisher for the book. Her declining health was painfully obvious, but she and I continued to work—the bond that had developed between us, and the reason for it, stronger than ever. My final trip to Alabama was right before Christmas 2000. All that time I had been writing. The project was moving forward, but the hot breath of the Grim Reaper—reality—moved ever closer. When I left her on December 22, Nancy and I said goodbye for the last time—and we both knew it was the last time. Nancy died January 13, 2001, before we could get the book into print, but she had seen and approved the completed first draft of the manuscript.

The end result of those four one-on-one sessions with Nancy, which included seven hours of audiotape, was *The Originals: The Women's Auxiliary Ferrying Squadron of World War II*, published in July 2001 by Disc-Us Books. The story of Nancy Love's original WAFS was, at last, told. Nancy Crews's wish was fulfilled. My WASP novel, *Flight from Fear*, also from Disc-Us, followed—published in 2002. In 2008, I made good on the rest of my promise to Nancy Crews when the University of North Texas Press published *Nancy Love and the WASP Ferry Pilots of World War II*. The following year, 2009, the University of Alabama Press published *Nancy Batson Crews: Alabama's First Lady of Flight*. I had told my mentor's story as well.

What now?

Back in the summer of 2000, a few months after my first visit to TWU, I received a call from the archive. Dorothy Scott's twin brother, Edward, had donated Dorothy's letters written to her family while she was on active duty as a WAFS/WASP between November 21, 1942, and December 3, 1943. A window to Dorothy Scott had opened. Was I interested? I was in the throes of writing *The Originals* and Nancy was dying, but, yes, I was interested.

The WASP 2000 biannual reunion was to begin at TWU in Denton in late September and then move to Sweetwater, Texas—where the majority of the WASP took their training. I returned to TWU in late September for the reunion and to read Dorothy's letters. Sitting in the research room in the library—surrounded by WASP memorabilia, books about the WASP, and archival boxes containing collections of papers and photographs—I "met" Dorothy. Now I know how the California prospectors felt when they found gold!

Some of her letters lay unfolded in the archival file folders, but most were still in their envelopes. The paper was crinkly but intact and fragile along the folds. Experiencing the letters was like taking literary communion. They beckoned to me to "take, read."

The first page of the first letter bore the wing insignia of the Air Transport Command above the letterhead, which read: New Castle Army Air Base, Wilmington, Delaware. Below the letterhead were the hand-printed initials,

W.A.F.S.

Thanksgiving, 1942 [November 26]

Dear Mom:

To attempt to set down in writing all the events of the past two weeks seems a Herculean task but here goes.

I left Pullman [Washington] Saturday morning after calling Spokane and finally getting a "clear enough" report. There I captured a CAA inspector and a WACO and took a test ride for my horsepower rating. What a ride! Dodging clouds, all aerobatics and hedgehopping and he did most of the flying—but I got the rating.

After that it all blurs into a mess of telegrams, phone calls and frantic haste to get here by the 21st.

I was to fly, but Dad and I figured just enough time so we drove. The drive was tedious mostly but was broken at Colo. Sprgs. by seeing Ed—his girl [Ethel]—and car trouble. Most of our visit with Ed consisted of him overhauling the car motor. Also there we ran into amazing luck getting two new tires! That's still beyond my comprehension. (We ruined 4 old ones en-route.)

Then here at Delaware finally (Friday evening) we called in and I was told to report next A.M. Dad and I drove out and were shown around. Then I took a flight test and passed (hallelujah!) and was set for the rest—a board interview and a physical. Both passed very well and I was officially a WAF.

This took two days so meanwhile Dad left for N.C. and I moved into B.O.Q. 14 (Bachelors Officers Quarters).

Then I started attending classes and getting acquainted. And life settles into routine—but what a routine! Yesterday Dad returned from seeing Don and left today for home.

Not too far into my reading, I sensed that Dorothy was reaching across the years to me through her letters—an extraordinary reaction given that I am not a believer in "out-of-body" episodes. Nevertheless, I took a deep breath and dove into the soul of this young woman, by then dead for fifty-seven years. She began to speak to me through her pen and ink scrawl, through her utilitarian part-cursive, part-printing, through her descriptions of her love of flight, and through her easy narrative of what was happening in her life. I was back in 1942.

The opening line in that Thanksgiving 1942 letter—"To attempt to set down in writing all the events of the past two weeks seems a Herculean task but here goes"—is an understatement if ever there was one. Dorothy Scott had indeed stepped onto a roller coaster of life experience that took her first to Spokane for a compulsory horsepower rating, then—en route south—to Colorado Springs to visit her twin brother at Peterson Army Air Base, and finally on a cross-country motor trip east to Wilmington, Delaware, with her father. Where she was going from there, who knew? But she was ready for the ride.

The rest of this letter to her mother can be found in chapter 2.

Dorothy's letters became an extraordinary research tool for me, and I leaned on them while working on *The Originals* and, later, the Love biography. Then, just as the Love book was published in January 2008, I was invited to Texas by the Dallas Historical Society to present a paper on the WASP Squadron of the 5th Ferrying Group stationed at Dallas Love Field during World War II. The theme of that meeting—and of *Legacies: A History Journal for Dallas and North Central Texas*, a publication that was to follow in the spring—was "Dallas Goes to War: Life on the Homefront." My presentation also would be included as an article in *Legacies*.[2]

Out came Dorothy's letters, by far my best resource on the WASP stationed in Dallas because that is where she spent all but the first six weeks of her service. Dorothy's ongoing narrative gave me the meat for my presentation. I quoted liberally from the letters.

While in Texas to present the paper, I stayed with Dawn Letson, then the coordinator of the TWU Woman's Collection. Driving back to her home in Denton after the Dallas festivities were over, she asked me if I would consider editing Dorothy's letters for the WASP Archive. Remembering my initial stab of interest eight years earlier, I was thrilled at the suggestion. "I'll go you one better," I said. "I'll write her biography." The letters made it all possible.

Dorothy had haunted me since I first read her letters in 2000. An impromptu trip in May 2005 to her hometown, Oroville, Washington, whetted my appetite. I was in Seattle doing WASP oral histories for TWU and decided to drive over the Cascades to see where Dorothy hailed from. The town clerk in Oroville remembered Ed well and gave me his address in California. He and Ethel had moved there to be near their two sons. The bad news was, she thought Ed had since passed away. I wrote to Ethel Scott hoping to make a connection. Some months later, I received a letter from Tracy Scott, Ed and Ethel's elder son. His father had died New Year's Day 2002.

Tracy had found my letter at his mother's. We established contact, but with Ed gone, I had lost the only person who would remember Dorothy well enough to talk to me about her. Tracy and I did, however, exchange e-mail addresses.

Then Dawn made her suggestion early in 2008. I immediately reestablished e-mail contact with Tracy and, in September 2009, went to California, where I arranged to visit Dorothy's grave and also meet her nephew. Tracy and his wife, Jane, proved to be a tremendous historical and family resource in the writing of Dorothy's story.

On March 10, 2010, in Washington, DC, I was honored to represent Dorothy Scott's family when the Congressional Gold Medal for service to their country was awarded to all the WASP. I also had the privilege of laying Dorothy's symbolic red rose at the new US Air Force Memorial during a ceremony held March 9 to commemorate the thirty-eight WASP who died while flying for the Army Air Forces in World War II.

My journey has been an incredible one: learning about the WAFS; learning about the WASP; and watching as those who survive continue to be honored—belatedly—for their unique service in our nation's finest hour, World War II.

For several years, I have been blessed with the job of editing the *WASP News,* the official WASP newsletter. I also serve as a WASP oral historian and have done some sixty interviews for the archive. Both jobs are performed under the auspices of TWU. And, through friendships with some of the surviving WASP, I have been privileged to attend numerous events like the biannual WASP Reunions, AirVenture at Oshkosh, and aviation conferences such as Women in Aviation with several WASP who have become personal friends.

It is my privilege to write about them, and Dorothy's story is an integral part of that.

Dorothy has given me a different perspective on the WASP in general and the original WAFS in particular. I've known these women only in their elder years. I met them when they were in their seventies; those still with us are in their nineties as of this writing. Many of my friends—including all of the original WAFS I knew—have passed on. Of course, I never knew Dorothy. I was six years old when she died. But through her letters I have come to sense "who" she was as a young woman, and I think we would have been friends had we met in a common time.

Oroville is a small town in north central Washington near the Canadian border. Dorothy had two brothers, and the three of them rode horses over the hills of Okanogan County and swam and boated on nearby Lake Osoyoos. Hers was an outdoor life. She dreamed of flying and, at age twenty-one, took to the air. She proved to be an excellent pilot and hoped to make flying her life's work.

Dorothy loved music. Movie musicals and operettas like Rudolph Friml's *Rosemarie* were her soul food. She dreamed of becoming an accomplished violinist, of living in the highest penthouse, and of having "one husband, four children, and two Collies."

An athletic young woman who kept up with her brothers, Dorothy also was a gifted writer, though it is doubtful that she ever thought of herself that way. The discerning letters that have given us her life's story, plus a few other pieces she penned, are the tip-off. The epilogue of this book contains her college junior-year English essay. It earned her a rare A-plus.

Because she died in service late in 1943, most WASP never knew her. Her closest WAFS friends, Helen Richards and Betsy Ferguson, died in 1976 and 1981, respectively, before interest in the women fliers of World War II became *de rigueur.* But a couple of references in some early WASP books mention her friendliness, her unabashed enthusiasm, and her sincerity. The fledgling women ferry pilots, who came from the Army training facility to the 5th Ferrying Group in Dallas between May and August 1943, came to know her as a capable flight leader and a superior instrument pilot. Those who arrived in September and October knew her as a most empathetic liaison into life in the Ferry Command.

That is the Dorothy you will meet in these pages.

Finding Dorothy Scott

NEW CASTLE ARMY AIR BASE
WILMINGTON, DEL
W.A.f.S.

thanksgiving 1942

Dear Mom:

To attempt to set down in writing
all the events of the past two weeks
seems a herculean task but here goes:
I left Pullman Saturday morning
after calling Spokane and finally getting
a "clear enough" report. There I captured
a CAA inspector and a Waco and took
a test ride for my horsepower rating.
What a ride! Dodging clouds, all aerobatics
and hedge-hopping and he did most
of the flying but I got the rating.
After that it all blurres into
a mess of telegrams, phone calls and
frantic haste to get here by the 21st.
I was to fly, but Dad and I figured
just enough time so we drove. the
drive was tedious mostly but was

(over)

Dorothy's first letter home—written to her mother five days after she arrived at the WAFS squadron in Wilmington, Delaware—is but a prologue to what lies in store for her as a ferry pilot for the Air Transport Command. The letter is breathless, as Dorothy must have been, given all she hoped for in the new life she had chosen.

Introduction

Women in Aviation, 1903–1941

Dorothy Scott and her sister WASP did not enter World War II ready to fly by happenstance. Events in America, dating from December 17, 1903, when Wilbur and Orville Wright first flew at Kitty Hawk, ushered in a century of flight. And American women were quick to engage in this exciting new phenomenon.

Bessica Raiche did not hold a pilot's license, but on September 16, 1910, she flew her husband Frank's homebuilt aircraft, and she did so with no prior instruction or experience. Sufficiently impressed, the Aeronautical Society in New York chose to hold a dinner in her honor and award her a gold medal with the inscription First Woman Aviator of America.[1]

Blanche Stuart Scott, the only woman to whom aviation pioneer Glenn Curtiss ever gave flight instruction, was the first American woman to actually put an aircraft into flight, but it may have been by accident. Curtiss blocked the throttle of her biplane to keep it from gathering sufficient speed to take off. She was taxiing the aircraft when something, possibly a gust of wind, lifted the aircraft from the ground and it flew to an altitude of forty feet and then settled gently back to earth.[2] Sources place the date between September 2 and 12, 1910, but most likely it took place on September 2.

In one account, Scott takes credit for intentionally removing the block from the throttle, unbeknownst to Curtiss, and taking off.[3] Not the first woman to take the initiative to get what she wanted, gutsy Blanche never did get her pilot's license but continued to do stunt flying until 1916, when she quit by choice.[4] One of her favorite stunts was flying upside down under bridges.[5]

The Aeronautical Society of America credits Raiche as the first woman to pilot and solo an aircraft in America. The Early Birds of America gives that honor to Blanche Scott. The Early Birds of Aviation is an organization devoted to the history of early pilots. The organization was started in 1928 and accepted a membership of 598 pioneering aviators.[6] Bessica Raiche herself said: "Blanche deserved the recognition, but I got more attention because of my lifestyle. I drove an automobile, was active in sports like shooting and swimming, and I even wore riding pants and knickers. People who did not know me or understand me looked down on this behavior. I was an accomplished musician, painter and linguist. I enjoyed life, and just wanted to be myself."[7]

The first four American women to obtain pilot's licenses from the Aero Club of America and the prestigious Fédération Aéronautique Internationale (FAI)[8] were Harriet Quimby, #37, on August 1, 1911; Mathilde Moisant, #44, on August 17, 1911; Julia Clark, #133, on May 19, 1912; and Katherine Stinson, #148, on July 24, 1912.[9] Katherine's younger sister, Marjorie, was not far behind. The sisters later trained English and Canadian pilots to fly in World War I.

Early female stunt pilot Ruth Law (licensed November 12, 1912) was known for her flying over the Statue of Liberty with lights and fireworks displaying the word Liberty from the wings of her Curtiss Pusher, an early aircraft with engine and propeller behind the pilot's seat.[10] When America entered the Great War in 1917, the *New York World* hired her to make a 2,500-mile cross-country flight selling Liberty Bonds.[11] Law volunteered to train US military pilots during World War I but was used instead to recruit military pilots. She refused to accept the US War Department's rejection of her request to wear a uniform while performing this duty and eventually secured the right to wear the uniform of a noncommissioned Army officer while flying on recruiting tours for the military.[12]

In 1916, Neta Snook was the first woman admitted to the Curtiss-Wright Aviation School in Newport News, Virginia. There she took flight instruction and learned aviation mechanics from none other than Eddie Stinson—Katherine and Marjorie's brother, the heir to the pioneering Stinson Aircraft Company of San Antonio. But a shutdown due to flying restrictions, brought on by the United States' entry into World War I, ended that quest for her license before she could solo. She bought a wrecked

Canuck, the Canadian version of the Curtiss JN-4 Jenny—the signature American World War I trainer aircraft—and rebuilt it. Finally she soloed the Canuck and earned her US pilot's license in 1919.[13] More important to her, in the summer of 1920, she passed the test for the far more prized license issued by the Aero Club of America and the renowned FAI. "Now I was a recognized pilot before all the world," she said.[14]

Neta, who was living in Iowa, took her Canuck to California where she could fly year round. She landed a job as an instructor at Kinner Air Field in Glendale, where they offered aerial advertising (towing banners and flying billboards) and flight instruction. As a pilot with a background in mechanics at Curtiss-Wright, Neta proved an invaluable asset. In December 1920, Amelia Earhart heard about Neta, and she and her father went to Kinner to check Neta out. Amelia wanted a woman instructor.

Amelia arranged to return the following day to work out the details. However, the following morning she was delayed because her father needed her to do some work in his office. She called Neta and asked if after lunch would be convenient.

"That will be fine," Neta told her. "There's too much fog for flying anyway."

"Good," said Amelia, "then maybe you'll have time to tell me how you learned and why you wanted to fly. I've been dying to know."[15]

Amelia took her first lesson on January 3, 1921. For one dollar in Liberty Bonds per minute in the air, Neta Snook taught Amelia to fly. They also became friends.[16]

Amelia Earhart received pilot's license #6017 from the FAI on May 25, 1923.[17]

On June 3, 1928, Amelia Earhart flew the Atlantic Ocean as a passenger in the trimotor Fokker *Friendship*. Wilmer "Bill" Stultz was the pilot and Lou "Slim" Gordon the copilot and mechanic. Amelia kept the flight log, which became her story of the flight, the book *20 Hrs., 40 Min.* Amelia became an instant celebrity as the first woman to "fly" the Atlantic, albeit as a passenger.[18] To a friend, she likened her usefulness on the flight to that of "a sack of potatoes."[19] She vowed to fly the Atlantic herself someday.

In 1929, just before the decade closed out, two crowning achievements cast a spotlight on America's best-known women pilots of the day. On Sunday, August 18, 1929, Amelia, along with Louise Thaden, Ruth Nichols, Phoebe Omlie, Blanche Noyes, Gladys O'Donnell, and fourteen others climbed into their aircraft, started their engines, and took off from Santa

Monica, California, headed cross country for Cleveland, Ohio. They made history.

The occasion was the First Women's Cross-Country Race, christened "The Powder Puff Derby" by humorist and aviation enthusiast of the day Will Rogers. Already brewing among the competitors in the race was the idea of forming an organization of and for women pilots. During a quick stop in Kansas City, one of the racers, Neva Paris, ran from airplane to airplane to tell the competitors that there was a meeting planned under the grandstands in Cleveland after the race.[20]

On Monday, August 26, Louise Thaden won the Heavier Aircraft division of the just-over-2,700-mile race in 20:19:04 flying time. Gladys O'Donnell and Amelia Earhart were right behind her. Phoebe Omlie came in first in the Lighter Aircraft division.[21] Six did not finish the race. One, Marvel Crosson, died when her aircraft crashed near Yuma, Arizona, August 20.[22]

At the gathering beneath the grandstand in Cleveland after the race, Phoebe Omlie suggested forming a group and Neva Paris, the detail person, pulled it all together. The group, she said, "would promote good fellowship among licensed women pilots, encourage flying among women, and create opportunities for women in commercial aviation."[23]

Neva and three others signed a joint letter that was sent to all 117 women in the United States listed as holding pilot's licenses as of the fall of 1929. A meeting date was set, and all were invited to attend. Of the 117, 26 gathered on Long Island November 2, 1929, at Curtiss Airport, Valley Stream, New York. The 26 created what became known as the Ninety-Nines, the International Organization of Women Pilots. The name incorporated the final tally of charter members—ninety-nine. Membership would be open to any licensed woman pilot and the purpose was "good fellowship, jobs, and a central office and files on women in aviation."[24]

Neva Paris was named temporary chair, but on January 9, 1930, on her way to the winter air races in Florida, her aircraft spun out and crashed near Woodbine, Georgia. She died in the crash. Opal Kunz, another of the Powder Puff participants, was appointed temporary chairman in her place. Louise Thaden, determined to get the group going, took over as secretary; Blanche Noyes agreed to be treasurer. In 1931, Louise was offered the presidency, but she turned it down. In the first formal election, Amelia was elected president. Louise believed Amelia—who was far better known than any of them—could be a more vocal and effective spokeswoman for the women pilots. Louise then served as Amelia's vice president.[25] On January 13, 1930, when she heard of Neva's death, Opal Kunz wrote: "It should be remembered by all of us that this club was really founded by Neva."[26]

The Ninety-Nines, still going strong today, brought together like-minded women in 1929 and gave those women of American aviation (later women all over the world) a platform from which to speak, act, fly, and become friends.

In 1932, Amelia Earhart made good her pledge to herself and became the first woman to fly the Atlantic Ocean solo. But the question remained, could women make it in commercial aviation?

The most common job available to women was demonstrating and selling aircraft in the private market. Earhart, Thaden, Noyes, and Nichols all sold aircraft.[27] Louise Thaden sold twenty-five aircraft between 1929 and 1931.[28] "Demonstrating new airplanes is not all it seems on the surface, particularly if the 'demonstrator' is a woman and the 'demonstratee' is a man," Louise wrote. "There must be some psychological reaction which reacts on the male in the form of an urge not only to show the female the prowess of the male, but in the process of turning the airplane wrong side out and inside front. In all justice, it should be said that the least experienced of the males are usually the worst offenders."[29]

Twenty-year-old Nancy Harkness went to work in 1934 for Robert M. Love at InterCity Aviation, the flight service he had founded at East Boston Airport. Bob Love hired Miss Harkness to demonstrate "the WACO [pronounced Wah-ko] line of airplanes to prospective customers." Miss Harkness, who held a transport license, also took passengers on flights-for-hire and flew charter flights.[30]

Aviation historian Deborah G. Douglas writes, "It was the oldest gimmick in the book. Women pilots were used not only to persuade reluctant buyers of new aircraft, but also to sell the idea of aviation to the nation—after all, the logic went, if a woman can do it then it must not be so difficult."[31]

Teaching flying was another avenue for women pilots. The Stinson girls and Neta Snook were among the first female flight instructors.

Wing walking was another way women made a living in aviation. Phoebe Fairgrave started off as a wing walker in the early 1920s before she married Vernon Omlie. To relieve the boredom, she sometimes did the Charleston on the top wing of a biplane in flight.[32] Wing walker Jessie

Woods and her pilot husband, Jimmie, founded the Flying Aces Air Circus in 1928. It became the longest running air circus in US history—ten years. She walked on the wings of aircraft in flight, parachuted off aircraft, and dangled below them, with her knees holding her to a rope ladder.[33]

The onset of the Great Depression, following the stock market crash of October 1929, certainly quashed women's opportunities in the aviation job market—or anything else. The effect of the Depression on men's jobs was even worse.

In 1934, Helen Richey became the first woman hired as a pilot (actually copilot) for a commercial airline. "This marks a new era for women pilots," said Amelia Earhart, president of the Ninety-Nines. But Helen soon realized she was primarily being used by her employer for publicity purposes. The all-male pilots union denied her application for membership and complained to the Department of Commerce, protesting her work as a copilot. Helen stood five feet four inches tall, not a big woman. The male pilots insisted that she didn't have the strength to handle an airliner in bad weather. Consequently, she was limited to fair-weather flying. In ten months she flew fewer than a dozen round trips while male copilots flew more than a hundred. Frustrated, she resigned in November 1935.[34]

Phoebe Omlie landed what may have been the most important job of all. In 1932, she was Franklin Delano Roosevelt's pilot during his campaign for president. After he was elected, he appointed her to serve as liaison between the National Advisory Committee for Aeronautics and the Bureau of Air Commerce.[35] Phoebe also got to know Eleanor Roosevelt—who in 1936 named her one of the ten "most useful women" in America.[36] Phoebe wasn't as well known as Amelia Earhart, but she was every bit the leader Amelia was. Throughout her career, Phoebe wielded her influence to give other women a chance to prove themselves as capable as men. She was listened to and frequently used her privileged platform to argue the woman's side when faced with a wall of clueless masculinity. A case in point follows.

In 1935, the thirty male members of the Bureau of Air Commerce's medical division "declared unanimously" that women pilots were "not physically or psychologically suited for flying a regular run." Their information came from an article in the *Journal of Aviation Medicine* that stated: "out of ten women who had been killed while flying, eight were menstruating." Carroll Cone, assistant director of the Bureau of Air Commerce, wanted women pilots grounded for that nine-day monthly period. He gave Phoebe the job of writing the regulation.

Phoebe, who probably had to stifle the urge either to laugh or maybe scream, deftly quashed the request by suggesting that the information in the article was sketchy and that enforcing such a regulation would be extremely difficult. Why not, she countered, let her gather more information? Phoebe did more than gather information. She arranged to have Dr. Emma Kittridge of the Women's Air Reserve[37] appointed as a Department of Commerce examining doctor. She also recruited Dr. Clara Gross, of the Women's Medical College in Philadelphia, who was interested in the project.

Funding was a problem. Phoebe contacted Eleanor Roosevelt, who sent her to the assistant secretary of the Department of the Treasury in charge of public health—a woman, Josephine Roche. Unfortunately, Roche's hands were tied, as funding had to come through Congress. From there, Phoebe ran into some rather prim responses from several women from whom she sought help. Apparently the subject matter was "too delicate" for some of their ears, thoughts, and—most important—action. Finally, Phoebe herself volunteered to be the guinea pig. Cone's dismissal of the doctor's research done on her was, "this doesn't prove very much, you're just a healthy horse."

Though no funding was forthcoming, the bureau endorsed Phoebe's research plan. Perhaps her gumption, level head, and high standing with the men in charge were sufficient reason. No doubt some skillful persuading went into the mix. The two women physicians went to work. Examinations of women pilots began and went on for more than a year. No regulation was ever proposed, and the idea died a slow death.[38]

The sort of mentality that existed among men in 1935 did not die. It would resurface during World War II to affect Nancy Love's Women's Auxiliary Ferrying Squadron when those women began to fly for the US military.

Amelia Earhart wrote the following to Gene Vidal, director of the Bureau of Air Commerce in a personal letter dated November 17, 1935. "May I say at this time how much I feel the Department has advanced in its outlook in the last year or two? Instead of being a strictly regulatory body, it has become a real help to the [aviation] industry with its progressive policies. . . . The employing of competent women pilots has broken down a barrier, which had up to the present regime had [*sic*] appeared almost insurmountable. My particular thanks for the last."[39]

In this atmosphere, Phoebe Omlie was on her way up with the Bureau of Air Commerce. In 1935, she was appointed special assistant for intelligence at the National Advisory Committee for Aeronautics. With Amelia's help, Omlie convinced the chief of the Airport Marking and Mapping Section of the Bureau of Air Commerce that American towns and cities needed to be identifiable from the air. Grants were awarded for air marking through President Franklin D. Roosevelt's New Deal program, the Works Progress Administration (WPA).

The program had a twofold benefit. Not only did it provide a safety element for all pilots—private and commercial—it also created jobs for the unemployed of the Great Depression. Men would be put to work painting the names of towns on roofs.

Omlie hired Louise Thaden to run the Air Marking program. Louise hired two rising young women pilots, Nancy Harkness of Boston and Helen MacCloskey of Pittsburgh, to work with her selling air marking to mayors and councils of those cities and towns. When Nancy left to marry Bob Love, January 11, 1936, Louise hired Helen Richey, who was out of work.[40]

Blanche Noyes joined the Air Marking Group in the summer of 1936 and remained with the government until her retirement. In recognition of her thirty-five years of government service for air safety, Noyes became the first woman to receive a gold medal from the commerce department.[41]

The flying bug was catching by 1930. The Ninety-Nines had been established. The ranks of women pilots swelled. The girls and young women who would become the WAFS and WASP in the 1940s began to take notice.

Dorothy Scott was ten years old in 1930 when her father built his new landing strip on the outskirts of Oroville, Washington, and put on the town's first air show. Her twin brother, Ed, said Dorothy was always the first one at the airport when a plane landed.

Sixteen-year-old Nancy Harkness took her first flying lesson from a barnstormer, August 26, 1930; soloed August 31; and received her private pilot's license November 7, 1930.[42] Twenty-six-year-old Jacqueline Cochran took her first lesson July 23, 1932; soloed August 1; and on August 11 completed her certification.[43] Evelyn Sharp took her first flight lesson on February 4, 1935. She was fifteen. She soloed March 4, 1936, and on November 9 that year earned her pilot's license. She had just turned seventeen.[44] Cornelia Fort, twenty, took her first flight in early 1940, so-loed April 27, and when she had fifty hours that summer, her instructor signed her off to take her flight test.[45]

The late 1930s brought the dream of flight much closer to the American public.

Aviation pioneer Robert H. Hinckley saw a way for the US government, business, and education to work together to produce a boost to the sagging Great Depression economy and provide the country with a corps of young trained airplane pilots. It was called the Civilian Pilot Training Program (CPTP). Upgrading civil aviation was the goal.

In 1938, Hinckley was appointed to the board of the newly created Civil Aviation Authority (CAA), successor to the Bureau of Air Commerce and overseers of the country's aviation resources.[46] His plan was to build the CPTP using available resources. He enlisted the nation's colleges and universities to teach ground school in their classrooms. He contracted with fixed-base operators (FBOs) at local airports, who had resident flight schools, to provide the flight training to those students.

This was President Roosevelt's New Deal at its finest. Flight training was expensive, beyond the pocketbooks of most ordinary citizens, but with the government subsidizing the training, the nation's young people could now afford to try their wings. Hinckley believed that flight instruction and the ground-school curriculum would provide vocational training that could lead to employment in the aviation industry that, like so much of the American economy, had been hit hard by the Great Depression.

The program could help revitalize the depressed light plane industry as well as give an economic boost to the FBOs—those who provided flying lessons, charter flights, aircraft sales and maintenance, fuel, and supplies. The program was designed to lead to a boom in private flying, which, in turn, was expected to open up a market for new airplanes.

It was the first full-scale federally funded aviation education program and one of the largest government-sponsored vocational education programs of its time. Hinckley, visualizing the future and potential of aviation, believed "CPTP would make America airminded."[47]

Though the United States in 1938 was a neutral nation, the danger of being dragged into Europe's unsettled state of political upheaval was growing. The timing of CPTP's inception does suggest that it was a military preparedness program, but the program was structured—at least at first—so that military service was optional. Hinckley believed patriotism was what would motivate men to enlist, if and when the need arose. Of course the trained pilots the schools created did become a pool of potential military pilots. And they were needed when the United States was drawn into what became World War II. Unfortunately, the program "suffered from a split identity [civilian vs. military goals] and that interfered seriously with its effectiveness."[48]

In the eyes of the US Congress, CPTP did have a twofold purpose. It offered both New Deal economic recovery and war preparedness.[49]

President Roosevelt signed the CPTP bill June 27, 1939. That year, he also named Hinckley chair of the CAA.[50] Congress passed the necessary appropriations in August. Amendments provided for two items of note: applicants would *not* be refused admittance on account of race, creed, or color—which ultimately paved the way for the Tuskegee Airmen;[51] and at least five percent of the trainees would *not* be from colleges or universities.[52] That put CPTP in reach of those young people who could not afford to go to college and those who otherwise, in 1939 America, would not have been considered for inclusion.

Before CPT was approved, trial programs were put in motion in February 1939 at thirteen participating colleges or universities, selected because of their "pioneer work in aeronautical engineering or because they had flight training programs." The full program was under way by October.[53]

What about the Women?

England had inaugurated a similar program, the Civil Air Guard, making flight training available to both men and women between the ages of eighteen and fifty.[54] Would American women get the opportunity to learn to fly? The answer was "yes," but with strings attached.

The first full year of CPTP training, 792 colleges and universities and nearly 200 noncollege organizations offered the program. Four women's colleges made the list: Lake Erie College, Painesville, Ohio; Adelphi College, Garden City, New York; Mills College, Oakland, California; and Florida State College, Tallahassee. For coed colleges and universities taking part in the program, the solution was to use a ten-to-one ratio—men to women—thus allowing a few young women to enroll. The number of women was small compared to the men who sought enrollment.

The course called for thirty-five to fifty hours of subsidized flight instruction and "controlled solo flying." Even after the student soloed, the instructor frequently rode in the backseat continuing to teach and monitor the student's progress. The average time it took for a student to prove proficiency was 38 hours, and that was the same for men and women. The safety record for all of the CPT programs in the country in 1940 was more than five million miles flown per fatality. At the end of the CPTP's first year there were 980 new women pilots. By June 1941, there were more than 2,000 new young women pilots.[55]

Dorothy Scott was in that last batch, earning her pilot's license in June 1941.

Then everything changed.

The shooting war had begun in Europe on September 1, 1939. After that, the possibility of the United States entering the war became increasingly likely. Over the next two years, the initial goal of the CPTP—to upgrade civil aviation—was forgotten.[56]

Though the military wasn't sold on the CPT program, political pressure pushed the two closer and closer together.

On May 16, 1940, President Roosevelt asked for the manufacture of fifty thousand airplanes. In June 1940, Hinckley announced plans to train forty-five thousand elementary and nine thousand secondary flight students.[57] Beginning in September 1940—a year after the war in Europe began—the male CPTP students were asked to sign a pledge that they would enter military aviation if they were needed for national defense.

The Air Corps, from the beginning, looked with disdain on the CPTP and gave it but faint praise, says author Charles Planck, "but never admitted the program meant anything important to the armed forces." In 1941, after the Lend-Lease Act passed, it surfaced that 25 percent of the Air Corps cadets and nearly 50 percent of the Navy cadets were former CPTP trainees. "The Air Corps awoke to its importance," Planck adds. By early 1941 it was tacitly understood that trainees would be available for military service if and when needed. By June 1941, the rate of CPTP graduates joining up reached two hundred a week.[58]

At that point, the axe fell. CPTP graduates would now be required to enlist as part of their agreement with the CAA. And that spelled the end for the women. Women flight students were excluded from CPTP.[59]

"The girls didn't take it quietly," writes Patricia Strickland in *The Putt-Putt Air Force*. "They SCREAMED, and all over the country outraged women as well as women's organizations, like the powerful General Federation of Women's Clubs, joined them." The cry was "intolerable discrimination" and the newspapers took it up. Eleanor Roosevelt asked for an explanation.[60]

Though this requirement was the military's doing, not the CAA's, the agency was caught between a rock and a hard place—the public outcry and the obstinacy of the Army—and it was an unfair position. The forthcoming explanation was this: Officials of the Budget, the Senate, and the House—who controlled the purse strings—said that male pilots had more potential usefulness to the armed forces and that the funding needed to benefit the Army and Navy. Consequently, the CAA had to make changes in the CPTP.[61]

A footnote in the source tries to explain it further and take the heat off the CAA. "The CAA," it says, "had never discriminated against women." Women were eligible to try for any pilot or mechanic certificate the government issued. Women flew under the same rules as men and were subject to the same penalties for violations. Like the men, they could fly for hire. Though, as of July 1941, women no longer could learn to fly through CPTP, women who qualified as instructors proved a boon to the War Training Service (WTS) that succeeded CPT. Some fifty women instructors found employment teaching male flight cadets.[62] Among them were several future WASP, including Dorothy Scott.

By the end of 1941, the number of CPTP graduate male pilots who had joined the Army or Navy had reached fourteen thousand.[63]

CPTP had succeeded in bringing the number of women pilots in the country from 675 in 1939 to nearly 3,000 by July 1, 1941.[64] Many of those freshly minted young women pilots ended up in the WASP.

With the Japanese attack on Pearl Harbor on December 7, 1941, America went to war.

Part One

Becoming an Original: The WAFS,
September 10, 1942, to August 4, 1943

Dorothy Scott, a Civilian Pilot Training Program student from the University of Washington, soloed March 17, 1941. She was learning to fly seaplanes on Lake Washington. *Courtesy WASP Archive, Texas Woman's University, Denton.*

Chapter One

The Race Is On

A family rivalry landed twenty-one-year-old Dorothy Scott's photo in the *Seattle Post-Intelligencer* on March 18, 1941. Dorothy had bested her father in a contest to see who could solo an airplane first.[1]

> Blonde and stately Dorothy Scott crawled out from behind the controls of a training plane on Lake Union yesterday morning, and with a note of triumph in her voice, trilled: "Dad will have to give me that plane now!"
>
> The young woman, a senior at the University of Washington, had just made a solo flight and by doing so had won a bet from her father, G. M. Scott, automobile dealer at Oroville.

Dorothy, a University of Washington senior, was enrolled in the university's spring 1941 Civilian Pilot Training Program. At the same time, her father Guthrie M. "G. M." Scott was learning to fly at Wenatchee, in central Washington, some distance from the family's home in Oroville. G. M. challenged his daughter to a race to see who could solo first. At the same time, he purchased a new three-seat J-5 Piper Cub and told Dorothy that the winner of the competition could claim ownership.

Dorothy won by seven hours. She soloed at 10:30 a.m. on March 17—the first University of Washington coed to solo in the spring CPTP course. Immediately after landing, she sent Dad a telegram informing him of her flight. The *Seattle Post-Intelligencer* photographer snapped a picture of her writing out a telegram telling her father the news.[2]

He soloed that afternoon at 5:30 and immediately called to tell her. The telegram with her news had not yet reached him.

To the victor . . .

That daughter and dad were best friends made the celebration all the sweeter.

Dorothy sought acceptance in the CPTP in late 1939 when it was introduced at the University of Washington. She did not get in that first class but kept trying and was accepted for the 1941 spring semester class. She, one other coed, and eighteen young men were sent to nearby Lake Union to learn to fly floatplanes. The other twenty students learned to fly at the airport, where they landed airplanes with wheels on a runway rather than floats on the water.

Dorothy completed her eight hours of training in two weeks' time. The morning of March 17, when her instructor Everett Glenn was satisfied with her performance, he climbed out of the trainer aircraft and told her to take it up by herself. The *Post-Intelligencer* related the whole story.[3]

> After ten minutes in the air, she brought her ship in like a veteran, and wired her father the "bad news."
>
> Seven hours later her father telephoned from Wenatchee, where he is learning to fly, that he, too, had just soloed.
>
> "But I won, just the same. Now we'll be racing for our private licenses—and there's a chicken dinner involved in that. If he wins I have to cook him one, and if I win he has to buy me one."
>
> Miss Scott, incidentally, was the first University of Washington coed to solo in the present spring course.
>
> "I was a little scared at first, but I really got along better than if I was up with someone else. There was really nothing to it."
>
> Miss Scott says she hopes to be able to fly her plane across America to visit relatives and friends in various places this summer.

Two days after Dorothy's solo, G. M. wrote to her,

> PUBLICITY!—YOU have got it with a bang, and this time you roped me in with it. I just got a letter from the Firestone Tire man telling me that he is placing his bets on you to win. This morning I had occasion to phone the Ford Motor Co. The operator there said, "I see that you lost." Some people around here feel sorry for me that I lost the bet. Well it certainly made a good "story."
>
> Dad.

Left: Guthrie "G. M." Scott, 1913—Dorothy's father. *Courtesy: The Scott Family Collection. Right:* Katherine Faeth, 1913—Dorothy's mother. *Courtesy: The Scott Family Collection.*

G. M. was Oroville's Ford motorcar and Firestone Tire dealer.

The CPTP flight students at the University of Washington were due to complete the CPTP course—ninety hours of ground school and forty hours of flight training—in mid-June 1941. And Dorothy did just that. She actually earned her Class 1 Water license number 86188-41 on April 14, 1941, and her 2S Land license was granted on June 26, 1941. In all likelihood, G. M. had to ante up for that chicken dinner.

G. M. Scott was born in London, England, in 1884. When he was eight years old, his parents moved to America and settled in San Francisco. He only finished fourth grade, but in his teens he went to sea on a tramp steamer, crossing the Pacific as far as the Philippines.[4]

During the latter days of the Gold Rush in Alaska, he hopped a steamer north and ended up in Fairbanks. Sled dog teams were heading for Nome, and G. M. signed on. Later he would regale his children with stories of his dogsledding adventures.

The family doesn't know how G. M. and Katherine Faeth met. They were married in Seattle on December 22, 1913.

G. M. was a student of the American way. Business was the road to success. He returned to Alaska—Juneau, this time—where he bought a fishing boat, loaded it with salmon, and began to make trips down to Seattle to sell his catch. Katherine and their son Donald, born in 1916, lived on the boat with G. M. and made the runs up and down the coast. G. M. was so successful that, when the United States entered World War I in April 1917, his Army draft board told him to keep on fishing because the country needed the food he was supplying more than it needed him in the Army. But when the war was over, G. M. sold the fishing boat and in 1919 went back down to the States "in pursuit of riches," to use the words of his younger son, Edward. G. M. had an added incentive to settle down. Katherine was pregnant again.

An ad in the Seattle newspaper caught G. M.'s attention—here was an opportunity to buy into a Ford motorcar dealership in Oroville, Washington. He moved Katherine and three-year-old Donald to Oroville and settled there. In 1919, people in Oroville, like the rest of America, were putting World War I and its horrors behind them. On the horizon was a new decade, full of promise. G. M. was ready for it.

Oroville, population 1,013 in 1920, lay 162 miles northeast of Seattle on the wilderness side of Washington's lofty Cascade Mountains and three miles south of the US border with British Columbia, Canada. Remote was an apt description. In 1920, many babies were still delivered at home, but Katherine, now thirty-eight years old, was having a difficult pregnancy. She opted to go to a hospital in Seattle for the delivery. Dorothy Faeth and Edward Allen Scott were born February 16, 1920. Dorothy weighed 6 pounds 11 ounces; Edward, 6 pounds 1 ounce.

Katherine and G. M. were not expecting twins.

The Okanogan County newspaper related that

> G. M. Scott, local manager of Bowen Auto Company received the startling yet happy news Monday that he was the father of twins. Mrs. Scott is confined at the Seattle General Hospital and both herself and the new responsibilities of the house of Scott are doing nicely. Mr. Scott is the recipient of many congratulations and bears his blushing honors gracefully.[5]

When the attending physician, Dr. Woodword, was satisfied with mother and twins' progress, he released them to return home to Oroville. Each of the babies weighed in above the weight of many a single-birth infant, and both appeared in robust health.

Dorothy Faeth and Edward A. Scott were born on February 16, 1920. *Courtesy: The Scott Family Collection.*

Scott's Ford Agency and Service Station was located on Main Street. Two gas pumps—the old-fashioned kind with crown-like metal tops—stood sentinel out front. They offered regular fuel and eventually ethyl (also called high-test). Tires sporting decorative cardboard wings filled the plate-glass show windows, and Model T Fords flanked the garage and welcomed all comers. Scott Motors was a thriving business. The town drugstore was right next door.

Main Street Oroville, in the 1920s, still had vestiges of the western frontier, given the rugged mountains and dense forests that surrounded it. Oroville also had the distinction of being a stone's throw from the Canadian border. Mainstream civilization was far away physically, psychologically, and materially. Dorothy, Ed, and Donald Scott thrived as children. They attended the Oroville schools—first the old grade school down on Fifth Street, then they moved to the new all-brick building on South Main Street, and, finally, to the two-story high school on the hill overlooking the town.

The Scott kids were close growing up, the twins in particular. A classic wintertime photo shows Don and the family dog pulling the twins, clad in

Older brother Donald and the family dog take Dorothy and Ed sledding.
Courtesy: The Scott Family Collection.

snowsuits, on a sled. A good winter in Oroville could dump five-plus feet
of snow. Sleds, snowsuits, and galoshes were a fact of life.

Lake Osoyoos, which lies partially in British Columbia and partially in Washington State, dominated life in Oroville. The Scott family took
full advantage. Dorothy grew up around boats and fishing. She learned to
swim early and excelled at it, which led to Red Cross lifesaving activities
in her teen and college years.

The Scott family owned three horses, one each for Dorothy, Ed, and
Don. The horses were kept below the house in what later became the city
park in Oroville. When they got older, Don and the twins used to ride the
horses up into the Pasayten Wilderness area, some distance west of Oroville but still part of Okanogan County—a trip that old timers in Oroville
recall would have taken several days.[6]

Astride their mounts, bedroll and slicker tied on the saddles behind
them, seventeen-year-old Don and fourteen-year-old Dorothy and Ed
would have made their way through deep, shadowed valleys and across
pine-covered ridges. The challenge was planning and carrying enough

food for the three of them—even if they planned to hunt and fish to supplement their diet. The three also carried a substantial stash of oats for the horses. A summertime trip took all their ingenuity and wilderness skills. But this was the environment in which they lived—and thrived.

Depression years in the 1930s did affect life in Oroville, but things were not as bad there as many other places. The Scott family weathered the bad times, primarily because G. M. was the enterprising sort. He could run a business and he wasn't afraid of hard work.

Farmers from nearby towns who came into Scott Motors for repairs paid with farm products, as no one had any money. Cars were not selling, so G. M. bought a threshing machine and tractor and threshed wheat for hire. This brought in money for the farmers as well as for him. Many of the farmers told him that, due to his threshing methods, they had received more grain per acre than in many prior years. And that translated into more money. So Dorothy and her brothers grew into their teen years in the relative security offered by a small town that coped well with adversity and a father who thrived due to his work ethic.

A new thing called aviation entered Dorothy's life early.

The original Oroville airport was only three blocks from the center of town. In 1928, Okanogan County offered for sale several acres of land a mile or so northeast of town. G. M. bought the land "just for taxes." He hired some men to clear the sagebrush from the field and then hauled in several tons of gravel dug from alongside the railroad tracks that ran to the next town.

Fascinated with airplanes, G. M. planned to build a new airport. The field was level, and he thought it could be made into a lengthy landing strip. The end result was an all-gravel, 4,000-foot runway.

One day in 1930, a pilot named John Kammers—badly in need of fuel—landed at Oroville's old airport. Kammers knew G. M. had not yet added a fuel pump at the new airport. He parked his plane, climbed down from the cockpit, and walked into town to Scott's Service Station. There, he and G. M. shot the breeze. John then asked if his friend could fill up some five-gallon cans and truck them over to the runway and fill up his plane. G. M. suggested that, instead, the man taxi his plane up Main Street and fill it up at the service station.

He did.

The town had its entertainment for the day. Several townspeople gath-

Edward Scott (in the cap), Keno the family dog, and two of Ed's friends watch G. M. gas up the biplane parked at the pumps in front of the Ford Agency, summer 1929. *Courtesy: The Scott Family Collection.*

ered around for closer inspection of the visitor who dropped out of the sky. An enterprising photographer for the local newspaper captured all the commotion on film. In the photo of curious onlookers are fourteen-year-old Donald, ten-year-old Ed, a couple of his friends, and the family dog, Keno. G. M. can be spotted standing on the lower wing refueling the biplane. Kammers is sitting in the rear seat of the tandem two-seater open cockpit.

When G. M. did install fuel at his airstrip later that summer, he decided to put on an air show. He invited all the pilots he knew to come and bring their friends. Participating pilots flew passengers all day long. It turned out to be a great day for Oroville and aviation in north central Washington.[7] G. M. was one of Okanogan County's, and the state of Washington's, early aviation visionaries.[8] But he put off learning to fly himself. Odds are that the sheer cost of flying and keeping airplanes prevented him from doing so during the Great Depression. And he was looking at college educations for three children.

Dorothy, seventeen, graduated from Oroville High School in 1937. *Courtesy: The Scott Family Collection.*

John Townsley, a resident of nearby Tonasket, writes that the Oroville area was a hotbed of aviation enthusiasts in the second quarter of the twentieth century.[9]

The first airports were being built in Okanogan County in the '20s. I think Okanogan Legion Airport (named, I think, because the veterans in the American Legion were instrumental in building it) was the first in the early '20s. I know that Tonasket's airport was built with a grant from the Bureau of Reclamation in 1934, and that the current Omak airport was built by the War Department in 1943 as a hedge against a potential Japanese invasion. I have not found any mention so far of when Oroville's airport was originally built . . . gliders were being built in back yards and flown in the Oroville and Nighthawk areas between 1920 and the late '30s.

Dorothy hardly could help but be bitten by the bug of flight; his daughter's growing interest helped spur G. M. on. "My sister was always interested in airplanes, whenever one would land up at the airport, she was the first to go there to see it," Ed Scott recalled in an interview with Gary Devon, the editor of the Oroville newspaper in June 1993.[10]

From a blonde tomboy most at home playing with her brothers and their friends, Dorothy grew into an attractive, statuesque young

Dorothy Scott, a University of Washington senior, 1941. *Courtesy: The Scott Family Collection.*

woman. Photos of her—taken in her early twenties—hint at the extraordinary woman she seemed destined to become. Her Air Transport Command ID card, issued in late 1942 when she was twenty-two, gives the following vital statistics: color eyes, blue; color hair, light brown; weight, 140 pounds; height, 68 inches—or five feet eight.

The determined set of Dorothy's jaw is balanced by her softer woman's mouth. Her nose wasn't the sharp, defined Scott nose of her father, her twin brother, and [later] her brother's son, Tracy. Rather, she had her mother's nose, dominant but with gentler lines. Hers is a most feminine and lovely face graced with classical lines, yet the strong countenance and direct gaze of those penetrating blue eyes seem to telegraph a will to take charge that lurks beneath the surface.

As outgoing young women are inclined, given the right chemistry, to take the lead, Dorothy was a leader in her high school class of nineteen—typical in size for Oroville in the 1930s. Ed had been ill for several months earlier in their childhood and fell behind Dorothy in school. Dorothy and their mutual friend, Jim Zosel, graduated from high school in 1937. Ed graduated the following year. Dorothy was by far the dominant sibling.

Dorothy, a good student, truly began to shine once she arrived at the

University of Washington. She seemed to take the move from a small rural community high school to the university in metropolitan Seattle in stride. The self-confidence she would later exhibit in the WAFS was beginning to surface. A comparison of her rather demure high school graduation photo to photos taken in college and later, when in the service, reveals the transition to a poised young woman ready to take on the world. An air of self-assurance complemented her already natural good looks.

Sports dominated Dorothy's extracurricular activities. At the university, she swam and played intramural basketball. She earned her American Red Cross First Aid certification in December 1938 and held lifesaving certification as well. Dorothy originally enrolled at the University of Washington as a nursing major. But that changed.

Did she ever consider English as a major and writing as a vocation? Probably not. She seems too much the extrovert for such a lonely and cerebral existence. However, the writings she produced are full of humor, keen observation, and attention to detail. Words seem to flow from her pen or from her typewriter. A creative essay, "A Private Utopia," written for a 1940 English class at the university and a Mother's Day poem written for Katherine in May 1943, plus her remarkable letters home during World War II, comprise a telling portfolio.

The three-and-a-half months between when Dorothy was accepted into CPTP early in 1941 and completion of the course in June changed her focus on life. When she earned her private pilot's certificate that June, she should have been ready to take on the world. But in opting out of nursing, Dorothy had managed to mess up her schedule. When summer 1941 arrived, she did not have sufficient credits to graduate. She had been missing language credits since she entered the university. The lack of language credits was not unusual for someone coming from a rural high school, but she should have addressed it over the four years. She had not.

She also lacked the needed credits in physical education. This had to do with her original enrollment in nursing school, where she was to take health classes instead. With her interest in sports, this failure to make up the difference is surprising. Nevertheless, the bottom line was, Dorothy had finished four years and had not earned her academic degree.[11]

Her father may have been popping his buttons over her aviation prowess in summer 1941, but G. M. Scott—the no-nonsense businessman—surely was not pleased with the lack of a degree after four years of costly education. His philosophy always had been that college—something he hadn't had—was preparation for gainful employment and success.

Consequently, the triumphs in aviation turned a bit sour after June, but Dorothy did move another step up the aviation ladder by earning her commercial pilot's license that summer.

Flying had become the focal point of Dorothy's life. She wanted to make a living flying—no easy task for a woman in early 1940s America. G. M. wanted Dorothy to prepare for a career in business. He had opted for the American dream and become a successful businessman. She, he was convinced, was cut from the same cloth.

She and her father did take that trip they had planned to visit Katherine in Los Angeles. Dorothy's father and mother were separated by then. There had been domestic problems. Tracy Scott recalls his father talking about the rows between G. M. and Katherine and that his grandfather had "a well-recognized temper." But Katherine, by the late 1930s, had also experienced recurring battles with cancer. She had opted to move on to a less complicated, single existence and to the gentler climate of Southern California. Her sister lived nearby in San Diego.

In the summer of 1941, Dorothy was twenty-one years old, restless, and unsure what she wanted to do with her life—other than fly. When she and her father went to Los Angeles later that summer, they made a critical decision together. Dorothy applied to American Airlines for what was probably a secretarial or administrative-assistant-type job. Other than stewardess, not much else was available to women in the airline industry at the time. And Dorothy enrolled in Los Angeles's Woodbury College, founded in 1884 and one of the oldest institutes of higher learning on the West Coast.[12] Business education was Woodbury's forte. Dorothy would prepare for a career in business. G. M. was pleased.

Dorothy moved in with her ailing mother, a satisfactory solution for both her father and her mother. But Dorothy, who already had spent four years living on campus with other young women, longed for the social life and the freedom she had left behind at the University of Washington. She soon pledged Alpha Iota sorority, moved into the sorority house, and, seemingly, settled back into life as a college student.

Then on December 7, 1941, the Japanese attacked Pearl Harbor and the United States—up until then a neutral country—went to war.

US Army Capt. Donald Scott, either on leave or travel orders, visited his mother and sister in Los Angeles in early March 1942. By then, Dorothy was having second thoughts about her decision to enroll at Woodbury.

Nothing had materialized at American Airlines. She wanted to fly. Late in April, she wrote her father a letter asking to come home.

G. M. answered promptly:[13] [The all-caps in the typewritten letter on Scott Motors stationery are G. M.'s.]

April 27th, 1942

Dear Dorothy,

Your airmail letter of the 23rd received:

Yes, you can come home—BUT NOT UNTIL YOU HAVE COMPLETED YOUR COURSE IN YOUR PRESENT SCHOOL. My reasons are: If you come up here, or go to any other school but the one that you are at you will lose all the credits that you have earned. It is not like transferring from one University in this state to another in this state. I cannot afford to have you waste both TIME AND MONEY flitting from one school to another. However much I would like to have you home or nearer home still you have a job to do and you must finish it right where you are. Without your graduation diploma it is really hard for you to get started in a job unless you get one before you quit school.—If you can get a job with the American Airlines it will give you a most wonderful start in a growing big company, one that should be to your liking.

You ask me, "WHAT DO YOU WANT ME TO DO?"

Dorothy, it is getting to the time that you must prepare yourself for almost any eventuality that may come along. Please get the idea out of your head that you can make something out of FLYING. It is something that very few women have made a dollar at, something that if you had to get right down to brass tacks and really WORK AT you would be so sick and tired of it inside of a month you would CHUCK IT.

Herb is at it and from what I can find out is very tired of the same old training program every day. Knox is flying big planes from the west coast to the east and is getting to feel like a motorman on a streetcar just going round and round. I believe that business is what you are adapted for and so I think that it is what you should get into. Again I repeat that I like the idea of you getting into the American Airlines.

Please do not get peeved at me for this letter. I have got to look at matters from a cold business standpoint. Now that you have your application in [at American] you may any time receive a call to go to work at something somewhere.

It is no doubt very poor policy to leave LA just now—JUST TO FLY. REMEMBER, DO NOT LET YOUR ENTHUSIASM FOR ANYTHING

Nancy Love, founder and leader of the WAFS, Ferrying Division, Air Transport Command. In July 1943, she was named executive for the women pilots of the Ferrying Division. *Courtesy WASP Archive, Texas Woman's University, Denton.*

OR ANYBODY GET THE BEST OF YOUR GOOD JUDGMENT.
I went to Spokane yesterday to see Ed. He is getting on fine.

Dad

Dorothy finished the semester.

That summer, 1942, she returned to Washington and to flying and earned her flight instructor's rating. By fall, she had been hired to teach flying to military cadets at Washington State College in Pullman, Washington, over on the Idaho border. After Pearl Harbor, all nonmilitary flying, including flight instruction for the military, had been moved 100 miles inland from the coasts of the United States. Flight instructors were in demand, and women who could qualify were welcome. Dorothy had found a way to earn a living flying.

Dorothy was instructing in Pullman when she heard that the Army was looking for women to ferry liaison and primary trainer aircraft and that a woman pilot named Nancy Love was the head of the squadron being formed.

With the United States' entry into World War II, most of the male pilots who had been ferrying aircraft for the Army were reassigned to combat priorities. Ferry pilots were the men who picked up aircraft from the factories and flew them to training bases or to embarkation points for shipment abroad. They simply moved airplanes. Overnight, the Army's Ferrying Command, responsible for delivering those aircraft, was faced with moving what promised to be an ever-increasing supply of airplanes with a minimal corps of 386 flying officers and 548 enlisted men.[14] By late spring 1942, Col. William H. Tunner, newly assigned to command of the Ferrying Division (the new name for what had been known as the Ferrying Command), was desperate for pilots. In his search for them, he found help in an unusual place.

Veteran pilot Nancy Love already had suggested using experienced women pilots to fill that gap. In the summer of 1942, Tunner asked her to design a program to recruit, train, and oversee a squadron of handpicked experienced women pilots to perform ferrying duties for the Ferrying Division—but as civilians. She knew of nearly one hundred women who might qualify and was prepared to contact them all.

In September 1942, Love got the go-ahead from Maj. Gen. Harold L. George, commander of the Air Transport Command (ATC), the Ferrying Division's parent organization. She sent telegrams to eighty-three experienced women pilots. Her initial goal was a squadron of twenty-five, and eventually fifty. Getting the information via the telegrams, articles in the newspaper, and word of mouth, women from around the country began to respond. They came to New Castle Army Air Base (NCAAB) in Wilmington, Delaware, home of the 2nd Ferrying Group, for interviews, followed by flight tests and Army physicals.

As the women arrived and qualified, they began thirty days of orientation, which was designed to familiarize them with Army procedure. They began flying small liaison planes (L-2 Taylorcraft and L-4 Piper Cubs) and the PT-19A, the 175-horsepower primary trainer built at the Fairchild factory in nearby Hagerstown, Maryland. The latter was the reason the squadron was located in Wilmington. Ferrying Fairchild PT-19s would be their chief responsibility for the next several months.

This group of women, seventeen strong by the end of September 1942 and still growing, were known as the Women's Auxiliary Ferrying Squadron.

Dorothy Scott would join them in less than two months.

Barbara "B. J." Erickson in the cockpit of a C-47. *Photo from the B.J. Erickson London Family Collection.*

Chapter Two

Next Stop, Ferry Command

When Dorothy learned about the Women's Auxiliary Ferrying Squadron, she also discovered that a fellow pilot from the CPTP at the University of Washington, Barbara Jane Erickson, had gone to Wilmington, Delaware, to join them. Erickson was one of four coeds accepted for the first CPTP class at the university, spring semester 1940. Erickson had gone on to flight instructing for the CPTP and subsequently, like Dorothy, to flight instructing in eastern Washington. From there, she had gone to the WAFS.

Dorothy immediately wrote to Barbara asking for information about the program. Barbara answered promptly.[1]

Women's Auxiliary Ferrying Squadron
October 20, 1942

Dear Dorothy:

> Was very glad to hear from you and to hear that you are interested in the Ferry Command. It is all very new to me. I don't know much of the inner workings of the organization as yet but can give you all the information that I know and hope that it will help you to get what you want out of this flying business.
>
> The standard requirements are:
>
>> 500 hours certified flying time (minimum and no exceptions);
>>
>> 200 horsepower rating;
>>
>> 50 hours flying time during the past 12 months (any ship);

Commercial License;

High School Education;

American Citizenship;

Between 21 and 35 years of age;

2 letters of recommendation;

Considerable cross-country experience.

If you have these qualifications, write to Mrs. Love, WAFS, here at the Base and she will tell you the rest. You must pay your own transportation to the Base here and if you don't make it, they do not reimburse you. Not that you would not make it easy, but just to tell you the circumstances.

You must pass a flight test in a PT-19-A, in other words, a low-wing Fairchild, 175 horsepower Ranger. It is quite easy nothing more than the standard Commercial requirements, and forced landings. Then you must be passed by the Army Board, so that they OK your flying time and all of your credentials. If that is all satisfactory, you are fingerprinted and you fill out a bunch of forms, are sworn in and after all this is over, you are a Civilian Pilot for the Army Air Corps Ferrying Command.

You must stay here four weeks and take their training course. It consists of a minimum of 25 hours flying time, both in the PTs and the Cubs. Also, ground school every day from 9 until 12. Includes meteorology, navigation, military law and courtesy code, first aid, etc. It is all very interesting and they have very competent people lecturing for they are the officers from that particular branch of the service.

You have to live on Base in the barracks. It is the BOQ that the men used until we came here and is sure bare. There are about 50 rooms in the building and we all have our rooms to ourselves. We eat our meals at the Officers Mess here on the field, and find that the food is not too bad. We are still civilians, so we are not confined to the base after we are through with our work each day. But, there is this difficulty, we are about 8 miles from town and there is no definite method of transportation, so we don't get into town very often. We are usually through flying about 4 or 5 in the afternoon and from then on we are on our own.

I have two more weeks to go and then I am finished with the training and can go out on a trip. The first group of girls finished today and are due to go on a trip tomorrow. They don't know as yet what ships they are going to take or where they are going, but they sure are excited. Wish I was going with them, but guess that my time is coming later on.

Here is another thing, if you do not have 500 hours and have 200, you are eligible for Jacqueline Cochran's training course, which trains the girls for this Command. If you write to Mrs. Love and tell her your qualifications according to the above that I gave you, she will forward your letter on to Cochran and you might get into her course. That course is really a good deal and then you are sure of getting in here for that is the purpose of that course. Having your letter sent through Mrs. Love will help, so I would advise doing it that way.

I like it so very much here and have found it so very interesting. The other girls are very nice and we all get along fine together. I think that this is the real deal for us gal fliers and am so glad that we got the opportunity to do something like this. Everyone says that if the girls do a good job of ferrying these ships that we will begin getting to fly the bigger ones later on and also that there isn't much doubt that eventually we will get Commissions in the Army so that we can't leave for the duration.

Hope that I have told you all that you wanted and if there is anything else that you would like to know don't hesitate to write to me.

Best of everything—hope to see you here,
Barbara Erickson

By mid-October 1942, WAFS leader Nancy Love had just welcomed number twenty, Nancy Batson, into the fold. She needed twenty-five.

Erickson had told Dorothy that if she did not yet have five hundred hours—but had at least two hundred—she would be eligible for the program that famous race pilot Jacqueline Cochran was organizing to train young women with some flying experience to fly "the Army way."

At the time of Erickson's letter, Cochran was indeed well into setting up a flight-training facility and program for women through the Army's Flying Training Command. US Army Air Forces Commanding General H. H. "Hap" Arnold put his full backing behind the project, in writing, in a November 3, 1942, memo to the Army Air Forces Training Command, stating, "Contemplated expansion of the armed forces will tax the nation's manpower. Women must be used wherever it is practicable to do so . . . take immediate and positive action to augment to the maximum possible extent the training of women pilots."[2]

On November 16, the first class of twenty-nine women pilots reported to Houston Municipal Airport to begin training. Graduates of the program would join Nancy Love's WAFS and ferry Army trainer aircraft to cadet training fields around the country. Those entering Cochran's first class needed a minimum of two hundred hours to qualify.

Erickson's letter did tell Dorothy everything she needed to hear. She had found her answer. She knew what she wanted to do. She wanted to join the WAFS. She had just shy of five hundred hours and would need to get that 200 horsepower rating.

She wired the family the news. A quick, alarmed reply from Ed prompted her to write back immediately:[3]

203 Spaulding
Pullman, WA
Oct. 29, 1942

Dear Ed,

You sound like an old worry box—there's as much danger flying green students in old crates as there is in doing a job yourself in new planes. And money is no use to me. All I make now I put right back into renting WACOS [bi-wing trainers[4]]. Why not have someone pay me for flying them? I have no use for fine clothes or girl stuff—and there's lots of the world yet to see. You and Don have been around—I want to too.

There was the rub. Like many other young women born mostly between 1916 and 1924 who would make their way unerringly into the WAFS and what would become the larger WASP, Dorothy wanted to expand her horizons, stretch her boundaries, and—like her brothers—see the wider world that this phenomenon called World War II had dumped in their collective laps. More than twenty-five thousand young women applied to fly with what became known as the WASP, to do their part and help win that war. From that number 1,860 were selected for training and 1,074 graduated. Many, like Dorothy and Barbara Erickson, came from those college CPTP classes. They cared not one whit that they were being recruited to fly the smallest, least complicated of the Army's aircraft. Ultimately, the WASP would fly every aircraft in the Army Air Forces World War II arsenal. The women flew every aircraft assigned to them—including the relics and retreads headed for the boneyard as well as the fastest top-of-the-line pursuits. Most would, at some point, perform what Cochran herself termed "the dishwashing jobs"[5] of the Army. And they did it willingly, happily, and well. They were flying.

Jary Johnson McKay, a WASP from the second class to enter training (43-2), relates what Cochran told her class when they met her for the first time in December 1942: "Girls, I am going to tell you something and I want you to know this before you get into ferrying. It is not a glamorous life. You won't know from one day to the next where you are going to be sleeping that night."

Jary said she thought at the time, "What else is glamorous but that? I thought that was really strange that she thought that was not glamorous. Of course, that's the way it was. And it was glamorous!"[6]

Dorothy and Ed exchanged many thoughts they did not share with the rest of the family. Perhaps it was a twin thing. The two were good friends as well as brother and sister. She may have bristled at his questioning the safety and wisdom of flying for the Ferry Command, but still she could share concerns with him that she would not share with her mother, her father, or Donald.

She continued her October 29 letter to Ed:

> It looks like I'll not have to wait for another program to enter the WAFS. According to Barbara Erickson all I need is 500 hours and a 200 h.p. rating. These I can get by staying on here another week or two and fly the WACO. However, I have to wait for an answer from the officials of it before knowing where I stand.
>
> According to Barbara it is the real thing for girls in flying. We take a 4-week training course then are sent out on jobs all over the country. It will be all light ships at first but has a very promising future.
>
> If I go back east (Wilmington Delaware) I want to drive if possible. If I do drive, mom may go with me. I could meet her in Colorado Springs maybe.
>
> I'm getting pretty good pushing a WACO around, but lots of funny things happen—and some not so funny. I lost my Gregg pen during a slow-roll last week and this 98-cent substitute isn't so hot.

[The slow roll is a maneuver in midflight where the airplane wings roll 360 degrees around the aircraft's longitudinal axis, so that halfway through it is flying upside down. The roll continues until the airplane completes the 360 degrees. Dorothy was flying an open-cockpit airplane, so the pen was lost overboard when she was upside down.]

The day I lost the pen, I was wearing new shoes with leather soles that would slip off the rudder pedals at the most inopportune time. Once I was doing a snap roll and had just gotten on my back when my foot slipped, which made the plane dive out underneath like a Split-S or a loop. Good thing I had lots of altitude. Now I wear my rubber boots always.

[A snap roll is just what it sounds like, a rapid rather than a slow 360-degree revolution of the aircraft on its longitudinal axis in midflight.]

Yesterday I took a secondary student up with me and did snap rolls. He did some too. On return, he said his safety belt wasn't working—he hadn't had it on! Ye gods, good thing I did good snap rolls or gravity might have got him.

My students are all doing OK if the weather will let us keep flying. This a.m. I went out dual at 7 a.m. There was only a 2,000-foot ceiling so we did most low work, tho we did some stalls and pulled the nose right up into the clouds. We dove out quick-like, but some kids went into them and spun out—the dopes.

On the return to the field the wind had picked up to 30 m.p.h. so we had our hands full getting down. It surely was funny. If we closed the throttle completely we stood still, so we used throttle and dove it in. Everyone ran out to grab our wings to hold us down, but I held it O.K. by stick forward and throttle to keep the tail up. Everyone else did the same. Thank goodness no student was up solo.

I haven't heard from Pop yet about the Ferry Command but he'll let me go, tho it will leave him alone again, darn it. That's the only part that I don't like, but I can't let it keep me here. He can close the garage and spend his time visiting us kids. How far is Delaware from North Carolina?

[Dorothy didn't need her father's permission, she was twenty-two, but apparently she asked for his nod of approval anyway.]

This letter is too long. Send it to mom, please, cause I'd hate to write all these incidents again.

I saw Jim last weekend again and was surprised how well I liked him all over again. But it isn't enough to hold me here. He'll be going overseas soon anyhow. He gave me a picture of him so he's right up there with you and Don now.

[Jim Laferty, a cattle rancher from Chelan, Washington, was Dorothy's "first real boyfriend back in 1940," according to Ed.[7]]

I got the paper. I also got the *Oro-Gazette*. Maybe I'll write in some day and give them some "me" dope.

Bye,

Your Sis

Nancy Love's response to Dorothy was positive, much to Dorothy's relief. Love told her that if she could pass her 200-horsepower rating, she was to report to Wilmington on November 21, 1942. Dorothy immediately called the Civil Air Authority in Spokane and got an appointment to take a check ride in a WACO.

From what Dorothy told her mother in that Thanksgiving Day letter home, apparently the check pilot felt a great urge to show off a bit for his pretty but very determined student. "What a ride!" she wrote. "Dodging clouds, all aerobatics and hedgehopping and he did most of the flying." But Dorothy very definitely got what she came for—her 200-horsepower rating. That was all that stood between her and the WAFS.

As Dorothy had told Ed, she planned to drive east to Wilmington, but it was G. M., not her mother, who made the drive with her. That way they could split the driving between them. And, for G. M., it was a chance to visit his two soldier sons. Ed was in Colorado Springs and Don was now in North Carolina. Afterwards he would have a good sense of "where" both Don and Ed were when he wrote to them or received their letters. Likewise, he would get a good look at where Dorothy was going to be.

Dorothy immediately called her father to tell him she had passed her horsepower check ride and was due in Wilmington November 21. He met her in Spokane. Not only had she earned her rating, she now had 504 hours in her logbook—enough to fully qualify for the WAFS. They headed south in Dorothy's car through Salt Lake City and then east on Highway 30. They hit a little snow in Utah, but outside of that they had ideal weather on into Colorado Springs.

Dorothy and her father arrived in Delaware Friday night, November 20. She reported to New Castle Army Air Base the following morning. When her interview with Nancy Love was completed, Dorothy was hus-

tled out to the flight line for a check ride, which she passed easily. Then
G. M. left for North Carolina to visit Don.

Dorothy's letter to her mother, written Thanksgiving Day, November
26, 1942, picks up here:

Now for more details of this place. The post is new and not very large. It is
about 7 miles from Wilmington and I'm glad my car is here.

We WAFS have this one barracks that isn't quite finished. We have separate rooms with plain boards, army cots, one dresser, one wardrobe (open)
and one scatter rug. Aside from mice—walking noise—and mud it's fine.
My room is #13 so I ought to be lucky.

We can wear civilian clothes for dress but are issued all flying equipment—which is some array. (Military secrets, etc.) We wear khaki cover-
alls and leather jackets mostly.

We get up at 7, class from 8 to 11:45 consisting now of drill, meteorology, and navigation and later to include military law and first aid, etc. It isn't
at all hard for me and I enjoy it very much. After lunch (we eat in officers'
mess) we report to the field for flying—weather permitting. After 5 our
time is our own. There is the post theatre (15 cents) and officers' club (I
haven't been there yet).

The girls who have finished training go out on trips and are gone for
days. Most trips are south. They go in bunches.

The whole deal is exciting and wonderful. The more I see of it the better
I like it.

We get $250 per month (even in training (4 wks)) and $6 a day for
expenses while on trips. We pay up to 50 cents a meal and 4.50 a week for
our rooms.

The flying instructors and ground school are officers who are swell. All
the girls (total 25—I'm 25th!) are ok too. They are a little older mostly
and many are famous. I am not worried about my ability in comparison
though.

We pay out about $50 for dress uniforms for after we graduate.

To back up some. Ed is fine and I like his girl very much. Dad didn't like
the idea much before he met her but now it's ok.

I hope to go see Don soon—or vice versa—but Dad says he's ok too.
Dad saw Wash. D.C. between trains and visited Don quite a bit.

I have just returned from my first dual hop in an L-2B. We fly those and
PT-19-A's—which sound like bombers but are really much like the ships
I've been flying.

Now I must rush to get the last of the turkey—4:00 o'clock.

I'll write again soon.

For Xmas send me Airmail stamps or silk scarf.

By,

D. Scott.

W.A.F.S.

New Castle Army Air Base

Wilmington, Del.

By the time G. M. arrived back in Oroville, he had covered seven thousand miles via car and train. He dropped by the newspaper office and gave Mr. I. J. Doerr, the editor of the *Oroville Gazette*, a full account of the journey, which was published early in December 1942.[8]

It was two weeks before Dorothy had time to write again. By then she had heard from her mother several times—each letter full of questions. So Dorothy got busy and answered as many questions as possible.

December 13, 1942

Dear Mom,

Your letters of 9th and 11th show that I must be keeping you jumping.

Starting next week my life will be a matter of 12 hrs. here each two weeks and the rest of the time on the road. It's really hectic but wonderful.

You ask me about my experiences, they really accumulate but seem even common place to me now. I'll give some daily routine.

Saturday is parade day except that it was called off yesterday on account of fog. Usually the entire post marches out onto a runway and forms by squadrons with the WAFS last. If there are only 4 on the post we don't make a very large showing. We stand at attention and get inspected, then "at ease" while our leader calls down the line "present or accounted for, sir." Then we "right face, forward march" and go past the colonel (commanding officer) and his staff doing "eyes right." Then we march back to the hangar, fall out, and dash for a radiator to warm up.

Ground school is really unique. With only 4 of us in class it's very informal and varied. We get in on any special lecture being given officers so I've learned everything from tropical diseases to altitude flying.

Then we accumulate lessons in drill, manual of arms (with rifles) gas mask drill, Morse code, and even taking machine guns apart. It's not that we are going to use all this, but it's available so we learn it and do I like it! I can do a neat "present arms" or yank down a sub-machine gun using only a cartridge. I know sentry procedure and how the army is organized, and can put on a gas mask in about 3 seconds.

Then for my own information I explore airplanes in the hangars—all types from the Flying Fortress to our little liaison craft. Also I'm going to get Link Trainer[9] time after I graduate—(we can't before.)

The social scene also was of interest to Dorothy's mother, so naturally Dorothy had to report on that.

You want to know about the social life too. Well, mostly it's very casual and we "date" in bunches: We have a speaking acquaintance with lots of officers; we eat with them and see them around all the time. I go around mostly with a girl who is extremely good looking and popular, so much so it's often awkward for her. It helps me out to go double dating with her because it means the best selection of officers. I've had a few dates on my own but these fellows being ferry pilots are here for a few hours, then gone for days. They go to Africa and England, Florida and Texas.

Last nite we went to the mess hall to eat and meet 2 officers we'd dated before so we went to the post theatre with them. (It was "7 Sweethearts"—a musical of old Vienna—see it) then to the officers club where I found myself playing bridge with the Adjutant—(A top man here tho only a Lt.) He was too good at it though so I didn't enjoy it especially and left early. Often at the club we just dance and drink (I have one drink then just Cokes). This situation is only while we're training, then it be a matter of geography.

Dorothy's comment in her first letter about famous people prompted her mother to write and ask "what famous people?" so Dorothy responded with a list.

The famous people who you may or may not have heard of.

Mrs. Betty Gillies whose husband is vice president of Grumman Aircraft. She is tops in women flying clubs and has a multiengine rating and is second in command here.

Mrs. Nancy Love—read in Jan. *American* [magazine] under famous people. (our chief)

Mrs. Katherine (Rawls) Thompson—Olympic swim champion twice. Her husband is in the R.A.F. ferry division.

Pat Rhonie has much flying time, drove ambulance in France. Did a mural of flying in N.Y.

Cornelia Fort—was in Pearl Harbor the right time.

Jackie Cochran—runs training school in Texas for reserve WAFS. Very much disliked, is overbearing. She inspected this place the other day but I was flying and didn't see her.

Look Mag. for Jan. 15 (about) will feature us and I'm in the picture of the PT taking off and maybe some more.

Don will be here the 15th or 16th and I'm getting all thrilled about it. I'm trying to get red tape slashed so I can take him on one of my practice trips. They are trying to push us thru so we can start ferrying this next Wed. or Thur. But weather is tough so we'll not get in our 25 hrs transition minimum by then. (I'm glad otherwise I'd miss Don.)

The clothing situation is under control, though I can use scarves. I wear them all the time and after I start traveling washing will be a problem. They must be long ones—4' at least, and not narrowed at the neck (sq'd best). You see, my flying suit is fleece-lined which means wool and so I will pull my scarves up around my face so they must be large. Also, the PT's are open planes and the wind howls.

I'm going to ask Ed to come here and get my car, as I haven't enough use for it to keep it here.

Oh yes, we are not commissioned officers when we graduate, still civilians, the commission means like Don and is only a future possibility, so don't write to "Lt. Dorothy."

Dorothy

Thanks for stamps—send more.

Food for Christmas is nice.

Don did come for a visit and Dorothy did take him up in the PT-19, but she didn't have permission to do so. Taking a passenger up while on a practice trip was a no-no, and Nancy Love promptly called her on the carpet. Thoroughly chastened, Dorothy carried the sting of the reprimand on her conscience for long afterwards. She very much admired and respected her boss and wanted to stay in her good graces. Now she feared she had forever blown any confidence Nancy had in her or her leadership ability.[10]

Dorothy and the three other WAFS going through orientation in December were the last hired in 1942. Dorothy Fulton, Betsy Ferguson, Bernice Batten, and Dorothy Scott were numbers twenty-two through twenty-five of the original squadron. The other twenty-one women had completed orientation and were assigned to ferrying duty. They were hardly on base for a day before being sent out again. One group of six had left the base on a trip out west, December 4, and still had not returned by Christmas. Consequently, the final four admitted that fall barely met, let alone got to know, the other twenty-one. Then, as the four completed orientation, they were stopped from leaving on a trip because new orders had been received. A big change was in the air.

The twenty-five original WAFS were being split up. Five each would go to three other Ferrying Division bases to form new women's squadrons. Ten would remain at New Castle to ferry the PT-19s. Nancy Love was taking the first group with her to Love Field in Dallas, Texas. Nancy chose Dorothy to make the move with her. She also selected Betsy Ferguson, Florene Miller, and Helen Richards. They would be the first women to be stationed with the 5th Ferrying Group there, and as 1943 dawned, the five took leave of Wilmington.

Love Field was not named for Nancy—nor for her husband, Major Robert M. Love, Air Transport Command. Rather, it was named for 1st Lt. Moss L. Love, of Wright County, South Carolina, the tenth Army officer to lose his life in an airplane accident, September 4, 1913.[11]

Love opted to place Miller in command of the squadron rather than take the job herself. Nancy had other priorities to tackle. From Love Field, she soon would move to Romulus, Michigan, to oversee the formation of the women's squadron attached to the 3rd Ferrying Group. Later, she would do the same for the 6th Ferrying Group in Long Beach, California.

Building the new squadrons was her primary mission for her commanding officer, Col. William H. Tunner, commander of the Ferrying Division. The first class of twenty-nine women trainees—Jacqueline Cochran's recruits—had reported mid-November 1942 to a training facility located at the airport next to the Army's Ellington Field at Houston, Texas. The second class, numbering fifty-one, reported mid-December.

What drove Love, personally, was her desire to prove to her military superiors that women could fly more than just single-engine primary trainers. By transitioning, as the Army called it—moving up step by step through ever more complicated airplanes—she intended to fly anything the Army built. Nancy knew that if she did it, the other women could do it, too, and she planned to convince her superiors of that.

Love had established her credibility with her commanding officers. She had Colonel Tunner and General George's tacit approval to check out on any aircraft she thought she could handle.[12] Nancy's gift was an ability to lead. She would pave the way for the others.

Before leaving Wilmington, Dorothy wrote a hurried letter to her father about her transfer.

December 29, 1942

Dear Dad:

I'm being transferred to Dallas, Texas, immediately, to learn to fly larger airplanes. The WAFS are being split up to form the nucleus for bigger groups. (Shh—military secret—the works.)

I didn't go on any trips here—was on orders for one to South Carolina but was told not to go.

Leaving by car Jan. 1. Will leave my car at Coffeyville, Kansas, for Ed & drive on in my friend Betsy's car. This paper cannot be reprinted exactly but maybe Doerr [editor of the *Oroville Gazette*] could make a "Local News" off it please.

I haven't time to tell everyone I'm moving.

What-a-life—

Dorothy

I'll send details when I know more.

Chapter Three
Dallas!

Dorothy and Betsy Ferguson, two of the last four WAFS to join in 1942, struck up a friendship while working their way through the thirty-day orientation required of the women ferry pilots before they went on active flying duty. Betsy was the "good looking and popular" WAFS with whom Dorothy double-dated. Both were scheduled to make a delivery in late December, but their orders were canceled. They were given orders to proceed immediately to Dallas as part of the new women's squadron to be attached to the 5th Ferrying Group there.

Each had a travel dilemma that, when they compared notes, could be solved by a cooperative venture and traveling together. Dorothy wanted to get her car to her brother, Ed. Betsy wanted to go home and get her car and drive it to Dallas. Betsy lived in Coffeyville, Kansas—about three-fifths of the distance to Colorado Springs from Wilmington. They would drive Dorothy's car to Coffeyville—near the Kansas-Oklahoma border—leave it there for Ed to pick up at his earliest convenience, and they would drive Betsy's car on to Dallas.

The government issued them travel orders and gave them $6 a day for travel expenses plus nine coupons, each good for one full tank of gas. They left New Year's Day. The 1,250-mile-trip took them three days. Then, driving Betsy's car, they headed for Dallas on January 5, another 350 miles south.

Betsy was born Opal Hulet on August 19, 1912, in Arkansas. The Hulet family then moved to Coffeyville when she was a toddler known as Bitsy, which evolved into Betsy. As a youngster and on into her teens, pretty, blue-eyed blonde Betsy was never known to turn down a dare. She was a classic headstrong risk-taker. If anyone doubted that, she proved it for keeps when she married Lee Ferguson at age seventeen. The marriage was not for keeps, however, as they were married and divorced three times between 1930 and 1943.[1] Betsy was in the process of divorce when she joined the WAFS.

In their twenties, Betsy and her older sister Sally Duncan both fell in love with flying. They received their private pilot's licenses the same day: August 26, 1938. Betsy then became the first woman in Kansas to receive her commercial pilot's license. Sally followed suit. Both earned instructor ratings. In 1941, when Sally's husband, Hank Duncan, was granted a government-subsidized Civilian Pilot Training Program contract, he hired Betsy and Sally to teach college students to fly through CPTP and later the War Training Service programs at Coffeyville Junior College.

In the fall of 1942, with 873 flight hours to her credit, Betsy headed for Wilmington to join the WAFS. She was the twenty-third woman accepted by Nancy Love, arriving a few days before Dorothy.

The Dallas transfer had come as a complete surprise to both Dorothy and Betsy. Dorothy was thrilled to be part of establishing a new squadron and considered it quite an honor. "We keep hearing that Dallas is the most important base for the WAFS now," she wrote her father. "We don't know what we're in for, but it seems like twin-engine school and all heavier planes are a good possibility."

During World War I, the Dallas Chamber of Commerce negotiated with the Army Signal Corps (precursor to the Army Air Corps) to establish an aviation training school in the Dallas area. The chamber found a suitable site seven miles north of downtown Dallas on the south side of Lake Bachman.[2] The Army opened Love Field on October 19, 1917. The United States had been actively engaged in the war for six months.[3]

In June 1928, the City of Dallas bought the 167.10 acres for $325,000. Several airlines began building service out of Love. The first paved runways were completed in 1934. The air traffic control tower was commissioned in 1937.

When World War II came along, Dallas was the perfect locale for a military flight base. It was central to numerous aviation schools, manufac-

New Dallas ferry pilots Betsy Ferguson, Florene Miller, and Helen Richards at Love Field, January 12, 1943. Wearing uniform slacks and Army-issue leather bomber jackets, with parachutes slung over their shoulders, they are walking past a line of twin-engine trainers. Dorothy had just broken her collarbone and was not flying. *From the author's personal collection.*

turers and modification centers. The Army reactivated Love Field as a major military aircraft modification center and made it the home of the 5th Ferrying Group—the men, and later the women, who would ferry those aircraft. The women ferried to points all across the United States and into Canada. The male ferry pilots flew the globe.

Aircraft built in the Dallas–Fort Worth area, and ferried by the men of the 5th Ferrying Group, included the B-24 Liberator, built at Consolidated's Fort Worth plant; the AT-6 trainer and later the P-51 Mustang, manufactured at the North American plant at Grand Prairie; and the P-38 Lightning, which was modified at Love Field's Lockheed Mod Center.[4]

In 1943, the women of Love Field's 601st WASP squadron[5] began to ferry BT-13 basic trainers and the locally built AT-6 advanced trainers. They were sent TDY (temporary duty) to Wichita, Kansas, to pick up and ferry the Stearman PT-17, a bi-wing, open-cockpit primary trainer. Later, they went TDY to Wichita to check out on and ferry the twin-engine Cessnas and Beeches manufactured there.[6] Throughout 1944, the women also served as copilots on the B-24s, and those who had successfully trained as pursuit pilots ferried the P-51s and P-38s.

With the dawn of the New Year, 1943, more history was about to be made at Love Field. The first week of January, the men of the 5th Ferrying

Group and all other personnel at Love Field were about to encounter a new challenge: the arrival of their first five women ferry pilots. The job of welcoming them fell to base commander Col. Thomas D. Ferguson [no relation to Betsy].

Nancy Love's reputation preceded her. Her background and her standing with the powers-that-be in the Air Transport Command assured her warm welcome. One of Nancy's strengths was the ability to walk into any Operations office in the Ferrying Division and give help wherever and however needed—and with surety and finesse. Colonel Ferguson was aware of this.[7]

Nevertheless, Dorothy still had the feeling that, overall, their arrival came as a bit of a surprise. She wrote to G. M. on January 8:

> Honestly, the army is 99% red tape. We got here the 6th and since the post only seemed amazed to see us, we had to spend the night in town at a hotel. There we found Mrs. Love and 2 others, but the next A.M. we got moved into our quarters, the new nurses' quarters consisting mainly of fresh paint and muddy walks. This base is lots nicer than NCAAB mainly because the buildings are cheerful light grey.
>
> The first day was spent wading through red tape and black mud and meeting lots of the powers-that-be. The only objection I have to this place is that we're constantly on dress parade. Being the first WAFS here we're really noticed. Everyone is both friendly and curious. It's great to have Mrs. Love right along to do the talking. (My daily prayer is that I keep my mouth shut.)
>
> Now I'm in the Alert Room (transition room here) waiting again. I'll get a flight in today if I'm lucky. We start in BTs, which are about 400 wild hp [horsepower] and has me considerably worried. But everyone says they're easier than Cubs or WACOs. All of us except Mrs. Love are new to this high HP stuff, so we're all some disturbed by it all.
>
> These ships will be radio equipped so yesterday we had ground school on radio procedure. Our future is still unknown to me so I can't tell you much about it all except that we'll be advancing to higher ships.
>
> A lot is not to be talked about too so if my letters say nothing, that's why.
>
> I'm sure you'll be pleased with the way things worked out. Mrs. Love asked how you liked the idea of Dallas for me but I said I hadn't heard yet.

On December 15, Nancy Love had checked out on the 450-horsepower single-engine BT-13, the basic trainer used by male flight-training cadets that also was slated to be used by Jackie Cochran's young women recruits who by then were training in Houston, Texas. It was the next step up the ladder from the primary trainer, and now Nancy's girls in Dallas were going to be the first to follow her into that transition. Dorothy flew her first BT on January 9.

But there, Dorothy's progress came to a screeching halt. She and some of the other WAFS went horseback riding when they had some free time. The time turned costly as Dorothy, for all of her previous riding experience, took a tumble and broke her collarbone. How she must have relived that sinking feeling, that agonizing moment when she realized what she had done. She couldn't fly until it healed.

Nancy Love surveyed the damage and acted. She had Dorothy assigned to a Link Trainer instructor and asked that her injured pilot be given a thorough course in using the simulator to learn instrument flying. Dorothy would get a jump on the others in that department while she was grounded.

With that began a love affair between Dorothy and the "little blue box." Talk about making lemonade when someone gives you lemons. She proved adept at instrument training from the beginning, even though she fell behind in her aircraft transition for a good four weeks. The proficiency she gained in those otherwise lost weeks would stand her in good stead many times when she started ferrying.

The Link Trainer was for practicing flying on instruments only. When the door and hood are closed on the stubby little box, the student is left in the dark except for the lighted instruments and her navigation paperwork. She then practices flying without visual contact with the ground. Meanwhile, the instructor sits at a desk outside the trainer and follows her flight, which is projected on paper with a stylus.[8]

On January 3, Nancy Love checked out in the Dallas-built North American advanced trainer, the AT-6, the plane that followed the BT in transition. The AT-6 had retractable gear, a 600-horsepower engine, and cruised at around 160 mph. Following Nancy's lead, the WAFS would transition into the AT-6—as would the women training in Houston. After that, the women would fly the small twin-engine planes built by Cessna and Beechcraft that also were classified as advanced trainers.

Nancy flew an AT-6 to Romulus, Michigan, outside Detroit on January 13. Romulus was the location of the 3rd Ferrying Group and to be the home of Nancy's third women's ferry squadron. She went up to help her newly appointed squadron leader Adela "Del" Scharr get the squadron

Dorothy Scott, Betsy Ferguson, and Florene Miller dressed in winter flight gear. *Courtesy: The Scott Family Collection.*

up and running. The other WAFS stationed there were Barbara Donahue, Barbara Poole, Katherine Rawls Thompson, and Phyllis Burchfield.

Nancy got weathered in and spent nearly two weeks in Romulus. While she was there—when the ceiling lifted sufficiently for a flight in the AT-6— she checked out Lenore McElroy, a local flight instructor with thirty-five hundred hours. Lenore had not come to Wilmington to apply for the WAFS because she could not be stationed there. She was the mother of three teenagers and was married to a Romulus ferry pilot. Only if both of them could fly out of Romulus could she serve. Then Operations could schedule them on alternating trips. Now that there was a women's squadron in Romulus, that was possible.

Thus, Lenore became the twenty-eighth and final member of the original WAFS. Betty Gillies, who had replaced Nancy Love as squadron leader in Wilmington, had added two more women ferry pilots to the squadron when Helen McGilvery and Kathryn "Sis" Bernheim passed their flight checks and Army physicals on January 3—after Dorothy and the other four had left for Dallas.

On January 25, two days after McElroy was accepted, General Arnold's office issued a memo stating that, from that date, the Ferrying Division would employ only those women who had graduated from the Women's Flying Training School (WFTD) in Texas.[9]

Nancy Love's squadron of twenty-eight original WAFS was complete.

By January 25, 1943, 135 women, the first three WFTD classes, were in training at Houston's Municipal Airport. These women, upon graduation, were destined to be sent to one of the four WAFS squadrons to ferry the Army's trainer aircraft manufactured near those bases. A fourth class, already forming, would add another 152 fledgling pilots, more than doubling the number in training. The classes were designated by number and by the year in which they would graduate. The designation also carried a capital W denoting this was a class of women pilots. Class 43-W-1 led the way, followed by Class 43-W-2. Eight classes would graduate in 1943. Ten classes would graduate in 1944. Henceforth, the "W" is deleted because it is understood that we are discussing women pilot graduates.

On January 24, Dorothy wrote to G. M.:

> I'm flying the Link about every day now, and am doing ok. I can't reach the throttle with my left hand yet, but my instructor sets it for me before closing the hood and I get practice on timed turns and orientation procedure, etc. I do a lot of "book learnin'" too.
>
> Mrs. Love hasn't returned from Detroit yet, but when she does she's going to get one excellent report on our conduct here. Several officers have told us we're "just like the fellows" and we do need that rating! Mrs. Love is so concerned about how we'll be accepted here.
>
> A fellow killed himself off yesterday in an AT-6 by doing some illegal stunting over the city. He went into a woods at 250 per and burned up. What a mess. You should see our backyard junk pile. No, I didn't know the fellow.
>
> The other girls have been on only two trips in BTs. Today they were told

"we're all out of BTs for a while, so maybe you'll be checked out in AT's soon!" Golly, I hope they don't get too far ahead of me. Another two weeks ought to see me out of this brace, boy, will I be glad!

Did I tell you we're now getting inoculated against everything in the book? All of us are walking around with sore arms. Any more shots and a look would knock us over.

Dorothy did get good news when she saw the doctor January 29. She wrote to G. M. on January 30:

I saw the doc yesterday. He was pleasantly surprised at how well it's doing, better than he'd hoped for. He says I can start flying again next week—dual anyway, so I can finish checking out on the BT.

BT means basic trainer (as PT means primary trainer—what we flew in Wilmington) and AT means advanced trainer. The BTs are 450 h.p. with fixed landing gear but radio, trim tabs, and about 140 mph. They are low wing jobs with the "greenhouse hatch covers."

In the AT class are several types. That AT-6 is like the BT except that it has retractable gear, 650 h.p. and 160 mph. Also ATs are the small twin-engine planes built by Cessna and Beechcraft. They are for transitional training into big stuff. How far we go is limited to ourselves—just what we can handle. All the girls are still on BTs now tho.

I'm doing fine on the Link. Now I'm able to catch myself in any part of the range, find a beam, and fly home. I haven't been able to reach the throttle due to my brace but my instructor sets it for me and I fly at constant speed. As soon as I can do it I'll start using it for climbing and let down procedures. My biggest trouble is trying to watch everything at once; if I'm concentrating on the turn and bank, my air speed gets away (I'm going up or down) but I'm getting better all the time and have yet to spin in or hit the ground.

Mrs. Love got back this A.M. So things will move faster again.

Look magazine published a big article on the WAFS in its February 9, 1943, issue. All the women originally stationed at New Castle Army Air Base at Wilmington were featured, and Dorothy was in several photos. The magazine came out in late January, and the country finally learned something about the women fliers.

The squadron stood at twenty-five when the story was photographed and written in early December 1942. The Ferrying Division tried very hard to shield the WAFS from the glare of publicity. This five-page article accompanied by a dozen photos was the first of its kind sanctioned by their commanding officer Colonel Tunner and the Ferrying Division:[10]

> As men pilots leave for duty overseas, these members of the Women's Auxiliary Ferrying Squadron take their places delivering fighter and liaison planes from factory to training fields and embarkation bases throughout the continental United States. They live in wooden barracks, sleep on iron cots, fly day and night, sometimes in open cockpits, in zero weather, perform their hazardous duties with the skill born of hundreds of hours of flying time. These women are the elite of America's auxiliary services.

The statements were a bit of dramatic embellishment. At this point the Ferry Command had no plans for the women to ferry fighter aircraft. Also, ferry pilots were forbidden to fly at night and in bad weather.

In January 1943, after the *Look* magazine issue featuring the WAFS came out, the *Oroville Gazette*—in typical small-town newspaper style, particularly in that day and age—reported that Dorothy's dad, G. M. Scott, "was so excited about seeing Dorothy's picture in the magazine that he almost bought out the complete supply at the magazine stands, at least we had a hard time finding one to buy."[11]

G. M. sent her a copy of the newspaper article, and Dorothy wrote back:

> I'll admit the *Look* pictures of me were anything but good. However, I was the only one of the bunch who was *really* flying right then. I had just come down and was half frozen and didn't have any leather pants on—only the jacket so I had to stay in the background. I went out again immediately, which was when they shot the take off picture. Yes, I'm in the classroom shot too.
>
> *Look* hasn't sold out here but lots more Dallas people know us now. I hate to think of the deluge of fan mail the NCAAB branch will get. I'm pleased that we finally got some real publicity so people won't say, "How cute! What do you do—sell war bonds?"

Chapter Four
Back to Flying

Dorothy's January 30, 1943, letter to her father had given him too much information and she found it necessary to administer a mild scolding. Her enthusiasm for the coming transition into the BT and AT in that letter had spurred her very proud father to drift overboard in his bragging in the hometown newspaper, possibly to the point that she feared it could cause some repercussions. Dorothy dashed off a "cease and desist" letter.

Now listen, pop, don't go making a hero out of me or anything. The future is all too uncertain to talk about what I'm going to do, so best stick to history. Mrs. Love said it would be about a month before we get to fly ATs. Holy cats, when you think that Cubs were the thing just a couple months ago, the BTs are something. And also be careful about quoting statistics on these ships. If you read it in some magazine, OK, but not my dope on them.

I'd like to write Mr. Doerr and thank him for the write up, but it might be printed, and we're not allowed to have anything put in a newspaper unless it comes through Washington D.C., as did the *Look* article. I know Mrs. Love *told me* not to write the paper. So you thank him for me.

I now have 10 hours in the Link and my instructor told me she thought I could get safely home, if not artfully, in any instrument weather. However, each day I get another lesson and I get closer to being even more safe. A Link is not a plane. That will be something else again. Wait 'til I get 100 hours Link time. Today in the Link I really had my hands full doing precision climbs and glides at certain number of feet and minutes while also doing turns to certain headings by compass only. And the compass oscillates, so I have to do it by timing and fast math. Usually I use a gyro that doesn't oscillate.

Your daughter,
Who isn't flying anything at the moment!

On February 3, Dorothy's doctor told her that she could fly if she left the brace on, but the flight surgeon at the base said she could fly only with it off. She was grounded for another week. Still, she had the Link. The next day she did so well, her Link instructor insisted that she save the results for her scrapbook.

Dorothy went back on flying status February 11.

February 13, 1943

Dear Dad:

At last—I'm flying again. Wednesday I was put back on flying status, and I was receiving congratulations from nearly everyone. Thursday AM I reported in and started being checked out. 1 hour and 45 minutes later I soloed and that afternoon and the next day flew 5 solo hours.

I'd been grounded so long that just that wore me out 100%. Afterward I was told by my check pilot that the head officer had asked, "Are you sure she can handle it?" "I'm positive," he answered, but the head guy went out anyway and watched me! Horrors, I'm glad I didn't know until afterwards. He said I did fine. (You see, 3 hours dual is required and they counted my 1:20 time a month ago in it.)

It was wonderful to be flying again, I just sat up there feeling sorry for the people below me.

I flew to a neighboring field to shoot some landings and had a good time changing radio stations and calling in. The tower there must have fallen over at hearing a girl's voice because a little later I heard, "Army 214 from Hensley tower, what is the pilot's name please?"

"Dorothy Scott WAFS," I answered, and did not ask "why?"

One funny thing happened on my first solo. I taxied out to the waiting runway behind a B-25 and alongside a flock of BTs like mine. Well, I wanted to find out if I should stay behind the B-25 or go to the BT side so I called the tower and said "Dallas tower from Army 214 on the runway," and got told, "Army 214 cleared for take off." Wow! "Holy Cats!" I an-

WAFS leader Nancy Love flew this P-51/A-36 on February 27, 1943. She was the first woman to fly the high-performance Mustang, and in doing so she paved the way for 130 of her fellow women ferry pilots to do the same. *Courtesy WASP Archive, Texas Woman's University, Denton.*

swered, "I'm stuck behind all these planes!" They didn't answer, just cleared another ship. (All planes can hear all the tower says, tower gets planes, but no plane-to-plane hearing.) Now I'm smarter but I'll bet the tower was thinking—dumb women!

Anyway, now I'm waiting for orders for my first trip, and will likely go out Monday. The catch is that the rest of the girls are today starting to check out in AT-6s, but I can't because I have to have some trips first, so one of the girls and I will go on trips next week then it'll be AT-6s for me too. My shoulder did a bit of aching from unaccustomed use but it's ok.

Nuffs-nuff!
Dorothy

It was Florene Miller who offered to make the delivery trip with Dorothy so that she could catch up. That trip turned into a highlight for both of them.

Florene Miller had been Nancy Love's choice to lead the Dallas squadron in January 1943 because Nancy knew she herself would not remain on base long. A Texas native, Florene learned to fly when her father bought a silver Luscombe airplane in 1940 so that his four children could contribute

Delphine Bohn, in front of a P-38, assumed command of the WASP squadron at the 5th Ferrying Group, Love Field, in December 1943. *Reprinted with permission of Delphine Bohn Collection, History of Aviation Collection, Special Collections and Archives Division, Eugene McDermott Library, The University of Texas at Dallas.*

to the coming war effort by learning to fly. He knew aviation would play a big part. Florene could hardly wait to get home from college that spring and fly. She soloed at nineteen, acquired her needed ratings, and went on to teach flying with the War Training Program—the 1941 successor to CPTP. She was number thirteen to join the WAFS in September 1942.

Since Dorothy was the one who needed the practice, she got to do all the navigating on the trip and did just fine, even though they had radio trouble.

February 23, 1943

Dear Pop:

I must hurry and tell you about my trip yesterday. It's hard to believe so much fun could be had in so little time.

First, in the morning another girl and I were put on orders, just us two. We got all cleared, etc. and carried box lunches (courtesy Red Cross) and went to our planes. Well, first thing off is our radios were a new type. We finally figured them out ourselves, by guess-and-gosh, and took off. I did all the navigating and had enough to do what with trying to find the right beam. Nothing exciting happened but just the routine flying was wonderful. After 3 hours we got to our destination. I got their tower on the radio, but had too much static. Florene didn't get them at all so we came in anyway by watching traffic.

We landed and taxied in and before we could get out of our ships we were mobbed. It seems they could hear me fine and knew it was girls, so it being a new and somewhat remote post, it created considerable excitement.

The personnel in charge fell all over themselves trying to help us and we were "dated up for the rest of the week in five minutes."

However we asked for bus schedules and figured on a 7:15 one. (It was 5 then.) In the intermission we were escorted to the officers club and mess. During dinner we couldn't eat a bite for being introduced so much and talked to.

During dinner our "private escorts" a major and a captain, said we couldn't leave so soon so they'd fly us to Memphis, Tennessee, so we could catch an airliner home at 11 instead of 4 AM.

Swish! Before we knew it, it was all planned. With a few minutes to kill then, the Airdrome Officer "checked me out" in a motor scooter and we two went tearing all over the post, bumpy roads in scooters.

Then we climbed in BTs again (different ones) Major and Florene vs. Capt. and I. To do it up right we made a formation take off between smudge pots lining the runways. Remember, it was night! Oh pop, I'll never in all my life forget that ride! There we were nearly touching the next plane and guided only by small lights and the flare of the exhaust.

I was so busy watching the next plane that for a moment I forgot to look around, but soon I did, and the rapidly fading field looked like a million small fires.

We cruised in close formation for quite a ways, then we separated some. All of a sudden—swish, and we were in a snap-roll! I'd tightened my belt but did it even more, and from there to Memphis I had trouble telling when we were right side up and when we weren't. Loops, slow rolls, Immelmans, and everything else kept me plenty on the jump. I've never had such a ride. It was a very clear night but dark so the stars above looked a lot like the small clearing fires below and I had to check the instruments to believe anything.

After some time we approached Memphis, and that was a sight! From afar it looked like a patch rug painted with luminous paint, and as we drew near it got brighter and more definite. We came right over it at 6000' and spiraled down. All too soon we landed and shocked the natives by walking into the Terminal with flying suits on and a couple of handsome officers. They stayed with us until the plane time. When it drew up, who should step out but Mrs. Love returning from Washing. DC!

After that night ride anything else was anti-climax, so even my first airliner ride was a bit faded. It was too much like being inside a bus. But the worst part was, on the ground, I kept doing the pilot's work for him: taxi-ing, revving the motors, calling the tower, etc. And when what I thought was happening didn't—like with the ship's performance—I felt awfully disturbed.

Once in the air it was pretty tame and everyone slept nearly. We got to Dallas about 2:30 AM dead tired and we did some fast work getting to bed.

Thanks Pop.

Dorothy

Don't mention names or places to people please.

By mid-February, Nancy Love was on her way to the 6th Ferrying Group in Long Beach, California, to oversee the establishment of the fourth women's ferrying squadron there. Dorothy's classmate from the University of Washington, Barbara Erickson, was appointed squadron leader. Going with Barbara from Wilmington to fill out the WAFS contingent were Cornelia Fort, Evelyn Sharp, Barbara Towne, and Bernice Batten. Those five immediately began checking out in the BT-13s and 15s, which were built right there in the Los Angeles basin. It wouldn't be long before they began ferrying new BTs from the Vultee factory and delivering them all the way to Dallas.

Nancy opted to remain at Long Beach in order to check out on the variety of airplanes available to her there. As she built her aircraft repertoire, she also built opportunities for her pilots to check out on more and bigger and higher performance aircraft. At the top of her list was the A-36, an early version of the vaunted P-51 pursuit, as fighters were called then. In a single-cockpit pursuit, the first flight is a solo. Nancy soloed February 27, 1943. She also checked out on the workhorse of the Army Air Forces in World War II, the C-47.

Delphine Bohn, another of the original WAFS, was assigned to the Dallas squadron to fill the vacancy left by Love. Delphine was a West Texas girl like Florene. Born in 1913, Delphine grew up in Amarillo. Once she took her first flight, flying completely captivated her. She soloed in a Piper Cub in 1940, got her necessary ratings, and, like many of the WAFS, began through CPTP to instruct male cadets headed for combat. She was number fifteen to join Nancy Love's WAFS.

On March 1, waiting for weather to clear so they could go out on another BT delivery, Dorothy wrote:

Dear Dad,

We're waiting for weather to go out again. This time it will be due east for some ways.

In general, living has settled down to eatin', sleepin', and tearing around. Helen Richards and I have been going out nearly every evening, which is nice and saves us money—if not the fellows. I have about 250 in reserve. What'll I do with it? Buy bonds?

Last Saturday I wore my "civvies" and surely felt funny. We have to wear them sometimes to remember how to be just girls.

My shoulder's fine now—I've even gone bowling. I drove a car the other day—felt funny. I'll bet Ed's in "heaven" now—having a car to fuss over.

Dorothy

Helen Richards and Dorothy had become friends since arriving in Dallas. They hadn't really known each other in Wilmington, because Helen had arrived early. She was the tenth woman to qualify for the WAFS squadron. By the time Dorothy was accepted, Helen was out on deliveries and gone from base most of the time.

A Californian, Helen, too, was a CPTP graduate—from Pasadena Junior College, spring 1940. She had learned to fly at Alhambra airport in a J-3 Cub. When Richards finished her two-year college course, she took off for Floating Feather airport near Boise, Idaho, where she earned her commercial and instructor's licenses in 1941 and—like Dorothy—began teaching.[1]

When Nancy Love's telegram reached her there, Richards was running the flight school. By the time she reported to Wilmington late in September 1942, Helen had just turned twenty-one and had 964 flight hours to her credit. Helen, at five feet ten inches, was even taller than Dorothy's five feet eight. They made an impressive duo and regularly attracted the population of taller male officers stationed at Love Field.

Dorothy mailed a picture postcard of the Wilson Memorial Bridge in Jackson, Mississippi, to G. M. on March 3:

WAFS Cornelia Fort was the first American woman pilot to die on active duty during wartime. *Courtesy WASP Archive, Texas Woman's University, Denton.*

We went over this bridge—3,000 over it! We're headed still further east—Home tomorrow again. Swish!

Love, Dorothy

The WAFS may have been stationed in Texas and flying mostly southern trips at that point, but it was cold.

March 6, 1943

Dear Dad:

I've just finished another wonderful trip. Weather cleared Wednesday so after wrestling with cold engines and colder hands we got going. Boy! It was cold—about 15 degrees on the ground. We all wore our heavy flying jackets and boots and were grateful for the hatch cover. The cabin heater was effective by name only—no heat.

We landed first in Jackson [Mississippi] and stayed over night (R.O.N.), which means Remain Overnight.[2] We stayed at a nice hotel and saw a movie, and then Helen and I got the giggles and laughed so much the girls in the next room called us to be quiet. We needed excitement so we called long distance to the fellows we know here in Dallas and woke them out of a sound sleep. Then we ordered ice cream but couldn't get it, darn it.

The next day we flew to our delivery point—again too cold, and I did the navigating and did fine. It was nice to look out and see 3 more BTs in formation with me. Formation flying is lots of fun but keeps you busy so we fly pretty far apart most of the time. All the way it was quite smoky and got real bad close in so we drug the "iron beam" in. [Railroad tracks.]

We caught an airliner in Montgomery and flew to New Orleans where weather closed in and we had to wait until 3 AM to go out again. There we "saw the town" with the rest of the passengers. (7 more ferry pilots!) And did we do it up and down. First we got hotel rooms—but no one slept— and then cruised the town. We went to the old French quarter for dinner and it was as good eating as is claimed for it. I had grilled trout.

Then we walked around looking at historical spots and then to a night-club—where, nothing daunted, we danced in slacks until 2 AM when we returned to the field.

We landed in Houston at 6 AM and immediately confiscated the benches and fell asleep. We looked like the county morgue. I slept an hour then ate with some of the fellows and then talked to the girls who are in training there to be future WAFS (they hope). There are about 200 there now and in 4 classes. The top class is in BTs now and will move on up before long (but we will too). They won't finish before May I guess.

We took off again about 10:30 and got back to Dallas about 1:00 after flying over a beautiful overcast. It didn't take us long to get to sleep and I woke up at 6 and went to a movie with Paul and now it's the next day and we're waiting for a visiting general.

This general will be in tomorrow so today the post C.O.s walked in un-expectedly to inspect our quarters. Thank goodness they were pretty neat except for flying equipment too prominent for their liking.

Dorothy

As the month of March progressed, Dorothy's flying was very much back in sync with her fellow WAFS. Her next communiqué to her father was a postcard. "Busy with loop the loops today—will write soon's I get <u>around</u> to it!"

To: Sgt. Edward Scott and Ethel
373rd Air Base Sqdn. AAB
Colorado Springs, Colo.
March 9, 1943

Dear Ethel:

Your folks visited me yesterday and left films I'll try to see soon.

I like your family very much—maybe you'll be meeting our mom soon.

Dot

Ed and Ethel were married January 10, 1943, in Colorado Springs. No one from the Scott family could attend the wedding, but Ethel's mother was there.[3] Dorothy, having met Ethel in November, was delighted to have Ethel's parents visit her in Dallas.

March 25, 1943

Dear Dad:

It seems like I've skipped several days since writing last.

We've been on orders all this week to take AT-6s east, but the weather has been just fierce. It rained awfully hard last nite, and when I stepped from the sidewalk to the street getting into Penn's car, I went in up to my knees. Driving home we were about floundered all the way. Parts of the streets were over a foot under water.

Last Saturday I got in my solo AT-6 time and did a fine job, for which I was grateful because I hadn't been any too pleased about my dual work— but it was only because of a conflict of flying technique.

After getting in an hour-and-a-half solo I went to the Link again—but took my chute with me since it was en-route home. I've been living it down ever since as the only pilot to wear a chute in a Link. (I got a top grade too.)

Then at lunch the same day I talked a captain into a ride, so Florene and I spent the afternoon riding in the nose of a B-25. It was quite exciting and at last I can say I've attained my goals of being a "hostess on a bomber" because I passed out gum and water to the crew. It was just a local hop of repeated landing and takeoffs for checking out new pilots. It's really something to lie on your face peering down thru glass at that ground coming up fast.

Saturday nite was another dance, which was lots of fun and kept me up late enough to enjoy a leisurely Sunday doing nothing but eat a steak dinner with Paul and listen to the radio programs.

Monday we were put on orders but weather has held us here all these days. It'll be nice to fly AT-6s on trips because they'll cruise at about 175—oh boy! It's funny tho how speed means nothing but a figure on estimating arrival time and fewer refuel stops.

What I like is working all the extra gadgets.

Our commanding officer has finally returned from an extended trip to South America and we're glad to have him back—his subordinates are jerks. Best tho, we heard via the grapevine that since we're doing so well we'll be put on twin-engine stuff right soon—and do I like that!

It has seemed to me that all single-engine stuff is pretty simple, pursuits and all, but twin-engine flying is a real job because of the change in such a plane's job—that of cargo carrying and more people.

There are now four nurses here so we no longer enjoy the blessings of having everything like we want it. Our own barracks are now being built—slowly-and-not-too surely—so it'll be a great day when we get into our own.

Yesterday we were visited by a *National Geographic* reporter who we entertained by dragging her around in the rain. Her story should be pretty good.

We've been dressing up in our winter flying equipment lately and getting "shot" by the post photographer who then gives them out to the news stories thru the Public Relations dept. so we never know what or when we'll be plastered in something else. They don't allow us to give out any stories or let outsiders take pictures.

These AT-6 trips still won't be to L.A. or Colorado, but may go to Wash. D.C. sometime. I'll get leave sometime this summer and hitch-hike to Seattle in nothing flat.

Do you think you can get down this way any time this summer—I hope so.

We may get really signed on in this army before too long—then we'll really be under gov. orders. Oh well, it's like that in every way but name now.

Dorothy

March was a transitional month for the WAFS. The three new women's squadrons were up and functioning well, most of the women were beginning to transition up with the end goal to make them eligible to fly a greater variety of aircraft. Nancy Love and Bill Tunner could look on their creation—and responsibility—favorably. It appeared that the women in training down in Houston would be ready to join the "originals" by the first of May, thus doubling the WAFS's strength and thereby their usefulness. Maybe things seemed too rosy, but no one forgot that the reason for all of this was the war and the war still was not going well for the United States and its Allies. At the end of every successful day and achievement was the cruel fact that war—and everything they were doing—was about death, preferably of the enemy.

On March 21, 1943, death took one of the "originals."

On Sunday, March 21, 1943, Cornelia Fort and six Long Beach male ferry pilots took off to deliver BT-13s to Dallas. En route, somewhere over sparsely inhabited West Texas, the seven agreed to some formation flying. The WAFS were not trained in formation flying. Their instructions were to stay 500 feet away from any other airplane. Apparently—and unfortunately—Cornelia chose to ignore the order.[4]

The official Army accident report, dated April 6, 1943, reads:[5]

On March 21 at approximately 15:30 CWT [Central War Time] seven ships were proceeding East in formation, in the vicinity of Merkel, Texas. Of these seven ships, one BT-13A flown by Civilian Pilot Cornelia Fort and [a] BT-13A flown by F/O Frank E. Stamme, Jr., were involved in a mid-air collision.

It appears that the landing gear leg of F/O Stamme's aircraft broke off the left wing tip of Pilot Fort's aircraft, and peeled approximately six feet off the leading edge of the wing toward the center of the aircraft. At this point, the aircraft apparently pulled free of each other. An examination disclosed that the left wing tip of Pilot Fort's aircraft was wood, and the right wing tip was metal. This would account for the ease with which the left wing tip broke off at the time of contact with the other aircraft.

F/O Stamme's aircraft did not go out of control. Pilot Fort's aircraft apparently went out of control, and after executing a series of rolls, went into an inverted dive, slowly rotating to the left. There was apparently no attempt to recover or to use the parachute. The emergency latch on the hatch release was found to be locked.

Judging from the condition of the propeller blades, power was completely retarded after control was lost.

Cornelia had perished in the crash. She was twenty-four years old.

Word spread quickly through the WAFS's ranks. Cornelia was well liked and, though she was quiet and kept to herself, all her fellow WAFS knew she was a solid flier and an extraordinary person. Cornelia, from the beginning, planned to write the history of the Women's Auxiliary Ferrying Squadron. She had kept diaries of her entire aviation career and already was preparing to commit those jottings to a memoir about the squadron and its exploits—once the war was over. Cornelia had witnessed, first-hand, and had already written about the bombing of Pearl Harbor. As a flight instructor at Honolulu's John Rodgers Airport, she was flying with a student on the morning of December 7, 1941. They were shot at by a Zero but managed to land safely in a hail of bullets.[6]

Now Cornelia had become America's first woman pilot to die on active service to her country. Just days before, a Women's Flying Training Detachment trainee—Margaret Oldenburg from Class 43-4—and her instructor had crashed flying a PT-19 near Houston where the women were stationed.

Nancy Love and Cornelia's squadron leader at Long Beach, B. J. Erickson, along with Maj. Samuel C. Dunlap also from the 6th Ferrying Group, flew a C-47 overnight to Nashville March 24–25 to attend the funeral. B. J. wrote to her parents that Major Dunlap did most of the flying and that she and Nancy traded off flying copilot while the other slept on the floor in the navigator's spot.[7]

They checked into a hotel, cleaned up, ate breakfast, then they went to see the family. Since the Army would release no information until the April 6, 1943, accident report was made public, Nancy and B. J. were as much in the dark as the family regarding details of the accident. All did their best to cope in a difficult situation.

Because the Fort family was among Nashville's elite society, and because of Cornelia's popularity with a wide assortment of friends, the funeral in Christ Episcopal Church was very nearly a state occasion. Nancy, B. J., and Major Dunlap—all in uniform—were asked to lead the processional up the aisle of the church, after which Cornelia was buried in Mt. Olivet Cemetery next to her father. B. J. and Nancy could read on his tombstone that Mr. Fort had died on the very same day as his daughter—March 21— three years earlier. The inscription on Cornelia's footstone reads, "Killed in the Service of Her Country."

Nancy didn't speak at the funeral. She shied away from public appear-

Their first delivery of AT-6s: Dallas ferry pilots Helen Richards, Dorothy Scott, and Florene Miller get ready to take off, March 1943. *Courtesy: The Scott Family Collection.*

ances and felt ill at ease handling such an ordeal. But she wrote to Cornelia's mother.[8]

> My feeling about the loss of Cornelia is hard to put into words—I can only say that I miss her terribly, and loved her. She was a rare person. If there can be any comforting thought it is that she died as she wanted to—in an Army airplane, and in the service of her country.

The WAFS, unlike men in combat, did *not* live with death as a constant companion, unless one looks at the element of chance. Anyone can die tomorrow—or today. But they were *not* serving in a foreign country, they were *not* near the front lines, they were *not* under fire. What they were doing was ferrying airplanes from one place to another. Given the fact that accidents happen, any one of the ferry pilots—male or female—could crash and be killed at any time. However, the fact that they were professionals and good at what they did went a long way in protecting them. That is why Colonel Tunner insisted on accepting only the qualified—the best. He wanted impeccable credentials, he wanted the most hours and experience he could get from his people *before* they set foot in one of his airplanes—*before* those expensive airplanes were placed in those pilots' care.

Nancy Love didn't want to "think" about the possibility of an accident happening, the possibility of one of her girls dying. She didn't dare. In March 1943, the women ferry pilots were on the threshold of flying the Army's newest, hottest airplanes off the assembly line. Her answer was, personally, to take every precaution before ever leaving the ground and hope that her pilots did the same.[9]

Cornelia's death wasn't the end of Nancy Love's and the WAFS's trials in March 1943.

To date, there was no transport system in place to return ferry pilots to their home base after they delivered a plane, which meant that days could be wasted as these pilots made their way home by any means possible. Male ferry pilots were allowed to hop—or hitch—a ride in a military airplane. WAFS were required to return via commercial airliner, train, or some other mode of public transportation.

The regulation specified that WAFS were not "to solicit rides in bomber-type aircraft either for local flying or for cross-country flying without specific authority from the Group Commander." This was to protect their reputations. The problem was not concern over the moral character of the WAFS—rather, that the newspapers would publicize this fact and give gossipmongers a chance to question the women's reputations.[10]

"If the WAFS are to succeed, our personal conduct must be above reproach," Nancy Love told her women pilots early on. "There cannot be the faintest breath of scandal. Among other things, this means you may not accept rides with male pilots. If a male pilot and a WAFS were seen leaving a plane together there would be suspicions that they were playing house in government property."[11]

Until March 1943, the ability to hop rides was the only real distinction between male and female ferry pilots. On March 16, the Ferrying Division initiated a move to prohibit its women pilots from serving as copilots with male pilots on bombers. On March 25, the women of the 3rd Ferrying

Group in Romulus found themselves even more severely limited in what they could fly. Down came four policy changes:[12]

(1) Romulus women would fly only light trainer aircraft. No transition into basic or advanced trainers or twin-engine aircraft. (2) Women would not be given assignments as copilots on bomber ferrying missions. (3) Women would not be allowed to transition on any high-powered single-engine or twin-engine aircraft. [Numbers 2 and 3 meant women couldn't "build time" or work on transition in different airplanes as copilots to male pilots other than their instructors.] (4) Women would make deliveries on alternate days from the male pilots. AND, they were to be—if at all possible—sent in opposite directions. This was a further protection of their reputations.

Nancy Love objected emphatically to this directive, wrote one historian.[13]

Nancy Love was, in fact, livid.

But there was more still to come. On March 29, the Air Transport Command banned women from flying when pregnant and for one day before through two days after their menstrual period.[14] The no-flying-while-pregnant was not the problem. Not flying during your period was. Eight or nine wasted days per month per WAFS—and when all of them were badly needed.

One of the original WAFS, Esther Manning (married name Rathfelder), was pregnant. However, Betty Gillies, Esther's squadron leader at Wilmington, already had solved the problem. Betty let Esther fly until she couldn't get the stick back in the cramped confines of the PT-19s she was ferrying. Then Betty grounded her and put her to work as operations officer.

Nancy Love took matters into her own hands and went over the heads of both group and Ferrying Division commanders and appealed the menstrual period ban and the prohibition on transition directly to her personal friend Gen. C. R. Smith, Chief of Staff of the Air Transport Command. She risked Colonel Tunner's ire by ignoring the chain of command.[15]

General Smith saved the day. The Ferrying Division, he said in his letter of April 17, 1943, had imposed flight limitations on women pilots without consideration of individual professional qualifications. "It is the desire of this Command that all pilots, regardless of sex, be privileged to advance to the extent of their ability in keeping with the progress of aircraft development."[16]

With this, the WAFS would be allowed to transition into bigger, more complex airplanes. The WAFS had an almost perfect accident record. Cornelia Fort had been exonerated of any blame in her fatal accident. There was no pilot error on her part. And the only other accidents had been a couple of bent propellers following ground loops.

The ATC flight surgeon thought pregnancy was a disqualifying condition for flying, but he agreed with Nancy that the menstrual period should be regarded as an individual problem to be regulated by the local WAFS leader and the station flight surgeon "when his assistance was required."[17]

On April 26, Colonel Tunner withdrew the March 29 directive relative to WAFS not flying during menstruation and the March 17 order forbidding a woman to fly copilot with a male pilot. The WAFS now could transition on multiengine and high-powered single-engine aircraft in keeping with their individual experience and ability. Still tiptoeing around the morals issue, the directive did say that normally the WAFS would be given transition on cross-country checkouts by other fully qualified WAFS "when and if available."[18] For a while, Nancy wasn't exactly in Colonel Tunner's good graces.

One more major occurrence took place in March 1943. The women's flight-training program began its move to Avenger Field, Sweetwater, Texas. Houston lacked the facilities for the coming expansion of the program. By late May, the move to Sweetwater would be complete.

Dorothy left on her first AT-6 trip on March 27. After delivering their AT-6s to Dothan, Alabama, the WAFS had to get to Tallahassee to catch an airliner back to base. The flying officers at Dothan offered to fly them there in the AT-6s. En route, Dorothy's pilot let her take the stick and perform a number of aerobatic maneuvers.

"He said my Immelmans were better than his!" Dorothy wrote from Tallahassee that evening in a hurried note to G. M. on Hotel Floridian stationery:

> Waiting on a government car to the field. We delivered in Dothan, AL, and then were flown here. Enough of those rides and I'll be an expert aerobatic pilot. Those AT-6s do wonderful for that stuff!

The rest of the trip back to Dallas turned out to be no picnic for the pilots who had delivered to Dothan. They managed to catch the special airliner from Tallahassee to New Orleans, where more Dallas-bound male ferry pilots joined them. They all had to wait until 3:30 a.m. for another flight to Houston. From there, some sixty ferry pilots climbed aboard a train for Dallas, arriving back at Love Field at 2:00 in the afternoon.

On March 30, Dorothy learned from the transition officer that the women were going to get first chance at the new AT-17 that was coming—a twin-engine Cessna! Things definitely were looking up.

Two names had cropped up in Dorothy's March letters home. She and Helen had met two young men, Penn and Paul—no last names. The four had become good friends, and were now running together and double dating.

On April 24, the first twenty-three fledgling women ferry pilots graduated from the Army's Flight Training School in Houston. Six were assigned to the 5th in Dallas and arrived at Love Field on May 1, ready to fly. New WAFS were Mary Lou Colbert, Edna Collins, Byrd Granger, Evelyn Greenblatt, Ann Reed Johnson, and Sidney Miller. Life in the WAFS was about to change.

Chapter Five
The AT-6 and More WAFS

Dorothy's flight log for April shows BT-13 and PT-17 deliveries. By May, most of her deliveries were AT-6s. She wrote G. M. an explanation of how the WAFS picked up AT-6s they were to deliver.

> We get the AT-6s from the factory—but that's just 20 miles from here in Grand Prairie so we're all taken over by bus from here—30 at a time. We are also classed as the RST pilots—as they have only one hour's time on them when we take ours. Believe me, we check them good and treat 'em careful!

Iris Cummings Critchell, a graduate of Class 43-2 who became a Long Beach ferry pilot, says that the ferry pilots eventually were taking airplanes from the factory "with only a five minute prior engine run check recorded in the airplane flight Form 1. Seldom did the record show an hour's flight test time, which is what they had hoped to do. But the pace of production got ahead of them."[1]

On May 7, 1943, Dorothy sent Ed a jumbo postcard with a photo of an AT-6 over the San Antonio skyline.

> This is my favorite airplane, over a spot that's well known.
> Wanna be my cameraman?
>
> Your sis.

Dorothy was busy flying, which of course was what she wanted to be doing, and the dearth of long letters home was made up for with picture postcards or occasionally a short note on letterhead from various hotels

Florene Miller, Delphine Bohn, Betsy Ferguson, and Dorothy Scott talk with Lt. Joseph N. Drum (left) and Lt. T. K. McGuire. They were in Wichita, Kansas, June 14, 1943, to pick up PT-17s. *Courtesy: The Scott Family Collection.*

around the country. The ever-changing postmarks were clues to the ferry pilot's nomadic life—one that Dorothy now was leading.

Since she and the other WAFS had checked out in the AT-6, the airplane badly needed at training facilities around the country, they would deliver a lot of them over the next several months.[2]

The Dallas WAFS also made frequent trips to Wichita, Kansas, to pick up PT-17s at the Stearman factory there.[3] These primary trainers differed from the primary trainers the Wilmington WAFS were ferrying back east. The PT-17s were biplanes with 225-horsepower engines rather than the low, single-wing, 175-horsepower Fairchild PT-19s. But like the 19s, they had open cockpits with tandem seating.

In May, the six new Dallas WAFS were being incorporated into the ferrying schedules. They had flown the PT-19 and the AT-6 while in training at Houston. Ferrying the 17s gave them the opportunity to get their cross-country feet wet by first delivering something smaller and less complex than the AT-6. Before the Ferrying Division allowed a new pilot to deliver aircraft, it required each one to qualify in his or her own good time given individual skill level and experience. Dorothy's three PT-17 ferrying trips in April had given her experience, so she frequently was appointed flight leader for the new WAFS on trips.

In mid-May, Dorothy and three of the new WAFS took the overnight train to Wichita, where they sat for four days waiting for good weather. By the time the weather cleared, two of Dorothy's pilots were ill from their recent typhoid shots and had to be sent back to Dallas. Dorothy got new orders and replacement pilots for the two who were ailing, and four WAFS finally got off to make the delivery to Clarksdale, Mississippi. But their delays weren't over.

In Monroe, Louisiana, one of her pilots dragged a wing while landing. More delay. Waiting for the wing to be repaired, Dorothy met up with a captain in a twin-engine AT-7 who took her up for a spin and let her fly it. Then she took the captain up in her PT-17—which was strictly against rules, she found out later. When the damaged wing was repaired, the four took off again and finally delivered in Clarksdale, but not before Dorothy ran into one more problem. She described the problem to G. M. in her May 30, 1943, letter.

We got held up with the PTs in both Wichita and Dallas but finally got them delivered as I told you in my last letter. I think I forgot to tell you the exciting part.

I was leading the flight into Clarksdale and could not locate the airport. Then I saw a Cub land at the Municipal Field, so I went around and came on in. "CLUNK!" I set down in deep mud. The tail left the ground and nearly stood straight up. Boy! I put the brakes on, stick back, and gave it full throttle to blow the tail down. That was too close for comfort. Then I had to turn around fast and taxi back on the runway so the other kids wouldn't land. I found out where the right airport was and took off again without much trouble. I don't want to do THAT again.

As soon as I got back (7:30 AM) I was asked if I wanted an AT-6 trip, and, tho I didn't have to take it, I surely said, "yes" and since have been waiting for weather to leave.

While waiting, transition dept. called us old WAFS in and gave us AT-9 checks. Boy, what a plane. You bring it in at 120 mph—that's as fast as a bomber, and faster than a pursuit. I had a little trouble catching on to wheel landings but none with flying with a left hand wheel control and a whole new cockpit procedure.

In a few days' time, between the stolen ride in the AT-7 followed by the sanctioned check out in the AT-9, Dorothy had a twofold introduction to twin engines, and it was much to her liking. Flying a twin-engine aircraft meant that she controlled the airplane with a yoke—a half steering wheel—using her left hand instead of the familiar right-hand control stick common to single-engine aircraft; thus, her comment on the left-hand wheel control. With her right hand she had to work the throttles—two of them, one for each engine. Now, she could hardly wait for the AT-17 that had been promised by the transition officer.

Dorothy continued her May 30 letter to G. M., which included some big news of a different kind. No, it didn't involve a new airplane and it wasn't a man. It was a boat and two men. She and Penn and Paul had evolved into a threesome that liked a lot of the same things—and it had to do with water.

Yesterday I surely had a time, and of course did one of those crazy things that most always turn out swell—I'm part owner of a cabin cruiser! You know the two fellows I've been going around with for a long time. Yesterday we three were out fishing—tho we didn't fish because we came across these speedboat races.

We stopped and Penn started taking pictures. Before long I was being taken for a ride in a speedboat—boy, oh boy—and then we three were in-

Sgt. Edward Scott and Capt. Donald Scott with Dorothy Scott in Dallas, late in June 1943, for a Scott family reunion. *Courtesy: The Scott Family Collection.*

vited to go out to the first marker to get pictures of the races. This boat was the cruiser. First thing you know, we were boat-owners and it's a swell deal. We talked to lots of the racing fellows and they all said it was a plenty good buy. The owner wants a racer and we don't.

Anyway, we spent last evening cruising around, and pulled up alongside other boats so already we're socially well acquainted with the upper crust of Dallas.

I'm surely glad we've got it. All our fun had gotten narrowed to movies and dances, no swimming or picnics hardly, but not now.

We'll likely get going on that AT-6 trip soon. I can't understand so much bad weather.

Dorothy

Helen Richards, Dorothy's best friend in the Women's Auxiliary Ferrying Squadron. *Courtesy WASP Archive, Texas Woman's University, Denton.*

June 4, 1943

Dear Dad:

More fun. Right this minute I'm waiting to get a check out in a C-78—or AT-17—it will not take long because it is easier than the AT-9 to fly.

Oh, pop, this boat deal is super. We have such fun on it. I'm looking forward to you coming down late this summer and you'll like it too. You surely must envy me.

I'm considerably muscle sore from surfboard riding but I'm glad because I need toughening up. I'll probably spend most of my letters talking about our boat rather than flying. We have the nicest boathouse on the lake—white with red trim. The inside isn't so hot yet but we're going to fix it up too so we can stay at nite sometimes. We meet other boating people often and tonite are invited to dinner at a Dr.'s house, whom we met while out fishing.

During World War II, efforts on the part of people on the home front to invite servicemen—and women in this case—into their homes were widespread. Thus, Dorothy, Penn, and Paul were made welcome socially by a Dallas boating public that appreciated their service to the country.

She closed her June 4 letter with:

> 6 pm—now checked out on AT-17—fun! To do so had to miss a PT trip to Miami, Fla—later perhaps.

Class 43-2, which began training in Houston on December 16, 1942, graduated from flight training on May 28. Eleven of them were assigned to Dallas and reported in early June: Betty Bachman, Ruth Dailey, Frances Dias, Betty Eames, Jane Emerson, Kay Gott, Ross Kary, Avanell Pinkley, Helen Ricketts, Cappy Vail, and Betty Whitlow. That brought the squadron roster to twenty-two. With more nurses arriving at Love Field in addition to the new WAFS, the women's barracks was filling up. Helen and Dorothy decided to look for quarters off the base.

June 8, 1943

Dear Dad:

> Sunday three of us old WAFS were put on orders—PTs to Georgia. Bohn and Richards are with me this time. While waiting to leave for Wichita, transition asked us to check out on PQ-8s—those radio controlled Culver Cadets. However, we couldn't fly because of local thunderstorms, so I'm still waiting for that thrill. We fly those solo the first time, as there is no room for any second person.
>
> We left at midnite by plane for Oklahoma City—not Wichita because it was closed in so the airliner wouldn't land there. We stayed in the depot all night until 7 AM when we took a very crowded train the rest of the way. We got to Wichita about 10 AM and were in the air by 12:30. We stopped in Ok City for gas and went on to Dallas for over nite.
>
> Paul and Penn met me when I landed so we headed right for the lake and our boat and got in a good bit of swimming and boating before I went home to finally get some sleep.
>
> Then today (June 8) we got as far as Jackson MS. CAVU[4] [ceiling and visibility unlimited] weather but we couldn't go on due to thunderstorms in Georgia. We'll deliver tomorrow if weather permits, then get back in time for me to get a day off to get some sun-tan.

I'm flight leader this trip and do most of the navigating, 'cause I like to. We flew low over some of the bad flood areas near Vicksburg. Boy, the trees are all swimming.

Our next trip will likely be in AT-17s as soon as we all get checked out in them. Personally, the PT-17s and AT-6 are more fun. Today by pre-arrangement we three broke off for 10 minutes and looped and snap-rolled just for exercise. This seemed to be our last chance, because we don't do it when the new WAFS are along.

Don't you think I have lots of fun for one person?

Dorothy

G. M. received a picture postcard of the New Orleans Airport Administration Building, mailed June 9. Dorothy wrote:

> We had a super trip, but getting back is causing some trouble. These people are sun-struck. It's bus to Atlanta, then an airliner—then swimmin'!

Another PT trip awaited Dorothy upon her return to Dallas, and G. M. received another picture postcard dated June 14 and bearing the inscription, "Dogwood Tree in Bloom," Atlanta. Dorothy wrote:

> Back here again—this PT to Albany GA by myself. It's lonesome, but they are keeping me busy for sure.

On June 22, on a postcard showing the historical Old War Engine "Texas" in the Cyclorama Building in Atlanta, Georgia, Dorothy wrote:

> Twin-engine pilots ferrying PTs! Why we'd be ferrying these things if they were made any more.
> 2 AM Airliner waiting

Dot

Late in June, the Scott family held a long-hoped-for reunion in Dallas. Donald, now a captain in the Army Air Forces, flew in from North Carolina. Ed, a sergeant in the AAF and a Link Trainer specialist, hopped a flight in from Colorado Springs. G. M. took the train down from Oroville, and Katherine came by train from California.

Dorothy had no deliveries scheduled between June 23 and 29 while the family gathered. Everybody got to meet Helen and the other WAFS as well as Dorothy's partners in the cabin cruiser, Penn and Paul. But then she was on orders from June 30 through July 5. She was gone on a trip June 30 and July 1, but she did manage to have July 2 off, so the family planned an outing at the boathouse thrown by the three proud boat owners.

But G. M. left the morning of July 2—earlier than expected. Tensions existed between Katherine and G. M. They had lived apart for a number of years. Avoiding unrest when the goal was for the family to gather for a good time appears to be the reason for his early departure. Dorothy makes no such mention in her letters, but later correspondence alludes to his impatience to get away.

Maybe he didn't want to hang around indefinitely with Dorothy going out on a potentially long trip the following day. She could be delayed by weather or mechanical problems and might not be back for several days. Maybe by then G. M. had had enough togetherness.

When he got home, G. M. did drop by the newspaper office to give Mr. Doerr the story of the gathering, which ran in the July 9 issue of the *Oroville Gazette.* At the conclusion of the article, G. M.'s advice to anyone planning to travel summer of 1943 was: "If you don't have time to travel at this time, don't, as it is hard to find accommodations or eats anywhere you go and everything is crowded to the limit."[5]

A postcard showing a Texas longhorn steer with horns measuring 9 feet 6 inches went in the mail to G. M. from El Paso on July 5.

Here I am again—headed for Yuma in a UC-78 ("family car of the air" by Cessna). They're easy to fly—want one? We all rode the surf behind a speedboat and all fell off—ouch!

Dot

July 8, 1943

Dear Dad:

My, have I been busy since you left. Friday evening [July 2] we went out in the boat. It broke down. But we did ride the surfboard behind Red's speedboat and we all got knocked off hard. The boat needed a new coil.

Saturday, I got orders for a UC-78 trip to Yuma. I was thrilled, believe me! Just Delphine and me. We were flown to Wichita, where we hopped once around Cessna's field, then headed for Oklahoma City where we stayed all night in the nurses' quarters. So July 4th was spent in two long hops, one to Big Springs and then to El Paso where we stayed over again because Delphine's plane got a flat tire. We stayed at the Ferry Command hotel and I got to visit Juarez again—super steak!

Next day we delivered after a refuel stop at Tucson and was Yuma hot—whew! We were two lucky girls 'cause a captain flew us up to Phoenix instead of us having to take a train or bus. We caught the 8 o'clock airliner home and got here at 5 a.m. After some sleep we went in the boat, but no swimming because of a paralysis [polio] scare around now.

Ed left Wednesday morning for Ft. Worth, then back to Colorado Springs. Mom may leave today and Don will leave Saturday morning. He's seeing the Lockheed and North American factories and is really getting around. It's certainly been nice to have us all in one place. I hope your trip home wasn't too tiring.

Back at work, I found we all were grounded to attend ground school. Drill—8 to 9 a.m. Class 9 to 12. Class 1 to 5. One class was on gas masks, so we all went to the tear gas tent and some of the masks leaked—boy, those gals were red eyed, as we all were the rest of the day due to the stuff sticking to our clothes in the heat. Our shins itched and burned a long time—we were a sorry bunch.

It seems our ground school will be for about ten days and covers everything from "right face" to how to bail out of a P-38. We have exams at the end of each class but they aren't too hard.

The commission deal is still uncertain so we're flying a bit blind as usual.

Helen and I move to our house Sunday.

Dot

Chapter Six

The Statue of Liberty Is Green!

On July 11, Dorothy and Helen moved into a house on Stonegate Road in Dallas. Housing was hard to come by in wartime America, and many citizens rented out rooms and kitchen privileges, particularly to transients involved in government- and military-related work who were stationed in a community for a few months at a time.

Zimmy Sluder was such a citizen.

Zimmy's husband, Alex, was overseas—a major in charge of a P-47 group. He had been gone since fall 1942, and she wasn't exactly sure where he was. Zimmy and their daughter, Shari, had remained in Dallas. By summer 1943, when Dorothy and Helen moved in, Shari was five and ready to go to kindergarten that coming fall. Like many a precocious youngster, she was learning the letters of the alphabet. And she missed her daddy.[1]

With room to spare and an opportunity to add to the family income, Zimmy decided to rent space to these two tall, graceful, and very likeable young women whom she had met through base personnel who were friends of her husband. Initially, she was astonished to learn that they were actually pilots and that they ferried airplanes with a group called the WAFS. But as she got to know Dorothy and Helen throughout the spring of 1943, she saw the depth of personality and the love of what they were doing exhibited by the two young women and came to look on them almost as family. When they mentioned needing to find a place off base to live, she offered lodging in her house. And with that began a warm friendship.

As Helen and Dorothy settled in that summer, the three women shared

Weathered in at Birmingham, Alabama, while on an AT-6 delivery to Newark, New Jersey, July 1943. Three women ferry pilots from Dallas—Dorothy Scott, Helen Ricketts (WASP Class 43-2), and Byrd Granger (WASP Class 43-1)—with a Royal Air Force officer named Fredrick. *Courtesy: The Scott Family Collection.*

confidences and talked over problems, as women will. Dorothy—always bubbling—readily shared her excitement about trips she had just returned from, her enthusiasm over flying "under the hood," and each checkout in a new aircraft.

Two weeks after moving in to Zimmy's, Dorothy got her chance to fly her first trip to the docks at Newark, New Jersey, and therefore to New York City, across the Hudson River from Newark. Her carbon-copy hand-written letter to G. M., her mother, and her brothers was chock-full of her excitement about her adventure.

July 30, 1943, she wrote:

I just got back from the most adventuresome trip I've ever had! It was an AT-6 trip to Newark, NJ. This was a trip I've long wanted! We left Dallas early the morning of July 26th. I got up at 5 a.m. On the way out, I buzzed Helen's and my new house and also Penn and Paul out in the boat.

It went quite routine until we left Meridian, Miss., headed for Atlanta, GA. Over Birmingham we ran into a local thunderstorm so I radio'd in for a weather report. I deciphered the code to mean CAVU—or "perfect" weather, but actually it was so rough I couldn't hold the paper still. So "Phooey" tap I and tell 'em I'm comin' in.

We land ok and I walk into the weather hangar. "Ah yes," they said, "A special just came in—real storms."

Well, we stayed over nite (hmm—good steak) and cleared the next AM again. This time the report was low scattered clouds—very minor. A half-hour out, the "low scattered" had boxed in solid behind and below us. Again I tried the radio but no answer, so we turn around.

Whew! Going back to Birmingham, the area had fogged up nearly solid so I went on instruments. Boy! That was work. The other two kids hung on my wingtips and I followed that beam like a homesick angel. Just as we got over it I saw the field and headed in. Talk about being grateful at being on solid ground again! Those kids were a-thankin' me too—and I was a-thankin' Link.

We got off again that afternoon and made it to Richmond, Va. All the rest of the trip we had visibility only from 3 to 8 miles—which is seeing ahead not at all and down just some.

The next day was a gay one. We flew to New Castle where I got to see some of the old gang—when I'd left them in Jan. I hadn't even known what an AT-6 was for sure.

From New Castle I led them right over Philadelphia, then Wash. DC where I looked down on FDR and Wash. Monument, etc. Then we headed into New York and I got enough "lost" to fly over Manhattan's skyline and the Statue of Liberty. (It's green!) Then we delivered our planes and had 3 hrs 'til plane time. That we spent on a bus trip and subway ride.

Carbon is handy, I must do this more often.[2] Home again and more twin-engine time.

Dorothy

Dorothy's short snorter contained five bills, one US dollar bill and four foreign currency bills. Signatures of two fellow original WAFS are decipherable on the back of the US dollar bill: Betsy Ferguson and G. S. (Gertrude) Meserve. *Courtesy: The Scott Family Collection.*

More of Dorothy's short snorter. Ross Kary, WASP Class 43-2, signed the Bank of Canada bill. Dorothy's boss, Nancy H. Love, signed the top of the Banco Central De Guatemala bill and one of Dorothy's admirers added "Hi Babe" and his signature down the side. *Courtesy: The Scott Family Collection.*

Dorothy was flight leader on this trip. She and two new WAFS[3] had taken three AT-6s to Newark to be put aboard a Liberty ship[4] bound across the North Atlantic. Betsy Ferguson was leading a similar flight of three AT-6s. It was the first time any of the Dallas WAFS had made a delivery to the port at Newark. Up until then, their deliveries had been in the southern half of the United States, both east and west.

The six planes were destined for England, so they bore British insignia and were equipped with the British-style safety belts.

Dorothy and her two flying companions stayed overnight ("RON'd") in Birmingham. Betsy's flight didn't get away until later the morning of July 26. They RON'd in Montgomery and were behind Dorothy and her crew the rest of the trip.

The night of July 27, Dorothy and her two companions RON'd in Richmond, Virginia. There, they relied on the local Red Cross for food and transportation after securing their airplanes. Red Cross volunteers had organized in many towns and cities where ferry pilots landed regularly. Cokes, coffee, donuts, sandwiches, and carrot sticks were in good supply because restaurants frequently were not available. The volunteers then drove the pilots to their hotels and picked them up in the morning to get them back to the airport. Dorothy thanked them profusely and even wrote to G. M. about them.

"Boy, do I like the Red Cross! They fed us and transported us free this entire trip!"

As for New York City, Dorothy, good navigator that she was, was not lost as she flew toward it. Though she had never been there before, by looking at the charts she could judge just how far off the route she needed to stray in order for them all to get a good look at Miss Liberty. In spite of the haze that was omnipresent over the big city and its environs, the statue and the skyscrapers reached for the clouds above them in all their vertical glory.

During their three hours sightseeing in New York City, Dorothy bought a postcard showing the Brooklyn Bridge and wrote the following message to her father:

July 28, 1943

Look where I am! I am writing this while waiting for a 5th Avenue Bus on 5th and E. 42nd. We sure had adventures getting here.

They thoroughly enjoyed their excursion around New York, seeing as many sights as they could possibly squeeze in, but for whatever reason, in spite of the temptation to stay longer, they decided against spending any additional time, choosing instead to head for La Guardia and catch the first available American Airlines flight back to Dallas.

The winds of fate were blowing favorably for Dorothy and her companions that day. The flight that left after theirs crashed en route to Texas, and everyone aboard was killed. They, recipients of much good fortune, arrived back in Dallas safe and sound.

The winds of fate were kind to Betsy and her two companions as well. They, too, made it back safely to Dallas, but on the flight *after* the one that crashed. Betsy told the story this way to her sister Sally. "The New York taxi driver got stuck in traffic. I was really upset because I needed to catch a hop back to Dallas after delivering our planes. By the time we got to the airport, the flight had left." That was the flight between Dorothy's flight and hers—the flight that crashed. Betsy's outlook on life took a contemplative, later a spiritual, turn from that moment on.[5]

The work done by ferry pilots "involves hours of boredom interspersed with moments of sheer terror," says the legend of the Ferry Command.

Completing any ferrying trip depended on the weather and the often-interminable waits for the weather to break locally or to clear ahead. Ferry pilots frequently returned home in the middle of the night and had nothing available to eat other than that most welcome Red Cross fare. When possible, they caught airliners home because that was the quickest mode of transportation. The pilots of the Ferrying Division had top priority for seats on those airliners. So valuable was their service and their quick turnaround, they were, in fact, rated just below the president and his cabinet when it came to being given seats aboard an airliner. They could, and did, bump generals.

Some delivery points were large metropolitan areas, like New York, but many deliveries were made to out-of-the-way places, particularly out west. The Ferrying Division was in the process of introducing its own airline that would pick up ferry pilots at their delivery point and fly them back to their home base so that they could ferry yet another plane badly needed to fight the war.

As ferrying duties took her to many new places, Dorothy began to assemble her very own short snorter—a roll of banknotes, signed by various persons a ferry pilot flew with or met along the way—and it was a record of where the pilot had been. The tradition, begun by 1920s Alaskan bush pilots, "subsequently spread through the growth of military and commercial aviation. If you signed a short snorter and that person could not produce it upon request, they owed you a dollar or a drink (a 'short snort' [as] aviation and alcohol don't mix)."[6]

The men who flew for the Ferry Command—pilot or air-crew member—carried impressive short snorters and produced them with pride wherever they gathered. These men circumnavigated the globe during World War II, delivering desperately needed airplanes and supplies. They flew to Natal, Brazil, as easily as—today—we fly to Chicago. From there, they hopped across the Atlantic to Ascension Island and on to Dakar on the west coast of Africa. Some went on to the Middle East and others on to India where they flew The Hump.

The Hump was that perilous five-hundred-mile-long supply route across the Himalayas—the rooftop of the world—and then over the teeming jungles of Burma, and on to the remote interior of China. That was the Air Transport Command's most famous and most hazardous duty—delivering supplies to the land-bound Chinese Army, Americans, and other Allies fighting the Japanese. The guys who got that far sported super short snorters.

Stationed with the 5th Ferrying Group in Dallas, Dorothy was at the center of much of the Air Transport Command action. She and the other WAFS met many a young male ferry pilot who literally was off to see the world or just back from seeing it. She and the other women pilots loved to talk to the guys and hear where all they had been. When she was still in Wilmington, mid-December 1942, Dorothy had written to her mother:

> . . . these fellows being ferry pilots are here for a few hours, then gone for days. They go to Africa and England, Florida and Texas. I was telling a B-17 pilot this morning how one pilot was going to do his Xmas shopping in Florida. He said, "I did mine in Portugal." One Lt. I'd gone to movies and roller-skating with left for Africa a few days ago.

To build their own short snorters, the women—relegated to strictly stateside duty and an occasional trip to Canada—collected coveted foreign currency from the men. Dorothy's short snorter included dollar bills from the Bank of Canada/Banque du Canada, Banco Central de Guatema-

Short Snorter

Signed by WWII WASP

I'm not ready to come in yet, I just want some of those great pilots in there to sign my SHORT SNORTER BILL!

During WWII, a 'short snorter' was a little less than a full drink at a bar. But an aircrew member's 'short snorter' was a chain of paper currency, taped together, end-to-end, from various countries they had visited. The longer your short snorter, the more countries you had visited. Soldiers would have currency signed by comrades, much like an autograph book. As one note was filled, another would be connected to the first (usually by tape), with more added as needed. Long short snorters also meant free drinks at the bar, since the person with the shortest one had to buy the round. This tradition began during WWI and heightened during WWII.

Short Snorter cartoon by Dot Swain Lewis, WASP Class 44-5. *Courtesy of A. Z. "Chig" Lewis.*

la, Banco Nacional de Nicaragua, and Banco Nacional de Costa Rica, as well as a US dollar bill. The currency notes were autographed by men with whom she shared a Coke, a beer, a cup of coffee, dinner, a conversation, a dance. She had signatures of some of her fellow women ferry pilots as well. Short snorters were a badge of honor for the ferry pilots, and they carried them with pride.

The tradition was so popular, artist Dorothy "Dot" Swain Lewis, a Class 44-5 graduate, drew a cartoon showing a woman pilot flying up to the Pearly Gates flashing a dollar bill and telling St. Peter: "I'm not ready to come in yet, I just want some of those great pilots in there to sign my SHORT SNORTER BILL!"

The following explanation accompanies Dot's cartoon:

During WWII, a "short snorter" was a little less than a full drink at a bar. But an aircrew member's short snorter was a chain of paper currency, taped together, end-to-end, from various countries they had visited. The longer your short snorter, the more countries you had visited. Soldiers would have currency signed by comrades, much like an autograph book. As one note was filled, another would be connected to the first (usually by tape), with more added as needed. Long short snorters also meant free drinks at the bar, since the person with the shortest one had to buy the round. This tradition began during WWI and heightened during WWII.

And it wasn't just ferry pilots and aircrews that carried short snorters, it was service-wide. First Lady Eleanor Roosevelt was known to carry her own short snorter—and it remained dear to her when the war was long over.[7]

Dorothy was in good company.

Part Two

The Winds of Change

The WASP, August 5, 1943, to December 20, 1944

Jacqueline Cochran was named director of women pilots, July 5, 1943. *Courtesy of the Coachella Valley History Museum.*

Chapter Seven
Now We're WASP!

In July 1943, while the Scott family was gathering in Dallas and Dorothy was making her first trip to New York City, the tide carrying the women flying for the Army Air Forces in World War II began to shift. By mid-August the women pilots would have a new name, and the women in the Ferry Command would soon be facing an altered mission.

In May 1943, Jacqueline Cochran sent a letter to Army Air Forces Commanding General Hap Arnold listing all the reasons why she should be in charge of the entire women's flying program. Excerpts from that letter:[1]

> The group of women Ferry pilots has been more than doubled by the first small class graduated ten days ago. The next class . . . will make the Ferry group about 500 percent it's [sic] original size. By the end of the year, there will be nearly 1000 in flying service and in training. . . .
>
> My own idea is that before this group of girls is militarized, they should be moulded [sic] into a smooth running unit with problems relating to them in operations discovered and solved, and routines established . . . [and] when they are militarized "the Army Air Forces" should leave them a separate unit directly under the Air Force. . . . You need eyes and ears in who you have confidence to follow this women pilot program for you. They must be experienced, qualified eyes and ears, and they must be feminine. That's the job I would like to do, and which I think I can do well. . . . You and I had this job in mind for myself from 1941 on.

General Arnold apparently agreed with her, because he bought into her suggestion. What Cochran didn't say was that these women were moving into Nancy Love's territory—out of Cochran's control—and that was not to Cochran's liking.

On July 5, Cochran was named director of women pilots. Up to that point, her role was recruiting and selecting women for the army flight-school training program. The graduates of that training program were then sent to the Ferrying Division to serve as ferry pilots. Cochran had no say in how the graduates were used once they were in the Ferry Command. That was the job of the Ferrying Division and Nancy Love, to assign and use the women graduates as it saw fit. And it remained so.

The July 5 announcement appeared to give Cochran some kind of vague authority over all women pilots in the AAF.[2] The Ferrying Division was given no notice that the announcement would be made or any explanation of its implications once it was announced. The command and its staff were in the dark as to what, if anything, this meant to the WAFS in their employ.

On the very same day, July 5, Nancy Love was named executive for WAFS, answerable directly to the Ferrying Division's commander William H. Tunner, newly promoted to Brigadier General. A July 14 memorandum spelled out Mrs. Love's duties: advise Ferrying Division Headquarters and staff as to the best use of WAFS; plan and coordinate allocation of WAFS of the various ferrying groups; and plan and supervise training standards and a progressive air-training program to stimulate interest among WAFS in becoming qualified in more advanced types of aircraft. Nancy also was to formulate "rules and regulations governing conduct, morale, and welfare of WAFS."[3]

As far as transition was concerned, the WAFS—originals and new squadron members alike—could hardly contain their enthusiasm so ready were they to move on and up. The bigger, the faster the aircraft, the better. Getting checked out in order to ferry them was their primary aim. As far as conduct and morale were concerned, the group of women flying for the Ferry Command was functioning quite smoothly under Nancy Love. General Tunner and his boss, Gen. Harold L. George of the Air Transport Command, were most pleased with what and how the women were doing. They were, in fact, in the process of deciding to have the women ferry pilots transition into bigger and more complex aircraft: specifically the single-engine pursuits.

Then, while all the news out of Washington was still sinking in, on August 5, 1943, the Ferrying Division learned that one organization—Women Airforce Service Pilots (WASP)—would take the place of the two nominal women pilot organizations, the WAFS (Women's Auxiliary Ferrying Squadron) and the WFTD (Women's Flying Training Detachment), both operational and linked in their objective. Jacqueline Cochran headed that newly designated organization and the new name was of her choosing.

The acronym WASP was apropos because Cochran's ambitious vision, which had the nod from General Arnold, was to send graduates of the flight school to many different jobs and bases around the country. No longer would all the graduates go to the Ferry Command, only some of them. Consequently "women's ferrying squadron" no longer described what the women, as a group, did. Airforce service pilots, a more general description, did—and the acronym WASP was catchy.

Betty Gillies, squadron leader at Wilmington, recalled that, "We were WAFS until we woke up the morning of August 5 and learned that someone had changed our name while we slept! ALL WAFS WERE NOW WASP."[4]

This did not sit well with Dorothy and the other original WAFS, nor with many of the graduates of the flight-training school who were now flying under Nancy Love. These new WAFS had gotten to know her and recognized her vision for them. Nancy Love enjoyed great respect among the women flying for what was fondly called "the Ferry Command."

The pickup and delivery of airplanes continued as if nothing had happened, but the rumor mill worked overtime.

Ed had borrowed Dorothy's typewriter when he left to enter the service, but he returned it when he flew to Dallas for the Scott family reunion the end of June. Dorothy used it to type the letter transcribed below—complete with carbon copies for everyone. It was dated August 6.

Dear Family:

Holy Catz, but we've been busy. Remember how a few weeks ago I wrote that the ramp was deserted—well now it is crammed to over-flowing.

Let's see, I got an AT-6 to Newark, and Dad asks about our uniforms. They always cause comment but we don't think anything about it. One incident in Lubbock the other day, though, with some enlisted men—"Whaddya know, women in uniform pants!"

After the AT-6 trip, I had a solo one to take an AT-17 from St. Joseph to Lubbock, which I did with no trouble at all except that I stayed up all nite getting to St. Joe, so I slept all day and left the next. In Lubbock the MPs picked me up in mistake for a missing WAC. I had to show all my passes and orders, etc. I got quite a bang out of it, and then had a nice shot with them all.

No sooner did I get back than I got another solo job—an AT-6 to Memphis. That was a mere detail so I left yesterday AM delivered at noon and got back via airline in time for dinner. That brings us up to now. Already I'm on another trip. This one is as flight leader for two girls to take 6s to Dayton, Ohio, which is a little off the ordinary. Some of the girls are going farther west now in ships. I'll likely get one soon, so Mom, watch out for your darling daughter dropping in. Don, I doubt if I get your way. I considered phoning from our nearest stop, but it was still quite a ways.

Late news says that we first five are to go to instrument school soon. That's swell, I'll be glad to get an army instrument ticket, called "soup ticket" here. We're to fit it in between trips so at the present rate I'll get my ticket some time next spring.

Over at the North American factory in Grand Prairie where we get the 6s they said they are converting to P-51s mostly so by the time we're ready for them they'll be ready for us—oh joy.

Don, I appreciate the dope on the Camp Davis WAFS—I'm glad I didn't get in on that.

We are now on a 7-day week, 24 hr job, and it means just that. Penn and I have been so busy and will stay so, that we're going to sell the boat. One outing in 3 weeks doesn't pay.

The car deal still seems ok but I'll wait and see how things go. Selling the boat will put me quite a bit ahead financially so maybe I can buy an old wreck outright. Still, Ed's or Don's may be available some time soon. Things are just so certain I think I'll go into the fortune-telling business.

There's still no swimming here due to the epidemic, but the operettas every week are a big event. I haven't missed a one since that time you were here. None have been so good as those first ones though. *Naughty Marietta* was tops, and I'm looking forward to *Rose Marie*.

Our home-life is almost routine. I can even wash dishes without it seeming a rare event. With such hectic housing conditions, we consider ourselves very fortunate.

That's enough.

Dorothy signed the letter with everyone's pet name for her.

Dorothy
Dot
D. D.
Sis

One big piece of news in that August 6 letter is an indicator of great things to come for the women pilots of the Ferry Command. The North American plant in Grand Prairie, Texas, was switching over to the manufacture of the P-51—the high-profile, single-engine fighter aircraft that, in 1944, would nail down an Allied victory over Germany. It was the plane that all the male and female pilots longed to fly.

From Dayton, Ohio, on August 9, Dorothy wrote to G. M.:

Imagine who I saw today. While we were getting our things together at the Dayton airport where we delivered, one of the fellows mentioned "Lt. Gillis."

"Who did you say?" I asked. It turned out it was our old CAA friend who gave me my instructor's rating.

He was very glad to see me and we ate lunch in the Officers Mess and talked of old Washington days. He surely wishes he could get back there. He is in charge of the army operations in this center run by Northwest Airlines. He gets quite a bit of flying done, but like me can't seem to get to the west coast.

It was good to get these ships delivered. It has been a bit of trouble for me because I had a "dud" for once. This ship kept throwing oil on the windshield so I couldn't see ahead at all and had a dangerous time landing always. Also all of us had oleo pressure give way on the landing gear,[5] causing one wheel to drop when landing, which aggravates ground-looping tendencies. It looks awkward, one wing nearly dragging. Yes, the line crews are supposed to fix such details.

Visibility was again always low. I'm getting used to this blind flying.

On return I'm going to ask for another trip immediately, not take time off. Also I hope to see Nancy Love and Jackie Cochran as they should be in Dallas now.

The trip I want is one to California. Nearly all have gone out there now except me.

Airliner leaves at 6:30.

Dorothy

On August 21, Dorothy got a long-awaited checkout in the 1200-horsepower A-24.[6] She flew for two-and-a-half glorious hours and made eleven landings. Then, miracle of miracles, she was assigned a trip to Southern California the following day—to deliver an A-24. After much lobbying, she was going west. She could see her mother.

Dorothy also knew that Nancy Love was due to visit the squadron the latter part of August. She and the others hoped that Mrs. Love would bring an explanation of just what and who the WASP were and of everything else that was going on. Dorothy did not want to miss out on that. She made her plans carefully and left California with time enough to return to Dallas.

August 24, 1943

Dear Mom:

I know you'll be interested in hearing from me soon so I'll start from where I left you. It seems so funny to have seen you so recently and yet here I am at home again. I always get that feeling when I return from some distance.

The bus ride out to Burbank was uneventful except that the driver and I had a nice talk.

I signed my ticket and got on as the first call so as to get the choice of seats. Being so tired it was no trouble at all to curl up in the front seat and sleep clear to El Paso. There I cleaned up and got to eat breakfast on the plane. I like to eat on a plane. Then I finished my trip papers and soon Dallas was in sight.

Back here Nancy Love was just due in so I waited and she, Helen and the rest of us did some talking, and things will be altered some in the course of time.

We had steak for dinner and since I got so much sleep, we're going to do something tonite.

Dorothy

Nancy did, indeed, give her women pilots an explanation.

General Tunner and Jacqueline Cochran had decidedly different interpretations of the extent of her new role. Tunner considered Cochran to be an advisor to Air Staff. Her job was to recruit and see to the training of women pilots. And, of course, he was under the impression that they all were destined to fly for the Ferrying Division—if they proved qualified to do so—because that was the original purpose for training women. But Cochran took her new title, director of women pilots, quite seriously. Coupling this new entity—the WASP—with her title, Cochran took this as the next step on the way to a women's air corps under her leadership.

In mid-July 1943, she had taken twenty-five of the flight-school graduates (all but two from the newly graduated Class 43-3) away from the ferrying squadrons and sent them on a completely different mission. They were to learn target towing at Camp Davis, North Carolina. Six of the twenty-five—Betty Deuser, Dora Dougherty, Elsie Dyer, Isabel Fenton, Elin Harte, and Lois Hollingsworth—had originally been assigned to Dallas. This was the reason for Dorothy's comment to Don about Camp Davis in her August 6 letter to the family.

Cochran didn't tell the Ferrying Division what she was doing. She issued new orders—hers. The four WAFS squadron commanders released the women she requested to report to her in Washington, DC. After that, no one in the Ferry Command knew where the women had gone. This created a huge headache for General Tunner's administration, which was responsible for paying the missing women. It took weeks to find them and nearly four months to straighten out the mess and get them paid.

On August 30, Cochran sent twenty-five more, all graduates of Class 43-4, to Camp Davis to learn to tow gunnery targets.[7]

Though the Ferrying Division doggedly held on to the name WAFS after August 5, the usage began to disappear as the name WASP gained both official sanction and general popularity. Though Nancy Love's position with the Ferrying Division never changed, she was subsequently referred to as the executive for the WASP in the Ferrying Division, answerable to General Tunner. Cochran, with General Arnold's backing, was calling the shots for the growing WASP organization as a whole. Some five hundred women were in training at Sweetwater at any one time, and the number of women on active duty grew with every graduation.

Nancy Love was General Tunner's liaison in dealing with the growing women's squadrons within the Ferrying Division. By mid-August, 202 women were assigned as ferry pilots, and the number would rise to more than 300 by spring 1944.

In their August 24 meeting, Nancy shared as much as she could with the women who had gone with her to Dallas and those who had come since. Bottom line, they were to continue doing what they were doing—ferrying aircraft and moving up in transition as rapidly as they could. The originals were serving as flight leaders and role models for the new girls coming in. And graduates from Classes 43-1 and 2 were working their way into leadership positions in the squadron. The largest number of new graduates yet—twenty-six from 43-4—had just arrived.

The timing of Nancy's trip to Dallas coincided with something else big

Betty Gillies and Nancy Love, B-17 pilots, with the *Queen Bee* in Goose Bay, Labrador, September 1943. *Courtesy WASP Archive, Texas Woman's University, Denton.*

that was happening in her life.[8] She flew nothing less than a B-17 into Dallas on August 24.[9] This made her women pilots' eyes pop out with envy. She and Wilmington squadron leader Betty Gillies had spent the previous month getting their instrument ratings and learning to fly the Fortress. They had checked out in the B-17 ten days earlier and had just completed several Ferrying Division assigned deliveries of the big bomber. Tunner planned to have the two women—his top two women pilots—deliver a B-17 to England in early September as part of a two-hundred-plane armada of Fortresses.

When Nancy arrived in Dallas that day, she and Betty had completed their training and were ready to "fly the Pond." But when Dorothy and the rest of the squadron met with their leader, they were unaware that history might be in the making. Nancy and Betty's mission was a well-kept secret.

Tunner had been getting static from male pilots who objected to ferrying B-17s over the stormy North Atlantic to the United Kingdom and he saw a potential solution. "These flights had become almost routine and there was no reason for complaint. I decided to let a couple of our girls show them just how easy it really was," Tunner wrote after the war. "We had scheduled a blitz movement of two hundred B-17s to go over [September 3–4, 1943], and I assigned the two women to one of the planes."[10]

On September 1, 1943, Nancy and Betty left Ferrying Division Headquarters in Cincinnati in the B-17F—christened *Queen Bee*—on the first leg of a trip that, in a few days' time, would take them across the cold, unpredictable North Atlantic. With them was a four-man crew: a navigator, a radio operator, an aerial engineer, and an assistant aerial engineer. The plane was destined for the US Eighth Air Force in Great Britain. After some delays, they landed in Goose Bay, Labrador, September 4. Much of their trip from Presque Isle, Maine, had been under instrument conditions.

They never took off from Goose Bay. Gen. C. R. Smith, thinking the two women and their crew were well on their way, sent a wire to England alerting the commander of the Air Transport Command European Wing, Brig. Gen. Paul Burrows, that the plane flown by the two women pilots was on its way, and to notify General Arnold.[11]

The telegram was delivered while Burrows was having dinner with his boss, Hap Arnold. Burrows handed the telegram to Arnold, who immediately ordered the flight stopped.

The following is Arnold's message:[12]

Just have seen message from C. R. Smith . . . indicating that a B-17 with women crew will leave for England shortly. . . . Desire that this trip be cancelled and no women fly transoceanic planes until I have had time to study and approve.

Passengers Nancy Love and Betty Gillies boarded a C-52A in Goose Bay the morning of September 6, 1943. The flight was bound not for Prestwick, Scotland, but back to Presque Isle. They were going home. Two male pilots took their places and ferried *Queen Bee* on to Scotland.[13]

So ended the only attempt to have WASP pilots deliver aircraft across "the Pond." The women's role in ferrying aircraft for the country would grow and flourish, but all trips would be confined to the continental United States and Canada.

Chapter Eight

Under the Hood

Dorothy took a few days' leave the end of August and hopped a flight to Peterson Field in Colorado Springs to see Ed and Ethel and also her dad, who took the train down from Oroville. The primary purpose of the trip was for her to retrieve her car since Ed had acquired a car of his own. The Scotts enjoyed the brief respite together, then Dorothy took off early the morning of August 31 and drove straight through back to Dallas.

She dropped G. M. a note September 2 to let him know she arrived safely: "It rolled all the way here without a complaint. In fact it rolled so good I went the whole way at once and averaged about 50. It's 750 miles so I got here about midnight."

Instrument school and flying under the hood awaited her. The "hood" was a black cotton curtain pulled over the cockpit where the student sat. The instructor—or a check pilot—sat in the other cockpit, had a clear view, and kept watch for traffic.

September 8, 1943

Dear Dad:

> I'm buzzing right along in instrument school now and start tomorrow on the AT-11—twin-engine plane for instruments.
>
> I have another instructor who is ok. He said, "Some of your air work is a little rough, but I'd pay anyone $25 who could lose you on any range." Boy, he makes me work on let-downs (i.e., constant speeds and rates of descent). One thing was fun. There were a few cumulus clouds at 5,000

The twins, Ed and Dorothy. It was Ed who preserved her story by saving her wartime letters home. *Courtesy: The Scott Family Collection.*

today so we went up into them and I really flew instruments. It was funny being able to see out but still have to fly "under the hood." It was really good practice too.

I had one trip last Sunday. Since there was no hood time scheduled I asked for a one-day trip and got it. I took six new girls in PT-19s to Ballinger, Tex. It was funny to fly the 19 again, as I hadn't since Delaware days.

We got to our delivery point just ten minutes ahead of a terrific storm. I'd been watching it come and had an alternate airport picked out, but we got in ok.

My instruments all went haywire en route. Suddenly I noticed my airspeed drop off so I ducked the nose and gave it more throttle. It didn't move so I tested it in a real stall. It dropped back to zero so I guessed it was cockeyed. Also the altimeter stuck so I made my final approach at 2700 feet and 140 mph. I taxied in at 100 mph. Ho Ho.

Bye

A malfunction had caused all three instruments to give dangerous but obviously false readings. The altimeter should have replicated the field's actual elevation, 1,738 feet—not 2,700; the normal landing airspeed for a PT-19 is at best 90 miles per hour, not 140; and the taxi speed should have been about 20 miles per hour, not 100. Dorothy, being an experienced pilot, realized what had happened and coped with it.

Her letter of September 9, was to the whole family and, again, she used the typewriter and carbon paper so everyone in the family would get the news. In it, she alluded to two changes. The new barracks for the women's ferrying squadron were finished, and Don had been transferred to south Texas. Dorothy wrote:

Dear People:

Well, I'm still waiting around for my instrument test. It's supposed to be just a basic test (no radio) but my instructor says that I'm liable to get both cause I'm good enough to finish up right away. Either way will be fine with me because one way I'll get more hood time, and the other I'll get back onto trips sooner. Helen Richards got into the school yesterday.

Betsy, Helen and I are on the outs with Florene and Delphine. Yesterday Betsy found out she was thrown out of her top job and D. put in so she raised a howl. She had me there to listen in and so of course the whole deal blew up. Some bad words were flying around. I tried staying on the listening side only but too many sore spots were raised and soon I was talking some too. What will come of it all I'm not sure but I'm not in any worse light than before—maybe. Anyway I'm sure of not getting a staff job, which is good cause I'll get more flying and less politics.

Dad, I'm all moved out of Zimmy's, and all moved in the barracks—it's nicer too, real convenient.

Don, there's some good chances that I can get down your way in an AT-6 some time because a lot go to Victoria [Texas] and I can get lost 25 miles worth easy. It's funny how things work out. If I hadn't gone into instrument school I'd have gotten to take some A-24's to Camp Davis. Several of the girls have gone there with them. By the time I get one there now, you'll be gone.

Now I gotta go take that flight test. . . .

Well, I just finished my test. Whew, that is absolutely the hardest work in the world; first flying, then under-the-hood air work, and last, a test. I didn't do so good I thought, but I got a Fair on it so I pass ok.

My air work isn't so good as my radio work, so the next test will be easier. No radio this test.

I went to lunch at the mess and who did I see but Jacqueline Cochran. First time I'd seen her. She was eating with the CO so I didn't meet her but I will later today as she's coming here to the barracks.

Personally, I'm glad I don't "rate" too high around here as it's too much work mixing flying and politics. If they let me fly, I'll not quibble over becoming a "leader." Anyway, if we were elected by the kids I'd sure out rate our top kicks so that's consoling.

Dorothy

Dorothy was well liked by the women from the flight school who had begun to join the Love Field WAFS squadron in early May. And word was getting around the women of the Ferry Command that Dorothy Scott was a pretty neat individual and all-around gal, easygoing and likeable.

A few days later, Dorothy was taken out of instrument training, temporarily, to deliver an A-24 to New York City. She and Jane Emerson, 43-2, were assigned twin A-24s. Dorothy was flight leader. Her instrument work to date paid off in spades on this trip, because they ran into big weather trouble.

From: Hotel Henry
Pittsburgh, PA
Friday, September 17, 1943

4:00 PM

Dear Dad:

Before leaving Tulsa with my A-24, I had a factory man there give me a short review on cockpit procedure and Jane and I got off with no trouble.

We had to do some fancy relocating to get into Scott Field outside St. Louis due to a wrong beam heading (late change) but all was ok. From there we flew to Columbus, Ohio, and got in just too late to go on further east because of less daylight hours.

We RON'd there staying in the nurses' quarters and saw the post movie. Then today we got into trouble—weather again. We cleared for Harrisburg, Pa. via Pittsburg [*sic*]. Outside Pittsburg we ran into a few lowering clouds so we hedgehopped on and I called the Pittsburg radio for weather reports. As I received them in code we had to circle while I deciphered them. They read none too good so I decided to go to a small army field about 20 miles s.e. of Pittsburg, but the clouds really fell to zero, so I changed to fly down the beam to a field about 50 miles away on a heading of about 125 degrees. All this time telling Pittsburg radio my plans. Well fooey, but we really got boxed in all around and Jane was following me patiently. I had the radio relay my plans to her.

Seeing no way out now I asked the radio to advise a field. You see Pittsburg itself I didn't want due to local haze always, but this time they said their own field was the best bet, so I put my instrument lessons to work and beam-bracketed back. They kept asking my position but I knew it only approximately. However they kept in contact and really helped me out and we broke out as planned and they spotted us at the same time so we switched to the tower and came on in.

I'd felt fine all along but when I got out of the plane I felt like a wet dishrag. The weather has us stopped until noon tomorrow at least.

I had a hunch we might get stuck so I have a winter uniform on—and even pajamas! Boy, and it's cold! We nearly froze in the planes. They have an air scoop for keeping the engine cool—and one for the pilot too—no cabin heat (has a plug-in for a suit heating—if only I had the suit.)

P.S. I sure like that airplane!

Dorothy painstakingly sketched out the whole convoluted landing sequence for G. M. to add to the letter. On it she added: "Columbus had given us 5,000 feet clearance over 3 miles all the way. And even the reports read 'OK except local showers!' Ye Gods!" The envelope bears a Pittsburgh, September 17, 1943, postmark. Dorothy mailed the letter that night. She and Jane RON'd in the Hotel Henry. The letter was on hotel stationery.

The weather in Pittsburgh held them until noon the next day. After sleeping in, and with time to kill, Dorothy started a letter to her mother, also on Hotel Henry stationery. Both her parents now got a kick out of receiving her letters handwritten on hotel letterhead. Those, like the picture postcards complete with postmarks from her various ferrying ports of call, told them where she had been. On the way to the airport, she finished the letter to her mother with, "Gee it's cold up in this part of the country. I'm writing this now while riding to the Pittsburgh airport in an open GI truck."

Dorothy's reference to the beam and bracketing is what she was hearing in her earphones—the Morse code signals for the letters A and N—"dit dah" and "dah dit." "The beam" is when those two signals merge into a constant hum—"on the beam"—that was the directional signal to and from the local airport's radio range.[1]

Dorothy and Jane landed in New York after an uneventful two-hour and ten-minute flight from Pittsburgh on September 18. The weather had moved on east. Jane had never been to New York before, and since it had turned into an exceptionally clear day, they went to the top of Rockefeller Center and gawked like the accidental tourists they were. Then they wore themselves out pounding New York's sidewalks, gawking some more, this time from street level, finally stopping in an oyster bar in Grand Central Station where they could sit down.

Dorothy had bought a postcard to send to her dad. The description on the picture side read: "Looking South over Lower Manhattan and New York Harbor from the Observatories of the Empire State Building—1250 feet above the city street, New York City." She penned a brief note to G. M.—"We finally got in O.K. and now have four hours to kill. It's real good visibility so we are seeing NY from this place"—and dropped the postcard and her mother's letter in a Midtown mailbox.

They caught the 8:30 p.m. airliner back from La Guardia as far as Memphis, where they were grounded by bad weather. When they took off again, they were in the soup immediately and flew over the top of it all the way to Dallas. Dorothy found the view of the cloud formations so fascinating that she stayed awake watching them.

Sunday nite,

September 19, 1943

Dear Dad:

> Now, I have a secret for you. I went to see Capt. Wright who is head of it [instrument school] and we talked a while, and guess what—he wants me to instruct on instruments for him!! This isn't sure yet because he has to see the powers-that-be to get their ok, but it shows that I must rate with him. It'll be a

good deal for me besides instilling my book knowledge a bit more, because it will give me a good reputation on the post that I can sure use.

(next day)

I flew instruments in the AT-11 today, and did ok. When we landed, we found the army newsreel service shooting pictures of some of the girls coming out of another plane and getting into our AT-11s—the bums! So we watched a while. First thing you know, they had me doing a solo number for them in a PQ-8—the little target ship I mentioned earlier and flew for awhile the other day. I got back into my chute, climbed into the thing, started it, and taxied for a ways. So now I'm in the movies. It will be sent overseas and then maybe released here.

And, remember last February when I told you I took a *National Geographic* writer around for her material—in the rain? The October issue is out and has a "Women-In-Uniform" article and a short note about the WASP—and I'm quoted!

Dorothy

Dorothy had a lot going on in her life at this point. Both her leadership abilities and her proficiency with instrument flying had put her in line for some very interesting work. For Captain Wright to be so impressed with her work that he offered her a job teaching instruments was a huge compliment. Not only had Dorothy put in the hard work, she had proved to be very good at instrument flying. And the captain obviously saw in her an ability to pass her knowledge on to others. As he said, it wasn't a done deal, but he was carrying the idea forward.

On the other hand, photogenic Dorothy had a way of getting pulled into Army photos. With her tomboyish good looks, positive attitude, and ready smile, she easily attracted the male photographers.

A case in point, Dorothy made the front page of the September 24, 1943, issue of *The Flying V*, the official newspaper of the 5th Ferrying Group. She and two male ferry pilots—all dressed in khakis and carrying parachutes slung over their right shoulders—are striding through the entryway to Ferrying Group headquarters. The imposing sign—"5th Ferrying Group" supported by two sturdy columns—spans the road with buildings stretching into the distance behind them. A guardhouse with sentry can be seen to the right of the photo. The American flag flies high from the

Dorothy Scott was the cover girl for the September 24, 1943, *The Flying V*, the 5th Ferrying Group's official newspaper. The officer on Dorothy's right is Lt. Frank Harvey. The other officer is not identified. *Courtesy WASP Archive, Texas Woman's University, Denton.*

flagpole behind them. Superimposed against a white fair-weather cloud is a four-engine C-54 transport in flight. The young man on Dorothy's right is Lt. Frank Harvey. The young man on her left is not identified.

The issue was dedicated to the 5th Ferrying Group's first anniversary at Love Field, which was September 28. The story that accompanies the photo says that when the first personnel arrived September 28, 1942, they:

> ... found barracks that lacked windows, streets that were unpaved, equipment and office furnishings still crated in quartermaster warehouses. Less than 100 enlisted men were in the party that moved to the new base. . . . The women pilots appeared on the scene [in January] as WAFS and in late summer [1943] were designated WASP. Barracks were erected for occupancy by WACS but only two have reported for duty. . . . Only projects not completed at end of the first year are the chapel, the gymnasium, and runway improvements.[2]

Congratulations, printed on page two, came from Brig. Gen. William H. Tunner, commander of the Ferrying Division; from Col. Thomas D. Ferguson, the 5th's first commanding officer at the base, now in command of the Eastern Sector of the Ferrying Division; from the new commanding officer of the 5th as of September, Lt. Col. Russell W. Munson; and from Col. Robert H. Baker, former commander of the 2nd Ferrying Group in Wilmington, where Dorothy initially had served, and now commanding officer of the Kansas City–based Central Sector, Ferrying Division, overseer of the 5th Ferrying Group.

Things were going well for Dorothy, with one exception. Word had come down from headquarters that Helen was being transferred to Palm Springs. Rumors about a possible new base for the WASP there were confirmed. Looking into a possible transfer there, herself, began to weigh on Dorothy's mind.

SNAFU, TARFU, and FUBAR[3] were the nicknames for the Ferrying Division's "airline" used to get pilots back to base after they delivered their aircraft. It had evolved over time as the Ferrying Division searched for the quickest, most efficient way to get ferry pilots back to home base so that they could be sent out again. Commercial airline service was severely cut back because many of the DC-3 airliners operating before the war had been commandeered by the military. Deliveries often were made to out-of-the-way places, and taking trains and buses was time consuming and therefore inefficient. The quick turnaround and rapid return of these ferry pilots was critical.

Those DC-3s commandeered from the airlines, known as C-47s in the Army Air Forces, became the backbone of SNAFU. Airlines. The alphabet soup denoted the colorful, if irreverent, names the men gave to the pilot retrieval service. What became MATs (Military Air Transport) in 1944—and so known after the war—began with these flights to pick up ferry pilots.

From: Del Prado Hotel
Chicago, Illinois
September 25, 1943

Dear Dad:

It seems I must write you real often so I won't forget happenings.

In Dallas Tuesday I was put on orders again—and I'm just one AT-11 hour from my instrument rating. (Then I teach it—no secret.)

Anyway, here I am taking an A-24 to Windsor Locks, Conn.

We flew TARFU to Tulsa and stopped overnite. One fellow and I are together. This AM we got our planes and taxied out. At the end of the runway I had some trouble getting my brakes on for running up the engine. And no wonder—one wheel was afire.

A B-24 nearby saw it and radio'd.

My, was I popular for a while. Out came a fire truck, an ambulance and a colonel! There I sat very nonchalant. Well, it wasn't serious so I got taken back by the colonel and some mechanics brought back the plane. They checked it good and Don (the fellow) and I finally got off. (His radio had fizzled so he came back too.)

We stopped in St. Louis for gas then on to here. Weather butted in—we came into here ceiling about 500 and visibility about two miles—optimistically speaking.

Parked for the nite we grab a taxi, and partway to town we discover I go a different way (he has friends here) so I grab another at a street corner. Imagine my surprise to be told by the driver that I got on at Cicero (a district) right in front of Al Capone's place! He said his last nite's passengers spent the time shooting at street lites en route. It must still be full of small-time gangsters.

Tonite I really ate. It was very good because the last three days I've been living on soup as nothing else would stay down. I'm going to need a rest cure soon.

Much as I like the A-24 they sure get lots of ailments. This one, besides the faulty brakes has haywire gas gauges, short circuit in the radio, and a hood that I kill myself closing. However, I'm not freezing this time. I drug out my winter underwear, white uniform, flying suit and leather jacket—all of which I wear.

Chicago I haven't seen yet, too much fog and rain. Maybe it'll be bad tomorrow—I hope—so we can stay a few hours.

Three new girls were washed out in Dallas—poor check rides. The training center is shoving people through who shouldn't make it.

Dorothy

To wash out means to be eliminated from the program. Many young women washed out of the flight-training facility in Sweetwater, which meant they did not graduate and did not receive their wings. They were sent home. In this case, however, the women had received their wings and had been assigned to the women's squadron attached to the 5th Ferrying Group. The check pilots there judged the women to be lacking in the skills necessary to perform the duties of a ferry pilot.

Dorothy's statement in her letter to her father turned out to be prophetic. Those washouts went against the grain with Jacqueline Cochran and grew into a major confrontation between the Ferrying Division and Cochran and the Training Command.

Chapter Nine
Ferry Command at the Crossroads

At the end of August 1943, General Tunner learned that there had been "an excessive number of accidents and mishaps among women pilots, all of which involved graduates of the Women's Flying Training Detachment." That was when dissatisfaction with the actual quality of the newly graduated WASP first became an issue.[1]

On September 14, Tunner wrote to his superiors at the Air Transport Command (ATC) asking that he be allowed to eliminate those WASP "who lack an inherent flying ability and those found unsatisfactory." He also suggested changes to strengthen the training curriculum in Sweetwater to address those deficiencies: a minimum of three hundred hours total flying time; greater emphasis on crosswind landing and takeoffs and taxiing light aircraft in strong and gusty winds; a cross-country training trip of two thousand miles with several landings at strange fields and a minimum of two nights away from home base. He also suggested that the Training Command, and any other agencies interested in using pilots from "this particular training program, consult and coordinate with this Headquarters."[2]

The ATC concurred with Tunner's recommendations. On September 18, C. R. Smith, ATC deputy commander, notified the Training Command of ATC's decision. He sent along a copy of General Tunner's letter and a note stating ATC's approval of Tunner's plan.[3] The order went into effect with almost immediate repercussions.

On September 22, 1943, Jacqueline Cochran received a telegram on behalf of two Dallas WASP from Class 43-4.[4] It read:

There appears to be unfair checks and elimination among W-4 girls by Ferry Command this base. Would like to consult you at your earliest convenient [sic] some girls ready to resign.

Signed, Class W-4

Two days later, the three Dallas WASP pilots that Dorothy referred to in her September 25 letter home—all arrivals from the newly graduated (September 11) class 43-5—also were eliminated.

Jackie Cochran wanted to keep all her WASP even if the Ferrying Division could not use them. She hoped to build and command a women's air corps that would be part of the Army Air Forces. To do this, she needed large numbers of trained women pilots who could serve in many flight-related roles. With Hap Arnold's approval, already she had sent fifty women pilots to Camp Davis to learn target towing. She wanted "her girls" exposed to many AAF flying jobs, to learn different kinds of flying, and to see how they performed and fit in. The problem was that no one had bothered to pass this information on to the Ferrying Division or Air Transport Command.

The Ferrying Division was functioning under the assumption that *all* the women at Sweetwater were being trained to be ferry pilots and that, upon graduation, they were sent to the division ready to move to the next level of transition. Men who "washed out" of flight training were sent to the walking Army. As civilians, if the women could not make the grade, there was no place to put them and they would have to be dismissed. Confusion reigned. Cochran felt her girls were treated unfairly; the Ferrying Division felt its actions were warranted, as it was following Army procedure.

On September 29, Cochran wrote to the Air Inspector, Headquarters Army Air Forces, seeking redress. "The Training Command considers the accusations . . . of such a serious character that they should not go unchallenged."[5]

She asked for an investigation.

Two opposing forces were at work. Cochran showed her lack of understanding of, and respect for, the Ferrying Division's mission and its attempts to do its job under wartime circumstances. The Ferrying Division had its standards and had found some of the new pilots lacking necessary skills. The women were civilians, not military. The Ferrying Division had no authority to transfer civilians. It released them. Cochran was furious. She wanted and needed those women.

When the Love Field male check pilots washed out those five fledgling WASP ferry pilots in September, the system of sending training school graduate women pilots to the Ferry Command—that had been in effect since May—began to come unglued.

Several critical changes in circumstances impacted the Ferrying Division in September 1943, and the fallout affected the future of the WASP.

First, the Ferrying Division had just been made responsible for training its own future male ferry pilots. Up until then, the Training Command had handled all training. Now the transitioning of fledgling male ferry pilots would be the Ferrying Division's own responsibility. That created several problems. "Ferrying trainers was the foundation of the Ferrying Division's on-the-job upgrading program."[6] Currently, women ferry pilots were delivering nearly all of the primary and basic trainers.

The number of women ferry pilots was increasing rapidly. If all those women were held to flying only primary trainers, there would be no planes left for the men to fly and no way for them to transition up. There was more. Production of both primary and basic trainers was rapidly falling off. On the other hand, the production of pursuit aircraft was soaring as the US war machine switched gears to the offensive. Remember Dorothy's comment about P-51 production in her August 6 letter?

The Ferrying Division found a solution. Mastering the single-engine pursuit aircraft (P-39, 40, 47, and 51) was an unnecessary transition for male pilots who were destined to deliver four-engine heavy bombers overseas. Pursuit training was a side step. The same was true of the more complex twin-engine pursuit (P-38) and attack plane (A-20).

The primary goal now was to prepare male pilots to fly multiengine aircraft overseas. Women were barred from flying overseas. The women coming from Sweetwater were supposed to be "qualified to deliver at least the AT-6 type aircraft without personal supervision or additional training."[7] Why not point the WASP toward, and have them concentrate on, pursuit deliveries?

That was Tunner's decision—to build a sizable corps of women pursuit ferry pilots. Having women pilots qualify in Class P and specialize in that work, and secondarily qualify on the faster group of aircraft in Class IV, was desirable, if not essential for the war effort.[8]

There was a downside. The pool of experienced women pilots (two-hundred-plus hours) had been drained by the time Class 43-3 began training in January. The 28 WAFS plus the 109 women who would graduate from Classes 43-1, 43-2, and 43-3 totaled 137 women pilots. That number included nearly all of the qualified women in that pool. But—unknown to the Ferrying Division—Cochran began accepting for training women with only thirty-five hours—the number of hours then required for a private pilot's license. This represented a huge change in qualifications.

From the beginning, the Ferrying Division had fought the 200-hour requirement for women to be admitted to the program. The division wanted 300 hours. Men needed 300 hours to qualify, and the original WAFS had needed 500. But Cochran got her way in the September 15 and 22, 1942, showdown with ATC's General George when she was named director of the women pilots' training program. Two hundred hours stood as a requirement for the first women pilots to enter the Women's Flying Training Detachment in the fall of 1942 to be trained to be ferry pilots.[9] The rationale was, the women would receive an additional 120 flight-training hours, giving them more than 300 hours when they entered the Ferrying Division. That worked only briefly.

The Ferrying Division did not learn until April 1943 that the hours needed to enter the training program had been dropped all the way down to 35.

The 120 hours the WFTD women received in training, added to 35, gave them a total of 155 hours. The graduates were falling increasingly short of the 300 hours the Ferrying Division required for employment.[10] But it didn't matter because, by then, the Ferrying Division had been told, from the top through command channels, to accept the female training school graduates, period.[11] This, in spite of the Ferrying Division's belief that incoming male and female ferry pilots should be accepted using the same set of standards.

When the prospect of sending women to pursuit school arose eight months later in the fall of 1943, the Ferrying Division was faced with bringing women with only 155 hours upon graduation up to the 500 hours required, plus the necessary horsepower ratings, to attend pursuit school. And few primary or basic trainers would be available to them to help fulfill this requirement.

General Tunner's suggestion, in his letter of September 14 that WFTD graduates have a minimum of 300 hours total flying time, seems designed to address that problem.[12]

Class 43-4—152 women strong—arrived in Texas for training in February 1943. That was more women than had entered through the WAFS and the first three WFTD classes combined. Of the 152 trainees, 112 graduated August 7, 1943. The question might be asked, "How many had 200 accumulated hours, let alone the 300 hours the Ferrying Division previously required for admittance?" The occasional ground loop, bent prop, getting lost, misjudged landing, or unwise decision—flying into weather or running out of fuel on cross-country deliveries—became more frequent. The Ferry Command expected perfection of its pilots and did not readily tolerate these transgressions.

Trouble had been in the making. Now trouble had arrived.

On October 5, Cochran wrote to the Air Inspector again.

> It is imperative . . . that ATC be instructed immediately to keep these three women pilots [43-5] on its payroll until a decision can be reached as to whether their training has been adequate, or whether ATC is correct in its statement concerning the quality of these pilots.[13]

The day before, October 4, 1943, Dorothy Scott wrote to her family that girls were "flunking out of here [Dallas] after making it at their flight school. That's criminal since it's the school's fault, not theirs."

The Air Inspector began a several-weeks-long investigation across five bases employing WASP—three ferrying bases, Dallas, Wilmington, and Romulus, and also the training base at Sweetwater and Camp Davis. The investigating officer, Lt. Col. Dudley N. Outcalt, conducted interviews with forty-seven women pilots and did flight checks with twenty. When his report was released in late November, it said that the elimination methods at Dallas were unfair to the women. The check pilots resented them and applied the rules unfairly during check flights. The Air Inspector talked to some of the women at Dallas, who told him that the check pilots "rode the controls," making it difficult for them to properly control the aircraft. And the men yelled a lot. The Air Inspector's recommendation was to "admonish the commanding officer at Love Field for discrimination against WASP pilots."[14]

That addressed Cochran's complaint over the release of the five Dallas WASP. However, there remained a deeper problem. That was the lack of preparedness General Tunner addressed in his September 14 letter after receiving the report, at the end of August 1943, of the excessive number of accidents and mishaps and the dissatisfaction with the quality of the new women pilots. Obviously, this was not just a Dallas problem. This affected all four ferrying bases.

Iris Cummings Critchell, 43-2, recalls what was happening at Long Beach in August and September 1943:

> At first the evident lack of preparedness for long cross-country flights in newly arrived pilots in Class 4 puzzled the Long Beach transition department. Long Beach at that point had no knowledge that this was happening at other bases. The transition department's solution was to send a pilot whose preparedness was in question out on a BT trainer delivery flight with one of the squadron's already qualified women pilots. Over two months, I was assigned delivery trips with six of the new girls. The other experienced girls were doing this as well. Normally BTs are delivered solo.[15]

Iris, as part of Long Beach WASP squadron Commanding Officer Barbara Erickson's leadership team, was privy to scuttlebutt from the other bases. "Before the arrival of the Class 5 graduates, reports began to filter back that this lack of preparedness was showing up at all of the ferrying bases."

On September 21, 1943, the Ferrying Division requested of the ATC that it be sent only fifteen training school graduates per month. (This would mean approximately four new women per ferrying base.) The reason given was the "concern with the existing situation in regard to upgrading pilots." It should be noted that from fall 1943 through spring of 1944 excessive numbers of the division's male Class I and Class II pilots were backlogged, and upgrading them was a problem. Fewer incoming new women pilots—all of whom, it was hoped, would be fully qualified on the AT-6 and ready to transition up from there—would alleviate much of that problem.[16]

While all this was brewing, Dorothy continued to work on her instrument training with only ferrying trips to interrupt her efforts.

Chapter Ten
October 8, Red-Letter Day!

Freezing-cold cockpits at altitude and the Midwest damp took their toll on Dorothy. En route to Connecticut in the A-24, she ended up at a doctor's office in Cleveland. Diagnosis, ear infection.

October 4, 1943

Dear Family:

> I stayed in Cleveland two extra days swallowing "sulfa" pills and then—attired in some "long handles" (our pet name for long underwear) ordered by the Doc—flew on to Bradley Field, Connecticut, to deliver the A-24. Quite routine, but I did enjoy the autumn scenery up in New York, flying via Buffalo, Rochester, and Albany.
>
> I returned via airliner and had to report to the Doc here at Love Field. He promptly grounded me, not for ear trouble but for having taken sulfa drugs. There is a regulation saying no flying for six days after taking any sulfa—and I flew the very next day! My civilian Doc didn't know and I didn't either. It is supposed to make you see 'double' and act drunk at altitudes. Ho-hum.
>
> While I was grounded, I was asked to give speeches to the new girls—arrivals from Class 43-5—about trip procedure. Then I gave a lecture on flight tests to seven new girls who were ready to wash out after their earlier test rides. Their gratitude at getting set straight was so appealing that now I've been appointed ground training officer and will give all new girls the same dope. Those girls were flunking out of here after making it at their flight school. That's criminal since it's the school's fault, not theirs.

To address the backlash that began with Cochran calling for the Air Inspector, the command at Love Field sought an internal solution to what had, overnight, become a major source of contention. The new girls obviously needed help and guidance, an intermediary, someone who had already been through the adjustment period—someone they could talk to who could answer their questions, someone who had the ability to talk to people and make explanations in an understandable manner with an empathetic ear. Dorothy Scott became that someone, a liaison between the new girls and the "system"—the much-feared check pilots who had the power to send them home. Of course Cochran, by then, was in the process of getting the firings stopped and the Air Inspector brought in. Nevertheless, addressing the problem from within seemed prudent, and Dorothy proved to be good at it.

Dorothy wrote a second letter on October 4, 1943.

Dear Mom and Ed:

This letter is for you two (carbon to Ed) because somehow Dad gets written to and Don is too far behind.

Nancy Love is here visiting and is to take a plane back north and asked for me for copilot. That was a compliment but required a bit of work to get me back on flying status—the sulfa drug I took for the ear infection—but I'd already proved I could fly so I got on. Then the work really started. Boy, I wanted to please Nancy anyway so I worked myself to death. The plane was a C-47 or army version of the airliner. I hadn't even seen the inside of one, so I had some fast learning to do.

The trip with Nancy was a nightmare. I did all the paperwork, all the navigating, all the flying except for takeoffs and landings. And then I was busy with gear, flaps, etc.—all in an entirely new ship. Oh my! The navigating was hardest because I'd drawn the course both possible ways via the airways, but she decided to go direct, which eliminated all radio help. We had less than five miles visibility and no checkpoints for a hundred miles at a time.

I hit every point right on the nose, and so earned the compliment I got on my navigation when we delivered the plane. A copilot does a lot of gadget pulling and I had to learn their uses and location in no time at all. Imagine, there are five answers to give her after she says "gear down."—"Handle down, pressure up, green light on, got-a-wheel, and latch down and locked." Same with flaps, cowl flaps, mixture control, tail wheel lock, and a few more. You can see what a dither I was in. Besides, it was Mrs. Love, my boss, looking on at everything.

Well, she got an overdose of me this trip because she heard all my speeches to the girls in my ground training class and praised me for those. I'm glad, because she knew I could fly but didn't think much of my leadership qualities—not after the boner I pulled letting Don ride with me back in Delaware last December.

Enclosed is the front page of the post magazine. Everyone says it's good of me, I think so too. I sent dad a film print and I have one. This and the army newsreels have put me up in front. Alas I'm the writer for our squadron.

Instrument school will toss me from the student ranks to instructor soon—I'm terrific, yeah.—That and the new-girl training really will work me hard, but I want it that way.

Dorothy

Sis

Nancy did have her eye on Dorothy. She had detected competence and leadership qualities and wanted to observe and test them firsthand. The word on how well Dorothy got along with others had reached Nancy at headquarters in Cincinnati. The early take on Dorothy, when she arrived in Wilmington late in 1942, had been that she was "young and tomboyish" and that she "eats-sleeps-dreams-talks flying."[1] Back in January, Nancy had observed Dorothy in Dallas as she coped with her injury, worked through it, and focused on the Link Trainer and learning instrument flying. Now, the Ferry Command scuttlebutt regarding Dallas was, "You'll like Helen Richards and Dorothy Scott, both Originals. Dot reminds me of my younger sister, sort of a tomboy."[2]

Catherine "Cappy" Vail Bridge (43-2) remembers Dorothy well. "I was a member of the second class and was sent to Dallas after graduation from Houston. The first missions we had, when we got to Dallas, were orders that gave leadership 'command' to a WAFS—Dorothy or one of the others—while the rest of us followed like a gaggle of geese. I remember Dorothy as a modest and very helpful person. She became a good friend."[3]

Nancy's leadership needs were changing with the coming of pursuit

training and the shifting of the overall WASP program, and she was looking to her Originals and her early flight-school graduates—the women
with the most flying experience and/or maturity—to fill potential slots.
Nancy appears to have noticed a maturing on the part of her very young
pilot, and she most certainly didn't miss the enthusiasm Dorothy brought
to the job and life in general.

Six days later, out went another typed letter—jubilant in tone and again
with carbon copies to all:

October 10

From: Wasp Extraordinary

Dear Family

Friday morning, Oct. 8, 1943 (red-letter day) your esteemed relative became an army instrument pilot. Hurray! Mostly the feeling hereabouts was
"well, it's about time!" I took [the test] in a C-60, which is a big cargo plane
used here for hauling pilots en masse. I did a good job says my pilot and
everyone—so I'll take a bow.

With that behind me finally the deal was for me to instruct it to the
girls and some fellows perhaps. Well, Colonel Baker—who is C.O. for
this section of the Ferry Command and who used to be the head guy in
Wilmington when I was there—hears about me teaching and says "no!"
His argument (tho they don't argue) was that no new instrument pilot is
qualified to teach. It goes round and round and still is "no." That was surely
too bad because the instrument school had made a new nameplate for me
and hung it with all due ceremony, and I had a plane, students, and was
ready to go.

That was the situation last nite. This morning we have a review and so
get out before daylight and freeze to death before the head guys along with
the rest of the post.

And my last one was a few weeks ago in the afternoon wherein we all
sweated it out—this Texas weather! We did ok. I guess two of the new kids
don't stand at attention very long without fidgeting a lot.

Right after the review, I got with Delphine and a check pilot [on a
C-47]—like I flew with Nancy Love—and we spent the rest of the morning
in the air. Now I'm Delphine's copilot on a trip coming up next week. After
that, I'll go as first pilot. Back here, instrument school calls up and says for
me to hike right over with a student to fly instruments! I recover from a

faint and do so. Somewhere the wires got twisted. It was quite a deal.

Teaching is swell. I just love to talk anyway and to get a student in my power on the listening end is wonderful. The girl was Bernice Batten, the little short girl who joined when I did in Delaware.[4] (Dad and Don will remember her.) She sure tries hard and did ok too.

We landed after five p.m., so now I don't know whether I'm actually an instrument instructor or not. (Everyone here quits at five except pilots!) But now it doesn't matter because something else has come up.

Nancy Love came back on a one-day visit on another matter and I went to see her to inquire about some pilot-requests that had come into the office and of which I had not been included on the answers. Florene and I don't see things the same way all the time, so I ask Nancy direct. The deal is to go to pursuit school! Now this has been my pet for a long time so I ask if I get on and she says yes. Now what will [become] of this is anybody's guess. It may mean a transfer to a training school and then to a pursuit base so that's one possibility. What else is up to the gods and powers-that-be.

(Note!) Do not mention the above paragraph in any of your letters since wrong readers may be around. Never say much of such things in any letters—they're dangerous.

I'm really in favor of getting a transfer since I've been here a long time and there's lots of the world to see yet. Pursuit is ideal and leads to bomber transition—west coast—I hope, tho anything goes.

My big new job of organizing a ground school for all girls is well under control. I have an office, a secretary (who knows more than I do), a classroom, lots of students and subjects, and am getting instructors first so I won't have to do it. The trick to running something is not to let it own you or you're stuck with it—and I want to keep flying.

The day is now half-an-hour along (12:30 a.m.) on the dot so here's for some sleep.

By—
Dorothy
Dot
D. D.
Sis

In addition to working with the new WASP, Dorothy finished checking out on the two twin-engine Beechcrafts: the AT-7, primarily used for training

Dorothy Scott on the wing of an AT-6, Love Field, Dallas. *Courtesy: The Scott Family Collection.*

navigators, and the AT-11, used for bombardier training. Transitioning into small twin-engine aircraft qualified her as a Class II pilot—on the way up the ladder. On October 14 she was sent to Wichita to pick up an AT-11 and take it to Carlsbad, New Mexico. But first she had to bring it back to Dallas for the transition department to use it for twenty-four hours. The

Dallas runways were under construction. On her return, only one was available to her and it lay crossways to the prevailing wind—a crosswind landing being quite tricky and requiring piloting skill and know-how. It was her first such landing in an AT-11. She wrote to G. M. on October 21:

> When I came in with the 11, the wind was 30 mph directly across and it was my solo landing. Boy, it worried me plenty, but I did ok. The wind stayed up so strong, I couldn't leave the next day, but the day after that, I hopped to Midland for gas and then on in.
>
> Imagine my luck at Carlsbad to have a B-24 busted down there and getting repaired. It was fixed soon and I hitched a ride to El Paso. This was my first B-24 ride and I surely liked it. The crew was swell. I explored the plane and when we flew over 12,000-feet, I wore an oxygen mask. It was much like the masks we wore for gas attack drill. No, I didn't get to fly it at all. I could have, but was too busy getting all around from nose to tail and keeping from freezing to death.

In El Paso, Dorothy ran into two WASP heading for Dallas in BTs. She remained overnight (RON'd) there and rode back to Dallas with them. She ended up flying one of the aircraft, allowing the pilot to get some sleep in the backseat. From Dallas, she was sent right back out to Tulsa to pick up another A-24, this one headed for San Bernardino, California. She RON'd the first night, October 18, in Abilene, where some other girls were weathered in with PTs due to high wind.

> The wind was too strong for them, but not for me so the next day I headed out for El Paso. I had a lovely lonesome ride on in. I'd had trouble getting my gear down at each stop, since only one wheel would come down until I got tough with it. This time I was so busy getting both wheels down, I missed my heading and started to land on the wrong runway. The tower says "wrong approach, pull up and go around," so I do. (Was my face red.) We had to stay in El Paso over nite (a whole lot of pilots) since a front was moving just west of there,

Dorothy delivered her plane to San Bernardino the next day, caught the bus into Los Angeles, and phoned her mother to meet her. She had just missed Don. He had left the night before. She was disappointed, but she and her mom had a good evening together.

From: Palm Springs to Phoenix

October 22, 1943

9:30 AM

Dear Dad:

Mom and I went to Long Beach yesterday morning. They didn't have any planes for me so I'm hitchhiking back in this C-47. We stopped in Palm Springs over nite so I look up my friends.

Going into the Officers Mess I spotted Helen Richards. While talking to her Knox comes up and so I eat with him. In a minute or so I'm hailed by Ken Wickstrom (Mamer-Schuh pilot) and ol' Army. We spent the evening talking over old times.

Knox was to fly a B-24 that evening and I was going along but the plane was busted down. Knox has been meaning to write you, and will soon, but has been a bit busy flying to Australia and Hawaii. He's gone most of the time. He rates pretty high around here and earns it.

I have your last letter with me so I'll answer the questions. First, the "long handles" have come in handy several times lately, at Reviews, and A-24 trips etc.

I expect to get some kind of orders most any time so don't send me any apples or anything for a while.

I tell you some of my problems with the top girls in Dallas but not the whole story. Your advice on not talking is good in general but being a meek mouse has been a factor in me being pushed around. One or two good "soundings off" and things go smoother. When they deliberately keep me from getting Wash. and Calif. trips and keep me out of the transition I've earned I'm going to holler—and loud.

The best bet is to leave the scene entirely which I'm trying to do. But don't say anything about that stuff in your letters. I hate to have to burn them right away.

I'm the only Dallas girl with an instrument rating and Erickson is the only one in Long Beach. A few in Delaware have them. However, six of our girls entered the school right after I left and so more will have them soon.

I'm not sorry to not be taking it, as I need heavier plane time mostly. [She is referring to teaching instrument school.]

When letters are far apart bawl me out but don't worry.

By now,
Dorothy

I flew to El Paso in C-47, transferred to a B-24 and so returned to Dallas. Just finished dinner—first meal in two days. But I like this rush life. Let Mr. Doerr print most anything he thinks interesting except specific planes and places. (can use states ok.)

Dorothy missed her best friend and confidante, Helen Richards. She missed the camaraderie she and Helen and Zimmy Sluder had had that previous summer. In spite of her friendly, outgoing nature, Dorothy felt very much alone.

On September 14, 1943, General Tunner had told his superiors at Air Transport Command that—due to the large number of pursuit aircraft now being produced, coupled with the declining numbers of training aircraft being built—the Ferrying Division would begin training women pilots to fly and deliver pursuit aircraft.[5] At that point, Tunner had six original WAFS already ferrying a limited number of single-engine pursuit aircraft: Wilmington's Betty Gillies, Helen Mary Clark, and Teresa James were ferrying P-47s out of the Republic factory on Long Island; Barbara Erickson and Evelyn Sharp, P-51s out of Long Beach; and Romulus's Del Scharr had been ferrying P-39s out of Buffalo, though now she was in the process of being transferred from Romulus to Long Beach by way of Wilmington.

General Tunner was going to need a lot more women pursuit pilots. This development had resulted in the scuttlebutt Dorothy had heard and about which she had spoken to Nancy Love.

The Ferrying Division planned to establish a school for pursuit transition. Fledgling pursuit pilots—male and female—would be trained in Palm Springs, California. There, they would learn to fly the four single-engine pursuits—P-39, P-40, P-47, and P-51—in a focused, four-week training period.

The school would open December 1, 1943, in Palm Springs. The students would receive the best instruction available. Their instructors would be factory reps from the manufacturers of the airplanes and the airplanes' systems—people who knew their stuff.[6]

The requirements for entering pursuit school were an Army instrument rating known as a "white card,"[7] five hundred hours, and a Class III rating, meaning the pilot had been checked out in a heavy twin-engine cargo aircraft—a C-47 or C-60—or the Class IV twin-engine B-25 bomber. The original WAFS had to have five hundred hours to qualify for the program in 1942 and fly for the Ferry Command, so they had cleared that hurdle, but they had to meet the other two requirements. Flight-school graduates—beginning with the women from the first two classes and who met the three requirements—would be eligible as well.

Seven WAFS were given the nod to enter the first two classes at pursuit school: Nancy Batson, Barbara Donahue, Florene Miller, Helen McGilvery, Gertrude Meserve, Helen Richards, and Dorothy Scott.

In October, General Tunner submitted the names of fifty-six more women ferry pilots qualified to transition to more advanced type aircraft in preparation for pursuit school. Fifty-four were graduates of the flight-training school, and two, Dorothy Fulton and Sis Bernheim, were original WAFS.[8] Nine members of the first two classes to graduate from Houston were assigned to the earliest pursuit training classes along with the seven original WAFS. The Houston graduates chosen for pursuit school were Iris Cummings, Ruth Thomson, Lewise Coleman, and Carole Fillmore from Long Beach and Betty Whitlow, Betty Jane Bachman, Jane Emerson, Sidney Miller, and Cappy Vail from Dallas.[9]

The sixteen women headed for pursuit school were scheduled for instrument training at their home bases that fall. One path to logging heavy twin-engine time was to fly copilot in those transports being used to get ferry pilots back to base in the shortest time possible. It was on-the-job training at its best. Both the male and female ferry pilots were part of this transition plan, but it appears that the 6th Ferrying Group at Long Beach made the most concerted use of the opportunity.[10]

At this point, the Ferrying Division also told its Ferrying Group commanders that their pilots were *not* to be given pursuit transition at their home bases. Pursuit transition would be given *only* through pursuit school.

On October 24, Dorothy wrote G. M. from Monroe, LA:

> I returned from the LA trip and spent all day Sat. working at my ground school job. Today (Sunday) I was put on orders to take an AT-7 from Dallas to here. Due to weather, I didn't take off until 3:30 and landed here a couple of hours later.
>
> Boy, dad, that plane is wonderful. I was very careful because it is still quite new to me but I did everything just right and made an especially nice landing.
>
> Well, it took two hours from Dallas here but it is taking about 24 to return. There are no trains or buses until tomorrow (thank God) and an

airliner is going tomorrow also—guess which I'll take. (my orders ok airline travel)

So here I am. I went down to dinner and sat down at a vacant table. Up
comes an elderly man who says he is vice president of Delta Airlines and
would I join him and his secretary at dinner.

I would and did have a very nice evening talking to them both.

Delta has a lot of side-businesses besides 'airlining,' one of which is crop
dusting. They explained the specially-built planes they use for this and I'm
invited to see them tomorrow if I have time. I hope I do!

Since Mr. Wallman was nice enough to buy my dinner I invited him to
be my guest at the Officer Mess when he is in Dallas and it wouldn't surprise me if he does come—he said he would, of course.

The end of the month, Dorothy's ear and sinus trouble flared up again.
She was becoming concerned that this repeated problem could end her
Army flying career. On October 31, 1943, she wrote to her father, "For
a couple of super-healthy pilots, you and I are a washout. I just returned
from Detroit, grounded again with a sinus infection, to find your two letters stating you are now ill."

G. M. had allowed himself to get run down. He was considering coming south for the winter, maybe to Dallas. Dorothy tried to dissuade him.
She wrote: "Unless your doctor really advises it, I think that if he outlines
a diet for you and regular hours it should do the trick as well or better than
a month or two in a strange land."

Dorothy's trouble had started when she reported for orders in Romulus.

They gave us two PTs to take to Arkansas, but since they were open planes
and I'd caught a cold the day before, I was worried about it and reported
for advice to the flight surgeon. He promptly grounded me so I returned
via airline.

The whole deal shows that I'm getting run down so I'm in bed here
perpetually except for meals. Tomorrow I'm going to a nose and throat
specialist and see about preventing further occurrences of this, as if I don't,
I'll be eligible to be bounced—horrible thought. It makes me furious to get
hit by such a thing.

You asked about Penn and Paul. We've gone separate ways so I don't see
them very often. [One] isn't interesting and [the other] is always gone. In

case you are interested, I don't date anyone specially here (but there is the nicest bombardier in El Paso).

There are so many things claiming my attention now, ground school and "politics" here, getting checked out on the C-47 as 1st pilot, a new plane the A-25, getting well, and working on a trip to Washington where I can see you.

May I get them all soon; and you get well fast too. Don't work too hard at home cures and watch that hotbox apartment. Too much heat is bad too.

With the family gone from Oroville, G. M. now lived alone in the small second-floor apartment he had built on the back of the Scott Motors garage. That Dorothy worried about her father is obvious, but there wasn't a lot she could do about the situation given her WASP assignments and her wish to continue flying. The status quo would have to remain in effect for the time being—or, as they said during World War II, "for the duration." But Dorothy did put her mind to coming up with a solution.

Chapter Eleven
Pursuit School Bound

Grounded with a sinus infection and chafing at the inactivity, Dorothy was elated when word came through that she was being given a temporary nonferrying assignment. The Training Command needed input. Dorothy's work with the new WASP as they reported to Love Field, helping to get them up to speed in the necessary ground-school subjects and, in her own words, "educated on ferry procedure," had gotten the attention of some higher-ups. She was the one for this job.

Sixteen WASP graduates from Classes 43-5 and 6, instead of being sent to the Ferry Command, were assigned to South Plains Army Air Base in Lubbock, Texas. This was part of Cochran's expansion program. South Plains was the home of the Advanced Glider School. The young women were there to learn to tow CG-4A gliders at low altitude, mostly at night. The tow planes the WASP were expected to be flying were the single-engine A-25 and twin-engine C-60.[1] More commonly, the C-47[2] was used to tow the CG-4A.

The WACO-designed CG-4A glider[3] was the most widely used US troop and cargo military glider of World War II. Constructed of fabric-covered wood and metal, it had a two-person crew—a pilot and copilot—two fixed main wheels and a tail wheel, and could carry thirteen troops and their equipment.

The training program had begun October 21. In early November, Dorothy was sent to Lubbock to see how the WASP and their tow planes were getting along. She was to report her findings back to the Training Command.

Dorothy flew back to Dallas November 14 in a C-47. When she finished writing her report on the glider-towing program, November 15, she started a long letter to her dad. She had a lot on her mind.

> The time in Lubbock was most profitable, spent riding in the gliders and the tow planes. I had a whale of a good time and had a rest too, because of ground fog each morning. . . . They are considering using girls for tow pilots in planes no one approves of. Thank goodness I have enough material to put up a good stiff argument against the use of the A-25 as a tow plane. If we can use the C-60s or C-47s, it will be different. I don't think girls should tow on cross-countries anyway.

Dorothy did not relay her argument against the A-25 to G. M., nor did she say why she didn't think the girls should do cross-country towing. But apparently her recommendation against using the A-25 carried the proper weight, because only the C-60 Lodestar is mentioned during interviews done in later years with seven of the women pilots who served in Lubbock. One, Ann Karlson, 43-5, said that she flew the C-60 and, "I also rode in the CG-4 glider and learned to fly it."[4] None of the seven mentioned the A-25. Dorothy continued:

> Back here I found a lot of things cooking, some pertaining to me. . . . I discover I am to be sent to Palm Springs pursuit school for a month starting December 1. This presents a whole lot of possibilities.
>
> Now hang on to your hat because I am going to ask mother if she wants to come out for that period. It will do her a lot of good and me too. You see, I won't stay with her. I will stay on the post and see her only occasionally. You will no doubt disapprove on the grounds that she will worry me, but the reverse is true since I can see her only when I want to and she is a big help in so many little ways that add up to a lot—anything from sewing to sympathy.

Dorothy appears to walk a tightrope between her mother and her father. The middle child—the girl between two boys—she had become the focal point of the family. The peacemaker. The conciliator. The doer. Extroverted Dorothy had become the enthusiastic catalyst. She was in charge. The boys depended on her. Katherine and G. M. each depended on her. Dorothy organized the family get-togethers, taking the full responsibility for ventures now that the family was spread so far apart.

Dorothy had lived through the years when her mother and father were growing increasingly apart. She knew why her mother left. Years later, Ed and Donald—in talking to Ed's son Tracy—told him that G. M. not only had a terrible temper, he also was a tyrannical controller. When Katherine finally had had enough, she left. Dorothy appears to be the only one G. M. truly got along with. He adored her. They were pals—best friends.

Dorothy continues her November 15 letter:

Now for your part in this. You could easily be in Palm Springs too without straining your family ties too much, yet I don't quite feel that you could stay there contentedly considering how erratic my time allotments would be. Again, though I hate to say it and you will say it isn't so, I do more worrying about you and what you could do with yourself all that time. I'll be doing too much concentrated flying to do more than fall flat each night.

Right now I'm headed for that last C-47 time I need as soon as a plane is available. That will give me the Class 3 rating I need to go to Palm Springs; then I'm going to try to fly the A-24 and check out on the A-25 and get trips on them so as to get the single-engine heavy time I can use in pursuit school. If I get my way I'll get trips west and stop at El Paso and see Don. Anyway, here I am with two weeks and lots of things to do in that time.

Meanwhile I am in up to my ears in troubles here. Four WASP had forced landings all due to carburetor ice in PQ-8s, one of whom smashed her plane and broke her nose. Also our other troubles have magnified and gained momentum so that we all are treading on thin ice and may get some fast deflating.

You are probably wondering whether or not to come back here now. I shall likely be here a few days but of course can't be sure. Everything is in such a muddle I shant know what I'm doing one minute to the next.

Wire when you are coming so I can meet you.

Dorothy

Dad: I think it would be a good deal for you to drive out with me if you possibly can. This would be about Dec. 1 or earlier. Perhaps I'll not be given enough time for me to drive out so you could take my car, which I'll need there.

What Dorothy was seeing and hearing was something that Nancy Love was to hear about all too soon. But as of the last week of November, the problems were an internal matter affecting only the Love Field women ferry pilots.

With pursuit school looming as a future plum or a dreaded possibility—depending on each individual WASP's viewpoint—the rumor mill was rampant. Dorothy was well liked by the male check pilots and the mechanics who maintained the aircraft. No surprise there; she was outgoing and she got along well with men. She talked to them. They talked to her.

She was picking up on indications that some of the women pilots were either being pushed through transition too fast or that they were asking for transition they weren't ready for or weren't yet allowed to have. She also was hearing that some did not want to fly pursuit. They were being vocal about it and stirring up others. Added to that, with the four forced landings, one smash-up, and a broken nose to contend with, morale was sinking.

Frustrated by the way things were going, Dorothy decided to write to Nancy Love. She hoped Nancy would come to Love Field, answer the questions the women had about pursuit school and other concerns, and put their minds at ease. Since Dorothy had flown with Nancy the previous month, she must have felt enough of a connection with her boss to put her feelings in writing and wrote the following letter to Nancy Love dated November 26, 1943.[5]

> The way I see it is that you get all the "official" information and I get some of the undercurrent gossip, so if I tell you what I learn it might help you out. Darn if I like to appear as a stool pigeon, but if you don't know some of this stuff and should, this is OK.
>
> My main worries are that some of the girls refusing to go [to pursuit school] may spoil things for all of them, and too, that perhaps they aren't using the best methods of finding out who would be best to send. No one seems to have thought of asking the checkout pilots in A-24s and A-25s (rumor has it they're betting on how many will live through it all).

Unfortunately, Nancy Love was not in Cincinnati when Dorothy's letter arrived. She was at Long Beach to check out on two aircraft. On November 29, she requalified in the B-25 and, on November 30, she made her first flight, a solo, in the single-cockpit, twin-engine pursuit Lockheed P-38 Lightning—the first woman to fly it. On December 1, she was back for more to finish her P-38 qualification.[6] Thus Nancy paved the way for her women ferry pilots to transition into the P-38. Eventually, at least twenty-five WASP pursuit pilots would ferry the sleek aircraft.

G. M. did go to Dallas to spend Thanksgiving and the weekend following with Dorothy before she left, but he ended up not driving her. The four Dallas WASP bound for pursuit school were being flown to Palm Springs. Dorothy and G. M. took in a movie Sunday afternoon and then dinner before she went back to the base. The next morning, G. M. headed north, stopping in Colorado Springs to visit expectant parents Ed and Ethel. Their first child was due late in February.

Dorothy, Betty Jane "B. J." Bachman, Florene Miller, and Sidney Miller packed their B-4 bags, boarded a C-47 the morning of November 29, and reported in Palm Springs November 30 to begin pursuit school as members of the first class.

Chapter Twelve

December 3, 1943

In the late afternoon of November 30, Dorothy, Betty Jean, Florene, and Sidney landed in Palm Springs. Since her dad was now in Colorado Springs, Dorothy dropped a joint letter to him, Ed, and Ethel with a glowing report of her first day there:

Palm Springs Air Base Calif.
December 1, 1943

Sand, sand everywhere.

Tomorrow we start flying.

After me beating my brains out for a month trying to get to El Paso to see Don, I got there without any effort on my part. I left Dallas that next noon with a half-hour warning. The other three girls and I were flown in a C-47 by a major and captain who are running this thing—sort of. We flew to El Paso that afternoon and I called Don. He came down to get me and I stayed at his field in the WAC quarters. We had dinner downtown first, at the Officers Club—very nice. And he got a bang out of having his sister there in uniform, baggy slacks and all.

He had to stay at the field as OD, so I did too. Next a.m. I ate with him at the general mess (officers and enlisted too). I slicked up a bit more for this occasion (ahem). Then we went out pistol shooting until he took me to the field. There I showed him the plane and he met the whole party. He doesn't know we didn't leave until 2:30 that afternoon due to an oil leak.

Dad, while you and I were at the movie show Sunday afternoon, Florene was putting on one of her own. She was flying a P-47—which she wasn't supposed to—and coming in for a landing when she hit a power-pole. Sun in her eyes. It clipped off part of a prop blade, tore the fuselage, flap, and part of the elevator. She gave it the gun, flew around for two hours, and came in a heroine. The joke was, by hitting that pole she blew out all the field lights and radio contact.

Florene had trouble with her gear etc. etc. etc. and by the time she got the tower on her radio again it was after dark and they had all the jeeps etc. out, headlights on, lining the runway for her.

The pay off is, the lowly lieutenant who checked her out is going to be court-martialed. All higher up disclaim knowledge, the bums. And Florene is a heroine and comes on here to Palm Springs with us.

Two others are on a hot seat and Florene's a four-page glamour-girl with "lots of courage."

Anyway, we hopped on to here and started moving in. Helen and I are roommates, and there are 8 of us girls with 35 fellows. We spent today getting passes and entrance red tape then went to town. I'm surely sold on Palm Springs for its warm sun, beautiful mountains and quaint shops in town. This is on my "post war living" list.

Our barracks are two-by-four. No hot water.

First flights will be dual in BC-1's (AT-6 type aircraft). Then in order: the P-47, 39, 40, and 51. We are divided into A and B flights. Fly half day, school half day. I'm in A flight and must be on the line at 7:15 each a.m.

We have to wear skirts at evening mess—dern it.

Write soon and good trip home.

Dorothy

That was Dorothy's last letter.

Dorothy made her first flight in Palm Springs on December 2, with an instructor, in a BC-1A trainer. She logged an hour and made two takeoffs and landings. That was the extent of her flying that day.

The following day, December 3, she reported to the flight line again. Even though she had written that she was in Flight A and was to fly in the mornings, for some reason she was flying midafternoon.

A high, thin overcast limited the visibility to thirty miles. The desert temperature was a pleasant seventy-six degrees and the wind was a light four miles per hour out of the west-northwest.[1]

That afternoon Florene Miller and Nancy Love were standing on the flight line at Palm Springs, talking. Nancy had flown over from Long Beach in the P-38 she had checked out in two days earlier.[2] Presumably, she was there to talk to Florene about her ill-fated November 28 P-47 flight, and to say hello to her eight WASP pilots who had arrived for pursuit school.

Florene and Nancy waved to Dorothy as she and her instructor took off. Florene was due to go up next in the same trainer. While Dorothy was flying, Nancy and Florene continued their conversation.[3]

Dorothy, flying from the front seat with her instructor in the back, had already made several landings. Once again, she set up and entered her final approach, establishing a normal gliding attitude. Above and behind her, a P-39 student pilot swung from a shorter base leg into his final approach. Apparently the pilot in the P-39 could not see Dorothy's plane because of the position of the low winter sun and the banking attitude of his aircraft. He was above her and descending faster than she was. They were on a collision course.

The tower shouted a warning, but it came too late. The P-39 came down over the top of the trainer. The two planes collided in midair. The tail section of the BC-1 was severed. Both ships crashed into the ground a short distance from each other, with the BC-1 bursting into flames upon impact. Dorothy was killed, as was her instructor, 2nd Lt. Robert M. Snyder. The P-39 pilot, 1st Lt. Wilson A. Young, died as well. Young had been sent to pursuit school from the 7th Ferrying Group in Great Falls, Montana.

The time of the accident was 16:34 PWT (Pacific War Time)—4:34 p.m. in civilian time designation.[4]

The accident report that came out later noted, "It is also believed that the camouflaged aircraft in this area (Palm Springs) is a contributing factor to the accident." Among the recommendations listed on the form: "All aircraft used in Pursuit Transition be painted yellow."[5]

The pilot who had flown the P-39 just prior to Lt. Young wrote in his report that the radio in the aircraft was malfunctioning "during the time I was gunning the engine and during engine speed changes. During straight flight reception was O.K."

He also added: "When you are coming in on Base leg, from three o'clock on in the afternoon, it is mighty hard to see. Camouflaged ships against the mountains are hard to see. You are going directly at the sun and there is quite a bit of haze, and planes on final approach are usually in a shadow. Also the plastic windows are somewhat the cause of inability to see well. You can't see anything but a haze outside of your window until you get in a shadow."[6]

In the aftermath of December 3, Nancy assigned Florene to accompany Dorothy's body home to her mother in Los Angeles. Florene recalls, "Because I had been Dorothy's squadron commander at Dallas—and she and I had gone to Palm Springs together for pursuit school—I had to call her father and twin brother and tell them. I'll never forget that."[7]

Florene and Dorothy had been friends and had enjoyed good times together. They had been squadron-mates for a year, first at Wilmington and then at Dallas. They traveled to pursuit school together—two of the four Dallas women pilots sent to the first class. Even though they didn't, as Dorothy put it, "always see eye-to-eye," they were colleagues, and their destinies were irrevocably intertwined. Florene, Helen Richards, and the Long Beach WASP pilots who were not out on deliveries attended the funeral December 8 and the interment at Valhalla Memorial Park Cemetery in Burbank, California. Valhalla was chosen because G. M.'s father was buried there.

Valhalla Cemetery has a special section called the Portal of the Folded Wings Shrine to Aviation that is the final resting place for a number of aviation pioneers—barnstormers, daredevils, and sundry architects of aviation. There is a memorial to Amelia Earhart and others, honoring their accomplishments.[8] Dorothy is not buried in that special section, but it seems fitting that she lies in a place that memorializes famous pilots who have flown west.

Dorothy Scott, Nancy's WAFS number twenty-five, was gone. All that promise, all that ability, all that enthusiasm. Nancy never said a word to anyone, but those who knew her well knew that she was devastated. She was just beginning to really know this personable young woman and appreciate both her flying ability and her leadership potential. Nancy had met G. M. when he came to Wilmington with her in November 1942. She frequently asked Dorothy about her father.

Helen Richards took Dorothy's death harder than anyone in the women's squadrons.

But hardest hit of all was her family. The pain endured by countless other parents and siblings throughout the country and the world came down on the Scott family. Both Don and Ed, serving in the military, survived the war. It was their sister who was lost.

G. M. received these two letters after returning to Oroville.

On December 20, Nancy Love wrote one of the hardest letters she ever had to write.

Dear Mr. and Mrs. Scott:

Although I know that there is nothing I can say that will alleviate your grief at the loss of Dorothy, I do want to tell you how terribly we all feel about it.

Dorothy was one of the finest girls and best pilots we had. Her loyalty, efficiency and initiative were an inspiration to all of us and her loss is a severe blow, not only to the original group of WAFS but to the whole group. She delivered many airplanes while she was with us, and died serving her country—perhaps there is some comfort in that, in these times. She loved flying, and I think felt as I do—that if it has to be, the way to die is in an airplane.

If there is ever anything I can do, please let me know.

Most sincerely,
Nancy H. Love

On December 22, Ed wrote:

'Tis a bum Christmas. Not just for the Scott family. But for 1026 families whose sons went into battle in the South Pacific a few weeks ago. And whose sons shall never return.

I guess lots of American families have to give. It must be just an act of God. We have to pay, ever so dearly, for what freedom we can get out of life. And my sister was always one to be out in front. And I guess she just was cut out to lead the Scott family into eternity. God made her that way, and perhaps just for that reason. She'll be up there waiting, Dad—just like we last saw her—for the rest of her gang.

Well Dad, you'll be a Grandad soon.

The December 10, 1943, edition of the *Oroville Gazette* carried the story of Dorothy's death on the front page. It was a three-part article. Part one was the news story and obituary, and part two was a letter from G. M. Scott describing the accident from the Army reports he had received.

Part three was the heartbreaker. Dorothy, when she left to join the

WAFS, had promised to write, on occasion, a piece for the newspaper about her life in the WAFS. Her letter, written November 24 and posted from Dallas, arrived in the newspaper office about the time of her death. The editor, I. J. Doerr, ran it in its entirety.

Below is G. M.'s letter, followed by Dorothy's.

Dear Sir:

I regret to inform you of the death of my daughter, Dorothy. She died Friday December 3 at 4:30 p.m. Two planes collided in the air while coming into a landing at the Army Air Field at Palm Springs, California, 90 miles east of Los Angeles.

The cause of the accident—well it was just one of those unexplainable things. Three planes were circling the field for a landing. The AT-6 [*sic*] plane that Dorothy and an instructor were in was in the lead, the next plane was a P-39 Airacobra pursuit plane, the third plane was another AT-6.

The control tower operator first cleared Dorothy to land, then thinking there was space enough between them cleared the P-39—evidently forgetting that the P-39 landed 35 miles per hour faster than the AT-6. He gave his attention to the third plane, another AT-6. As the P-39 was behind and above Dorothy's plane and settling fast for a landing, the sun was low blinding the pilots. The P-39 pilot could not see Dorothy's plane. Result—a collision about 200 feet above the ground. The two planes crashed at once and burnt, two planes and three pilots. The pilots were not at fault.

Dorothy will be buried Wednesday at Valhalla cemetery, near Glendale, in the plot where my father is buried. Dorothy's girl companions in the WASP will attend the funeral in a body. Donald, Edward and his wife, Mrs. Scott and I are all here.

Thus ended the life of the best friend and the best pal I ever had.

I will return to Oroville as soon as I can clear up Dorothy's personal affairs.

Yours respectfully,
G. M. Scott

Dorothy's November 24 letter:

Dear Mr. Doerr:

The "semi-annual event" has come 'round again, and there have been several things happen since my last letter.

The WAFS have had their name changed to WASP (Women Airforce Service Pilots) because we are doing more varied jobs than merely ferrying. We were only 25 in number a year ago, but now are over 200. There are girls in innumerable bases doing "odd job" flying and so really releasing a pilot for combat.

My part of it all has mostly been a matter of more trips to more places in bigger airplanes. It seems funny that a year ago a WACO biplane was a "big" airplane, yet now that type is the smallest I fly, and I feel right at home in the army version of the Douglas airliner—the DC-3, known in the Army as the C-47.

The army training we get is something that couldn't be bought by a millionaire in civilian life. I'm now a full-fledged instrument pilot—and believe me it has come in handy a time or two.

Next thing coming up is pursuit school. We go to another base and attend a regular schedule of ground school and flying. It is lots better that way—and healthier.

Of course one might ask what good all this big plane flying will be in civilian life. Yesterday I asked a CAA man how to get my horsepower rating changed to show I'm qualified to fly planes as large as those I do for the army. "What's the use," he said, "there are no planes that big in civilian flying."

With so many girls at one base now, we can't all just fly; we have to attend to administrative work too. My job is ground school training officer. I see that new girls get educated on ferry procedure and all the extra subjects one needs such as radio, navigation, army regulations, etc.

Of course by this time I'm quite familiar with territory around New York and Florida and California, but still can't seem to get up into Washington. Maybe they think that if I did I might "get lost" for a few days. Eventually I'll get there even if it is after the war is over.

Since I could never seem to get home, my Dad made a point of getting down here again. It is always nice to see old friends. Most of the people I see that I knew before are those I flew with and are now in the Ferry Command also.

Well, eventually, I'll get home again by accumulating enough leave and then stubbing my toe or something so they'll have to let me go. Right now we're too busy, but I like it that way.

Please keep *The Gazette* coming. It is "home" for me as it is for so many people now scattered all over the world.

Dorothy Scott

Part Three

Women in Flight beyond the WASP

December 1943 to the Present

Chapter Thirteen
Aftermath

The story that Dorothy related to her father in her December 1 letter is the one Florene Miller Watson herself told many times of her harrowing P-47 flight that Sunday afternoon, November 28. Dorothy and her father were at the movies when it happened, therefore not eyewitnesses, but Dorothy heard about it upon returning to base later that evening.[1]

The flight made the Dallas Monday morning paper.[1] The P-47 hit a light pole when Florene came in for what should have been a routine landing. However, the late afternoon sun was in her eyes, temporarily blinding her. The impact damaged the propeller and tore open the fuselage of the airplane. It also took out all the lights and the radio at Love Field. What followed was Miller's fight to get and then keep the stricken airplane under control. It was late November and rapidly growing dark, and everyone in the tower realized there were no lights to help bring her in.

B. J. Bachman and Fran Dias (both 43-2) went to the control tower to find out what the commotion on the field was all about. "Everything was dark! Of course, the tower was out—the landing lights, everything—all the lights on the field were out," Bachman recalled. No one in the tower could see her, "but we could hear her occasionally. She flew around—it must have been two and a half hours. Her radio was damaged and we could hear by relays." Grand Prairie and Meacham Airport in Fort Worth were able to pick up Florene's transmissions and pass them on to Love Field. Her receiver was out, but she could still send.[2]

While she flew around to use up the fuel on board, the field personnel organized emergency lighting. Jeeps, parked along both sides of the runway, turned on their headlights, illuminating her path to land. And Florene brought the airplane in for a safe but heart-stopping landing.[3]

Given the Ferrying Division's earlier order prohibiting pursuit transition on base, Florene should not have been up in the P-47. But it turned out that she wasn't the only one. Other women had made or had sought so-called bootleg flights in the P-47. Florene had the bad luck to be the one who had a problem and thus called attention to it. What was interesting was that her flight, and the flights of others, ran counter to the recently released Air Inspector's findings. That report stated that transition was being denied the women pilots of Dallas by disgruntled male instructors.

Something wasn't adding up.

Before receiving the Air Inspector's report, the staff at Ferrying Division Headquarters already was discussing the high accident rate at Love Field, the latest being four WASP forced landings all due to carburetor icing in PQ-8s. These were the forced landings Dorothy had written to G. M. about in her November 15 letter. Staff concluded that the reason for the increase in accidents was that the women were progressing too fast on various types of planes.[4]

So what was the real story?

After Dorothy's crash, Nancy Love did not take the P-38 back to Long Beach. Presumably, she took the first available flight east to Cincinnati to meet with General Tunner and the Ferrying Division staff as they tried to begin to make sense of this cumulative, unwelcome, and now tragic turn of events.

On December 6, Nancy Love flew to Dallas to investigate the Air Inspector's findings, the reports of poor morale, and the ramifications of Florene's P-47 flight. Mrs. Love's subsequent report to General Tunner was that the morale of the squadron had been poor for several months. In fact, she confirmed her earlier suspicions that "this was largely due to maladministration." However, another cause of low morale "was the excessive accident and mishap rate of the Dallas WASP, the highest of any WASP squadron in the Ferrying Division." Contrary to the opinion of the Air Inspector, "this excessive rate was due primarily to pushing the girls through Transition School too fast, without making sure that they were fully qualified on the planes involved."[5]

This corresponds with what Dorothy had written to Nancy Love in her letter of November 26. Presumably, Mrs. Love found Dorothy's letter waiting for her when she returned to Cincinnati following Dorothy's fatal crash. One can only imagine the impact that letter had on her.

Contrary to Ferrying Division instructions, "three women were checked out in P-47s, even though it was known at the time that they were scheduled to go to pursuit school within a few weeks."[6] These transitions apparently were done without the knowledge of the commanding officer, "which would indicate that some, at least, of the check pilots, far from being resentful of the women pilot program, were willing to give the women 'bootleg' transition."[7]

Nancy was being pulled apart by conflicting realities. Florene's close call came only five days before Dorothy's fatal crash. But for Florene's safe landing of the stricken P-47, Nancy could have had two dead pilots on her hands in less than a week.

As it was, one of Nancy's original WAFS pilots was dead and another had barely escaped with her life. If, because of the back-to-back incidents, questions were raised about the women's fitness to fly pursuit, the new plan to have women pilots ferry pursuit could come tumbling down around her. Nancy had the reputation of her entire women's ferrying squadron to uphold. The less ruckus raised, the less attention called to the incident, the better.

Seven young women already were in Palm Springs learning to fly single-engine pursuits, and another eight were due to report December 10. Nancy moved on. Overreaction to the tragedy was avoided. The WASP continued to do their job—ferry airplanes—and women pilots continued to be assigned to pursuit school. The last two women pilots to graduate from pursuit school did so, ten months later, on October 15, 1944.

After discussing the matter with Colonel Munson, Commanding Officer of the 5th Group, Nancy relieved Florene of her command at Dallas and transferred her to Long Beach.[8] After Florene completed pursuit school, she reported to Long Beach for ferrying duty.

WASP author Byrd Granger writes, "It is a rule that any pilot who washes out an airplane must be transferred or discharged."[9] Florene had proven she was a good pilot. No doubt Nancy, who needed her good pilots—pursuit pilots in particular—took this into consideration. Florene was not the first, nor the last, WASP to be given a second chance.

Helen Richards and Iris Critchell, both graduates of that first pursuit school class, got to know each other ferrying out of Long Beach throughout 1944. "I made some flights with Helen," Iris recalls, "one in which we were both in the same airplane, so we had a few occasions to chat. She was not happy with Dallas. Helen was a skilled, knowledgeable pilot who kept her thoughts pretty much to herself, but she did say that the general situation in Dallas had not been to her liking. She managed to get transferred out.

"After the war, I saw a great deal of my friends and 43-2 classmates Ross Kary and Franny Dias, who also were stationed in Dallas. They, too, talked to me about the tenuous situation that had existed in the Dallas WASP squadron. They tried to spend as little time on base as possible. They knew things were not right and were glad to stay away and not be involved."[10]

These are echoes of comments that Dorothy wrote home to her family, in the fall of 1943.

On December 14, 1943, after concluding her investigatory trip to Dallas, Nancy Love returned to Cincinnati and wrote her report for General Tunner. He had trusted her to handle the situation—the problems at Dallas and the tragedy of Dorothy's crash. Nancy recommended that the transition department be more thorough in selecting suitable applicants for transition and to instruct those students on technical aspects of the airplane and on the proper flying of the ship. If a student did not display good judgment, a thorough understanding of the airplane, and good flying technique, she should be given more time on less complicated aircraft.[11]

Nancy felt strongly that no woman should be sent to pursuit school against her will; however, the WASP would be encouraged to go. There would be no squadron quotas for pursuit school. Each superior woman pilot was to be sent to instrument school, and if pursuit flying was her goal, she was to be given all opportunity to become a competent Class III pilot, after which she would be sent to pursuit school. Pilots judged to be borderline cases should be given further ferrying duties until considered qualified to fly more complicated aircraft.

Nancy also recommended that headquarters investigate transition policies and procedure at Dallas.[12]

Based on Nancy's recommendation, General Tunner immediately took steps to upgrade WASP training at all the ferrying bases. Ferrying Division pilots were supposed to have a minimum of one-and-a-half hours as first pilot in a C-47 in order to qualify for pursuit school—unless he or she had fifteen hours copilot time. Dorothy had commented on this very requirement in one of her letters. But Nancy found that some of the women had been sent to pursuit school without meeting this requirement.[13]

The problem, it turned out, was the old restriction on women copilots flying ferrying missions with male pilots put in place in March 1943. The restriction had long ago been rescinded, but apparently some COs either didn't realize it or ignored it.[14] This needed to be remedied quickly.

General Tunner, in a January 10, 1944, letter to his ferrying groups, suggested that qualified WASP be transitioned as rapidly as possible, in accordance with safe practices, so that they would be eligible for pursuit school.[15]

History would record that a total of 142 WASP qualified to ferry pursuit aircraft during World War II.[16] Nine original WAFS plus former Air Transport Auxiliary pilot Helen Richey qualified on base, before the ban was imposed, and 132 graduated from pursuit school. Two, Dorothy Scott and Alice Lovejoy (43-5), died in crashes during pursuit training.

On September 21, 1943, the Ferrying Division had requested of its parent organization, the ATC, that it be sent only fifteen training school graduates per month. This request was acted on by the Air Transport Command on November 24, and approved by Headquarters Army Air Forces on December 13, after the Air Inspector's report had been received.[17]

Class 43-6 (graduation day October 4, 1943) was the last class from Sweetwater from which the majority of graduates were sent to the Ferry Command. No graduates of Class 43-7 were sent when they graduated November 13, but several were sent later, after they earned additional flying hours. No members of Classes 43-8 or 44-1 went to the Ferry Command. At that point, the training at Sweetwater was being overhauled and lengthened. Per the Ferrying Division's request, fifteen graduates each were sent from Classes 44-2, 3, and 4. One woman each from 44-2 (Ruth Adams) and 44-4 (Maurine Miller) went on to ferry pursuit.[18] After that, due to further changes affecting the program, no more WASP were sent to the Ferry Command. All subsequent graduates were sent to other bases and duties, per assignment by Jackie Cochran.

The simple fact was that when the program was started in the fall of 1942, the women were to be trained to ferry trainer aircraft—mostly single-engine craft—with horsepower ranging from the 175 in the PT-19 to 600 in the AT-6. In the beginning, there was no thought of putting women into pursuit aircraft. But the war evolved and everything changed and by fall 1943, the one job women pilots were really needed to perform was to deliver single-engine pursuit aircraft to the docks for shipment abroad. Single-engine pursuit aircraft ranged from 1,150 to 2,000 horsepower and boasted speeds of 350 miles per hour on up to the 435 mph the P-51Ds could attain.[19]

By December 1943, the whole dynamic between the Ferrying Division and the Flying Training Command had changed.

Of course, Dorothy Scott did not live to witness any of this, but she helped lay some groundwork. She had done her best to help the new training school graduates adapt to life and realities at Love Field through her ground-school training assignment. She had cared about helping the other young women and performed accordingly. She had worked with the girls sent to learn to tow gliders. She had tried to clue Nancy Love in on some of the problems she witnessed in regard to the women's transition at Love Field. And she had exhibited the ability and the willingness to be an instrument instructor—in fact, to serve in any capacity in which she was needed.

Sadly, Nancy Love would lose one more of her Originals.

When Evelyn Sharp joined the squadron in October 1942 she had not yet turned twenty-three. Evelyn, who had been flying since she was fifteen and had done some barnstorming, had an astounding 2,968 hours to her credit. Of the twenty-eight original WAFS, only thirty-five-year-old Lenore McElroy, a longtime flight instructor, had more accrued time—3,500 hours. But in spite of her proven ability, Evelyn, nicknamed Sharpie, became the third of Nancy's original squadron to die in the line of duty. She perished April 3, 1944, when the left engine of the P-38 pursuit aircraft she was ferrying quit on takeoff.[20]

Diane Bartels, a Nebraska schoolteacher, received a National Endowment for the Humanities / *Reader's Digest* Teacher-Scholar Award to research and write the life story of Evelyn Sharp—all-American-girl, the pride of Ord, Nebraska. *Sharpie: The Life Story of Evelyn Sharp, Nebraska's Aviatrix* was published in 1996.

Three years later, Nashville freelance journalist Rob Simbeck told the story of Tennessee blueblood Cornelia Fort in the biography *Daughter of the Air: The Brief Soaring Life of Cornelia Fort*, published in 1999. Cornelia was the first of the original WAFS to die—March 21, 1943.

Through the efforts of these two authors, two of the three original WAFS who died during the war had been immortalized by 2000. With the publication of this book, *Finding Dorothy Scott*, the trilogy is complete.

All three of the original WAFS who died while flying for the Army Air Forces in World War II have had a hometown airport named for them: Sharp Field—Ord Municipal Airport, Ord, Nebraska; Dorothy Scott Memorial International Airport, Oroville, Washington; and Cornelia Fort Airpark, a small private airport located on the banks of the Cumberland River in Nashville, Tennessee. Unfortunately, the airpark was badly flooded in 2010 and it is now part of the Shelby Bottoms Greenway and Nature Park.[21]

Chapter Fourteen
Life Goes On

G. M. wrote the following letter to Katherine on company letterhead dated January 12, 1944.

Scott Motors
Ford V-8
Cars and Trucks
Oroville, Washington

Dear Katherine:

I have just received a long letter from Donald regarding your health. I sincerely regret to read of the recurrence of your misfortune. I had hoped and firmly believed that all traces of the disease had been removed in Seattle. To say that I am sorry is not enough. If there is anything that I can do to help, to make things more pleasant for you, please let me know.

Dr. Chessman is no doubt right in advising that you do not use X-ray or Radium or an operation. Judging from cases that have come before my observation I think that anything that you may do will only make matters worse, not help any. Will ask that you make yourself as comfortable as possible, and get all the pleasure that you can.

It is now a little over thirty years since you and I climbed the hill to visit Dr. Matthews one Monday morning. While in these thirty years we have had our spats, our quarrels, our joys, our sorrows, our ups and downs—I believe that we still have the same deep affection for each other that we had when we climbed that hill.

In these years we raised three of the finest children that ever lived, all honest, all truthful, all morally perfect, all ambitious. Edward is doing well for his country in his sphere. Donald is doing excellent.—Dorothy—well I am going to take the blame for her loss—possibly I should not have encouraged her fly.

Today Mr. B. D. Vincent the lawyer that was a partner of Mr. Adams twenty-three years ago passed by, I asked him to come in later as I wanted to talk to him. I told him briefly of Dorothy's loss, the Iowa estate left to ours and other children [Katherine's family was from Iowa], and that I had to make a new will. He suggested that you and I both make almost identical wills and, if you wish, will make one for each of us if we will let him know just what we wish. Probate cases have been his specialty since he left here, and as I believe him 100 percent honest I do not know of a better man that we could get to write these papers for us. Kindly let me know your wish in this matter.

With best wishes, I remain,

Yours,
[G. M. scrawled his signature at the bottom.]

Katherine's cancer had returned and the prognosis was that it was terminal. The men of the Scott family, having lost a much-loved daughter and sister, were now faced with the impending loss of another woman of their lives—wife and mother.

G. M.'s letters—this one to his estranged wife and the one he wrote to Dorothy when she wanted to leave school in April 1941—are the only written records of his thoughts and feelings. And, according to his son Edward, as passed on by his grandson Tracy, G. M. was a most typical husband and father of that generation and era and did not show emotion. The letters convey a rock-solid strength of character and conviction. Hot tempered and dictatorial he may have been, his guarded try for eloquence in the written word reveal his well-hidden but obviously deep feelings to the letter's recipient and the accidental reader.

In both letters, G. M. looks to the future, characteristically taking care of business, tying up—as is necessary at that point in their lives—loose ends. The light—Dorothy—has gone out of his life, out of all their lives. Now his wife, though they live apart by mutual consent, is dying. Both sons are away serving their country in wartime—the same circumstances that, already, have taken his daughter from him. He seems to feel, and acknowledge, the loneliness awaiting him.

Katherine died two years later, February 14, 1946, at Mercy Hospital, San Diego, California. G. M. learned of her death in a telegram from Donald. Since her sister lived in the San Diego area, it is likely that Katherine spent her last weeks or months there. Burial was in Valhalla Cemetery in Burbank, next to Dorothy. She was buried on February 16, Dorothy and Ed's twenty-sixth birthday. Her obituary in the February 22, 1946, *Oroville Gazette* said that she was born January 4, 1882, in West Point, Iowa, and had been in ill health for the past eight years.[1]

Life for the Scott family had, irrevocably, changed. The future now lay in that unborn child: heir to the past and to the future.

February 27, 1944, was a big day, bringing awaited and needed good news to the Scott family. A son, Tracy, was born, to Edward and Ethel Scott at Peterson Army Air Base in Colorado Springs, Colorado.

On February 10, 1944, not long before his son's birth, Edward Scott wrote the following letter to Nancy Love.

Hello,

I'm Dorothy's brother. And I'm sure you will be glad to receive the enclosure.

Perhaps it will take some more time to read it, but I'm sure you're glad it is so small. [Ed enclosed a copy of Dorothy's Mother's Day poem to Katherine.]

Our birthday is the 16th of this month and on that day I do hope you will be thinking of her. [Dorothy would have been twenty-four.]

I want to thank you now for that grand Christmas card and also the new hall, which has been named in her honor at Love Field Dallas, Texas.

Please drop in sometime at Peterson Field. I would so much like to meet the person my sister always thought so much of.

Ed & Ethel Scott

The irony of Ed's letter is that it arrived in time for Nancy Love's thirtieth birthday—February 14, 1944. Chances are, given Dorothy's death and Cornelia's earlier in the year, she never experienced a more unhappy one. We can only speculate the wrench she felt reading the letter from a grieving brother accompanied by that simple but artfully written poem.

Dorothy wrote that Mother's Day poem for Katherine in May 1943. The poem conveys the "listen to troubles or mend a blouse" message she wrote to her father when considering bringing her mother to Palm Springs for the four weeks of pursuit school.

Printed here with the permission of Tracy Scott—Ed Scott's son and Dorothy's nephew:

> Raising daughters may sound fine
>   Oh, of course it's not a bother,
> There's part of it though, is fore ordained
>   You can't turn over to father.
>
> It's not when they're young they worry you so,
>   You can always spank them then—
> It's later years when their interests turn
>   To careers, clothes and men.
>
> Keeping track of some daughters
>   Alike those in the Ferry Command,
> Would take a few tacks and lots of maps
>   Of this entire land.
>
> My mother gets her postcards mixed
>   Dates and places swirl:
> "Is Enid north of AT-6
>   Or ETA a girl?"
>
> "Is Stearman the boy in New Orleans,
>   Is Link part of a chain?"
> Mom, if you ever want to be happy
>   Don't give your girl a plane.
>
> Seriously though, airplanes or no
>   We think our moms are dandy
> To listen to troubles, or mend a blouse
>   They come in very handy.

Sometimes we let it slip-up
  And take our moms for granted
But that's all right, they understand
  And will be there when wanted.

So here's a toast to all our Moms
  On this, their day of the year
May they never regret they've got us
  And, gee Mom, I'm glad you're here.

Nancy Love was stoic by nature. She kept her emotions locked tightly away. That's how she was brought up by upper-crust Edwardian-era parents. The leader Dorothy had known, liked, and admired so very much led quietly and by example and did not seek personal recognition or the limelight. Nancy bottled up her feelings with the death of each of "her girls"—and ultimately she would lose three of her Originals and twelve women ferry pilots in all.

Evelyn Sharp was the third of Nancy Love's original WAFS to die in service. *Courtesy WASP Archive, Texas Woman's University, Denton.*

Nancy Love attended the funeral of the first of her Originals to die—
Cornelia Fort—but according to Nancy Batson Crews, whom Love personally selected to accompany Evelyn Sharp's body home after her fatal
crash in April 1944, Love never attended another one. She did not attend
Dorothy's funeral on December 8. She had flown to Dallas December 6 to
get to the bottom of what was going on with the 5th Ferrying Group and
the women who flew for it.

Barbara "B. J." Erickson London, who accompanied Nancy Love to
Nashville for Cornelia's funeral, vividly recalls Nancy's distress on the occasion. Nancy did not feel capable of speaking at the funeral, of handling
such an ordeal—very much in character for someone who did not like
being the focus of attention. "Nancy lived in an ordered world. Everything
she did was well thought out and concise. Those who worked with her assumed the same position," says London. "She did not emote, she handled
herself and the situation calmly."

What immense personal pressure Nancy must have felt knowing that
each of those three young women chose to join her program and had gone
to their deaths flying under her command. That they, themselves, made
the choice and willingly was not likely much solace to a leader like Nancy
Love.

Several of Dorothy's friends wrote to G. M.

Robert M. Garner, D.D.S.
Dallas, Texas
January 3, 1944

Dear Mr. Scott:

> I wish that I could be there in person to say this rather than write, as I find
> words hard to select to express my sincere regret to you in the recent loss
> of your daughter Dorothy F. Scott.
>
> Miss Scott as I knew her was in the relation of doctor and patient, how-
> ever I think that I knew her as well as some of my friends I have had for
> years. She was friendly and glad to find someone to talk to that was inter-
> ested in aviation and that knew a wing from the tail section. As her hours
> were long and she wasn't able to keep definite appointments, she usually
> had to take her appointments the last of the day and as that is my time to
> slow down we usually spent quite a bit of time gabbing about planes, flying

equipment, or in discussing new ideas that were developed into warplanes and that had been made public.

She came down one rainy foggy morning with a friend, Betsy Ferguson, and they consulted me for advice as to the selection of a medical doctor for Ms. Ferguson. As I had nothing to do, due to the hard rain keeping patients with appointments at home, I went with them to wait for one of my capable friends to get in his office. We spent about two hours gabbing of aviation while sitting there. You see, I'm just a long-winded Texan that likes to talk, and I talk when I get a chance. Now those few fleeting minutes seem priceless.

Dr. Garner and a friend, Dr. W. M. Jeffers, met Dorothy and her two ferry pilot companions Penn and Paul when they were out at White Rock Lake in their boat. He told G. M. how he happened to start talking to her.

Dorothy and the guys had tried to rent a rowboat for fishing. The "old fellow" who ran the boat rental concession was "too skeptical of people for his own good," Dr. Garner wrote. "If you know him, anything is okay, but if you don't then it is just too bad. He would not rent them the boat because he didn't think they would return it and it would cost him a dollar to have it towed in."

We were working on an outboard motor not 50 feet away and Miss Scott came over and talked to us. She said nothing of the deal with the old man, but after they left he came over and asked if we knew them. When we said "yes," then the matter changed. We did what we could, telling him that if ever they came back and wanted a boat to let them have it as they were willing to do all that was right. We added that they could, if they pleased, buy his whole damn house, boats and all. Think that it hurt him to know he had missed a chance to turn a couple of dollars right neatly.

I told her of this and I do not know if they ever went back, as they found a more congenial concessionaire across the lake nearer the Ferry Pilots Club. The old man is okay, but not quite the man to handle a boat concession on a public lake.

The doctor had seen the item in the *Dallas Morning News* telling of the crash in Palm Springs, but didn't realize who it was until one of his friends, who knew that he knew Dorothy, called the article to his attention.

Dr. Garner was a new father. His wife had just given birth to a nine-pound boy on November 18. He had been so overwhelmed trying to get things settled at home and at his office while living with a colicky baby and a two-and-a-half-year-old girl that he hadn't really read the story. "I had neglected news for sleep," he wrote.

> I wanted to write you as it seemed to me that you would like to know from one of her acquaintances in Texas that she was happy in her work to all outward appearances and just lived and thrived on aviation. If you have listened or talked to pilots very much, you will understand that death is one thing they do not discuss and brush aside as quickly as they can. Every pilot knows that it comes to all of us and to a pilot the odds are that it will come in a crash, crackup, or fall. They do not fear it and I personally believe they prefer it there in the cockpit to any place they can think of.
>
> As for myself, I would like to get mine while standing there at my dental chair plugging away on fillings and cleanings.
>
> I do not know if this letter will be to your liking but I sincerely believe that any word from anyone that knew her in places far from home will be gratefully received. When members of our own little circle are away, we like to hear of them and their doings no matter who brings the news.
>
> I knew Miss Scott for what seems so short a time that it now seems a fleeting moment. In that short time I picked her to be an honest, upright, straightforward, and clean American girl that had no use for the baser, or should I say evil, things in life. She was a girl that seemed happy to be able to do something to aid the war effort and was glad to do all she could. She never once decried her job or anything connected with it. I feel that the beginning of a long friendship has been interrupted temporarily, until such time as we shall meet again on the other side in that world we all hope and pray to be allowed to reach when our tasks on earth are done.
>
> May God be with you in this hour of great sorrow and console you and heal the aching wound in your heart.
>
> Until now I am just a name on a slip of paper to you. I am a dentist, 33 years old, married and the father of two children. A girl, two and a half, and a boy six weeks old. I have been in practice eight years and married seven. I wanted and tried to get into the Army or Navy but I couldn't pass the physical exam, so here I sit and let other fellows go out and do the work while I stay home and try to brace myself for the stares of people that give me that 'Why aren't you in uniform' look.
>
> Hoping and trusting that this letter may have filled one tiny void for you.

Zimmy Sluder wrote as well.

Dear Mr. Scott,

While rummaging through a snapshot album, I came across the enclosed snapshot, and thought you might like to have it. I took it from the porch of the boathouse last July.

Golly, Mr. Scott, I sure miss that daughter of yours. I guess I still can't realize she won't come bouncing in, out of breath, and all excited about the trip she just had—or the flying "under the hood"—or so many things she was always bubbling over to tell! It just seems that she's been transferred to another station, and one of these days we'll be able to get together for another of our "heart to heart" talks.

Her loyalty, sincerity, grand sense of humor, personality, love of music—all these things combined to make her one of the grandest gals I've ever known—and I was most proud and happy to be a friend of hers. One of my biggest regrets is that my husband, Alex, was never able to meet her. I'd written him of all the fun we had and what a swell person she was—and he was really looking forward to meeting her.

Speaking of my husband—he's been gone a little over eighteen months now—and has just received his promotion to lieutenant colonel. He's in charge of a P-47 group—"somewhere in Italy."

Shari is in kindergarten, and is able now to recognize the letters of the alphabet—and she's even learned to print her first name! Sure will be glad when her daddy comes home—she beginning to need a daddy around!

Where are Ed and Don now, and how are they getting along?

Helen was here on a P-51 trip in January when we received word that her father had passed away. After the funeral, they sold their home in Pasadena, and Mrs. Richards is now with Helen's sister in San Fernando. Helen was given a leave of absence, which we utilized by taking a two-week trip to Mexico—I think it did us both a world of good. The only thing though—we sure missed having Dottie along. The three of us had planned that trip as far back as last April, and it just didn't seem right that she wasn't there.

Mr. Scott, I hope you haven't minded my chattering on like this—it's just that it's been penned up for so long—it just had to come up—and being that you were closer to Dottie than anyone else, I had to write you. Please, if you have time—won't you write me—tell me what you're doing these days, and how you're getting along?

I'm sorry I missed seeing you when you were here—but I know how anxious you were to get back; maybe we'll meet again someday—who knows?

Please don't forget me.

Sincerely,
Zimmy Sluder

From Helen Richards, Dorothy's closest friend in the WAFS, March 24, 1944:

Thank you for the pictures. I cannot begin to tell you how grateful I am to have them, nor how I appreciate being remembered. When in Dallas a few weeks ago, I saw those you sent to headquarters there—the very first thing upon stepping into the WASP Alert Room of "Scott Hall." They are just grand! With these now, along with a host of precious memories—that, amazingly enough, seemed to increase each day—our Dottie shall be always close to me, until someday I shall be with her again.

The activities of the Ferry Command are very much the same as ever. It does look as if we may be getting those commissions any day now—soon as Congress gets through scrapping about it. And our new uniforms will be coming none too soon for me. The trouser seat on one pair of my beloved and much-worn Grays[2] gave way yesterday—most embarrassing!

Would certainly love to hear from you, Mr. Scott, whenever you have time to drop a line.

Thank you again, so much.

Yours truly,
Helen

Helen Richards's husband, Don Prosser, related in a 2004 interview that, after Dorothy's death, Helen threw herself into learning to fly the pursuits at pursuit school. She checked out on the hottest of them all, the P-51 Mustang, on December 24, 1943. She ended up logging 110 hours and 35 minutes in 1944 ferrying P-51s cross-country West Coast to East Coast—the most hours she flew in any airplane during the war. In doing so, she lived Dorothy's dream as well as her own.[3]

In February 1944, Helen took a month's leave from the WAFS squadron, 6th Ferrying Group, Long Beach, where she was stationed after pursuit school. That was when she and Zimmy went to Mexico.

"She was torn up by Dorothy's death and trying to rid herself of her grief," Prosser said. "But Helen could be tough as nails when she had to be. She showed little outward emotion. She bore it all inside where none of us could see it." Helen's solution, he added, was, upon return to active duty, to immerse herself in ferrying airplanes. As a result, General Harold L. George, commander of the Air Transport Command, issued her a commendation for ferrying the most airplanes one month during 1944. It was late March 1944 before she could bring herself to write a condolence letter to Dorothy's father.

Don and Helen Richards Prosser both became public school teachers, and they were the parents of two sons. Don, with Helen's help, was instrumental in starting a series of for-credit aviation courses at the high school where he taught. He and Helen also ran a flight service business. Both were instructors. Helen died in a plane crash October 23, 1976, while giving a biannual review check ride to a fellow pilot. She was fifty-five. Don Prosser married again and lived to age ninety. He died in 2009.

The name of the Oroville Municipal Airport was officially changed to the Dorothy Scott Municipal Airport "in honor and memory of Dorothy Scott, who freely offered her services to her Country and who gave her life in the Service."

Councilman Bernard M. Wills introduced the measure at the regular meeting of the Oroville Town Council. It passed with four in favor and none opposed. A resolution to that effect was signed by the town clerk, John Jacobi, and dated January 17, 1944.[4]

Chapter Fifteen
What Might Have Been

Without a doubt, the dedicated leadership of Nancy Love and Jacqueline Cochran is the single factor that won for the WASP the opportunity to fly the biggest and best of the US military aircraft during World War II. In the Ferry Command, each woman pilot was allowed to earn her way up in transition based on her ability. And once a WASP trainee mastered the AT-6 at Sweetwater, she could be sent anywhere to fly anything Cochran put in their collective sights.

The seeds were sown in the Golden Age of Aviation, the 1920s and '30s. The young women who became WASP lived those years and were profoundly affected—as were the men of their generation—by what aviation author Joseph J. Corn calls "the winged gospel." In his 1983 book by that name, Corn describes the years between the two world wars when there existed a fascination between ordinary people and their fantasies of flight brought on by stories and deeds of heroic fliers, male and female.

America was "airminded" in the 1920s and '30s. Pilots were popular heroes. People expected that they, too, would soon take to the sky, flying their own family plane or helicopter. The airplane symbolized the promise of the future.[1]

The women drawn to flight became, for a time, a small but vital part of the aviation world prior to and into World War II. "Americans . . . viewed mechanical flight as portending a wondrous era of peace and harmony, of culture and prosperity," Corn writes. "This was the promise of the 'winged gospel.'"[2]

The "three key tenets" of Corn's winged gospel were:

1. Airplanes would be doves of peace;

2. Aviation would foster freedom and equality;

3. The future would see a personal airplane in every garage.

The problem was, "By 1950, the three tenets had lost most of their credibility," Corn writes in the new epilogue added for the 2002 edition of *The Winged Gospel*, published *after* the terrorist attacks of September 11, 2001.

Numbers 1 and 3 are easy to identify. The doves of peace were a casualty of World War II and, by the end of the 1940s, the expected boom in private plane sales and using small aircraft as family runabouts for private transportation had collapsed.[3]

Number 2 is considerably more complex, and that's where the women come in. "The belief that aviation would foster freedom and equality . . . eroded in the face of continued discrimination and prejudice."[4] Helen Richey's fate at Central Airlines in 1934–35 was an early indicator that things hadn't really changed all that much for women. Granted, women pilots throughout the 1930s were involved with air racing, many became celebrities, and their feats were prominent in newspaper stories, but the big step—the step to employment at the airlines and in commercial aviation—proved beyond reach and would remain beyond reach for another forty years.

The time-of-the-month flap begun by the medical arm of the Bureau of Air Commerce, also in 1935, was another indicator. Flying at "that time of the month" would rear its ugly head again in March 1943 when, for the period of about a month, an order was issued by the Ferrying Division that the women ferry pilots were to be grounded for eight days a month. This time it was Nancy Love who brought sanity to the proceedings, as her friend and colleague Phoebe Omlie had done eight years earlier.[5]

And, of course, the elimination of women from the Civilian Pilot Training Program in mid-1941 smacked of inequality, but the fact wilted in the face of necessity for national defense.

Only the WASP's brief 1942–44 active-duty tenure showed promise of women advancing in the technical, commercial, and military sides of aviation. But, Corn points out, "By war's end, women pilots had been pushed out of the cockpits, and once again gospel promise succumbed to ugly, earthly realities."[6] The WASP were sent home December 20, 1944.

Of course Dorothy Scott didn't live to witness this. She died at the very apex for women in aviation—the highest point they had yet achieved in the history of flight. In December 1943, women pilots were accepted into, and were entering, the Ferrying Division of the Air Transport Command's pursuit school on identical terms as the male pilots. Dorothy was in that first group of 16 women pilots selected for and sent to pursuit school in December 1943. Some 130 of Dorothy's fellow WASP would succeed and graduate even though she did not.

The women ferry pilots assigned to the Ferrying Division of the Air Transport Command went on to establish a remarkable record. They delivered 12,652 aircraft over the twenty-seven months from late October 1942 to December 20, 1944 and, by September 1944, were delivering three-fifths of all pursuit aircraft coming off the assembly lines.[7]

But after the WASP, women would not return to the cockpits of military or commercial aircraft until the 1970s. And the fight was still uphill from there.

The demise of the "winged gospel" had a profound effect on women. The realities of the postwar world would see aviation's giant technological steps forward matched—unfortunately—by giant societal steps backward as the world wanted women out of the cockpit, out of the workforce in general, and back in the kitchen.

Dorothy's story, reasonably, could have lasted another sixty or so years. Ten of the original WAFS lived to ninety or beyond: Betty Gillies, Bernice Batten, Barbara Erickson, Teresa James, Del Scharr, Gertrude Meserve, Lenore McElroy, Barbara Donahue, and Florene Miller. Phyllis Burchfield made it to one hundred. By all rights Dorothy's story should have continued on the path flown by the 130-plus other women pursuit ferry pilots who performed so admirably throughout 1944—a service most vital to the Army and the country they all so proudly served.

Dorothy would have graduated from pursuit school in early January 1944, and immediately been assigned a P-51 to deliver to Newark, New Jersey—to be loaded aboard a ship that would take it to England. Those P-51s delivered to Newark by WASP were destined to accompany and protect B-17s and B-24s of the Eighth Air Force on bombing runs all the way to Berlin and back.

Yet another P-51 Dorothy might have delivered to Newark may well have been destined for Italy and the Fifteenth Air Force. One of the men stationed at Foggia would fly that Mustang as an escort for the heavy bombers on the crucial raids on the Ploesti oil refineries in Romania and back[8]—depriving the Nazis of the fuel they needed to wage war and, ultimately, bringing Germany to its knees. The P-51 was "a game changer" in the European war. Author Barrett Tillman writes: "As a weapon, the Mustang was tops. . . . With its speed, maneuverability, and range, it could take the fight to the enemy and engage him on better than even terms. At the same time, Mustangs protected American bombers from deadly Luftwaffe interceptors over any target."[9]

P-51Ds were the aircraft both the Long Beach and the Dallas WASP pursuit pilots were concentrating on throughout 1944. Their mission was to get them to Newark. From there, those aircraft were bound for combat over Germany.

This was the overriding reason the work of the WASP of the Ferry Command was so important. They were a crucial cog in the overall—and vast—machinery of World War II.

Dorothy had dreamed of being part of that. Dorothy's friend Helen Richards logged 110 hours in P-51s in 1944. Dorothy surely would have done the same.

And after a year of that kind of ferrying day in and day out—loving every minute of it but often being beyond exhaustion from the strain—Dorothy would have endured first the disbelief and then the shocking reality of the deactivation of the WASP on December 20, 1944, even though their services as ferrying pilots still were needed.

"Training men to take their places will require a million dollars, from four to six months' time, and even then will not replace the broad experience which the women have built up on pursuit-type aircraft," aviation columnist Gill Robb Wilson wrote in the *New York Herald Tribune* in December 1944.[10] But needed or not, the country simply wasn't ready for women to fly pursuit planes, or build bombers, or manufacture ammunition, or take over "men's" jobs in any field, even though their doing so meant releasing men to go fight the fight for democracy on foreign soil and in faraway waters and skies.

The war had put the world out of whack, and *mankind* wanted it put back to "normal."

Of course, they forgot to ask *womankind.*

Women would—after the fall of Germany May 8, 1945, followed by the Japanese surrender August 14, 1945—return to hearth and home, kitchen and *kinder.* Life and time went on, but the stage had been set. The Women's Movement arrived, and WASP numbered among those who heard the call, listened, and acted. Some wrongs were righted; progress was made, though inequalities still exist. A state of flux still seems to be the norm. But, today, women fly military combat aircraft, jet airliners, and spacecraft, and anything else they can handle—and that's pretty much everything. Names like Nicole Malachowski, Emily Howell Warner, and Eileen Collins immediately come to mind. Dorothy would be proud.

Chapter Sixteen
Recognizing the Thirty-Eight

Dorothy Scott was one of thirty-eight WASP pilots to lose her life flying for her country in World War II. She was one of three of Nancy Love's original WAFS to die.

Twenty-seven of the thirty-eight—including Dorothy—were serving as active-duty personnel. The other eleven were trainees at the Army's flight school for women. The first of the eleven perished on a training flight in March 1943 when the facility was located in Houston. The remaining ten died after the flight school was moved to Sweetwater in West Texas.[1]

Because the women were not militarized, they received no burial or other insurance benefits, their coffins could not be draped with the traditional American flag, and their grieving parents could not display a gold star in the window—the symbol for a family that had lost a son in service to the United States. Their remains were shipped home in pine boxes with the bill paid by their classmates or their squadron-mates who passed the hat to collect the fare.

The WASP were civilians, paid through Civil Service. But they were told when they were accepted that militarization was likely. A bill, HR 4219, to militarize the women pilots was introduced in the House of Representatives on February 17, 1944. The House Committee on Military Affairs scheduled hearings for March 21. Only Gen. Hap Arnold testified. The Ferrying Division was not consulted and played no part in the sponsorship of the bill.[2]

HR 4219 was expected to pass because Arnold wanted it, and Congress had never denied the Army Air Forces commanding general anything he asked for. Consequently, the uproar that ensued took everyone by surprise.

In January 1944, General Arnold had closed down the cadet flight-training schools. The loss of pilots in the European air war had been far fewer than anticipated, thus negating Arnold's previous calculations on number of pilots needed to finish the war. Addressing the shortage of male pilots two years earlier, in spring 1942, was the impetus for conversations that resulted in the WAFS and then the WASP. Now, in the spring of 1944, no longer was there a shortage of male pilots.

A negative media campaign against the WASP erupted. Responsibility for it is laid to three sources: a lobbying effort created by those newly laid-off male civilian flight instructors who would now lose their deferments and be subject to the draft—therefore, they wanted the WASP's jobs; complaints from Army Air Forces cadets (and their families) earmarked for flight training who were being released to the "walking army";[3] and from Army Air Forces combat pilots who had flown their missions and had recently returned from overseas. They wanted the WASP's jobs because, in performing them, they would earn sought-after flight pay.[4]

The "walking army" assignment those men appeared destined for was the expected war on the Japanese mainland. There were sufficient forces to conclude the European war, but the generals were looking forward to finishing the war in the Pacific. For that, the Army needed ground troops.

Lobbying the media and Congress, the men were heard. The politicians in Congress listened and were far more concerned with the complaints from the press and the pressure groups than they were about doing right by a group of women. Is anyone surprised? The women pilots were portrayed in the press as low-time, thirty-five-hour wonders, glamour girls—"Airport Annies"[5] out for a lark at the expense of the American taxpayers. It was nasty, and it worked.

WASP Byrd Granger (43-1) notes in her book, "A freshman in Congress, Rep. James Morrison (LA) inserts comments in the *Daily Congressional Record*:"

Wanted: Female impersonators . . . How about some of these thirty-five hours female wonders swapping their flying time for nurses' uniforms? But that would be downright rub-and-scrub work—no glamour there—and we do mean glamour.[6]

When the bill went to Congress for a vote on June 21, 1944, it died an ignoble death.

Training of future classes of WASP was canceled in late June, but those classes already in training were allowed to finish. WASP on active duty continued flying their assignments where they were based, though rumors began to fly as to their ultimate fate.

The events of the summer of 1944 resulted in General Arnold's seeming to do a one-eighty on the subject of militarizing the WASP. Between D-Day June 6, the August 24 liberation of Paris, and early October 1944, it was the course of military events in Europe that took a 180-degree turn. Once again the Army Air Force's losses had proved far fewer than expected. Now it appeared that unless the WASP program was deactivated, the women would be keeping men out of the air rather than allowing them to use their flying skills elsewhere. Arnold acted accordingly.[7] October 8, the women were told they would be officially disbanded on December 20, 1944.

This doesn't mean that what was subsequently done to the WASP was right, but it was expedient, and it was done swiftly and unconditionally. These are the events that happened, and the rationale followed as they unfolded.

From a different perspective, letting the trained women fliers of the Ferrying Division go would be costly to the government and—given more thought and fewer egos and personal conflicts—could have been accomplished so much more beneficially to all concerned. As it turned out, money would be spent shuffling and training enough men to replace them.

Nancy Love's ferry pilots—at least the work they were doing—was at that point essential to the war effort. Again, as Gill Robb Wilson pointed out, training men to replace the WASP pursuit pilots would cost a million dollars, several months' time, "and still not replace the broad experience which the women have built up on pursuit-type aircraft."[8]

The rapid movement of critically needed pursuit planes to the docks on the East Coast—by women pilots trained to fly them—had become a vital cog in the 1944 war machine. By the fall of 1944, women, 117 of them, were ferrying three-fifths of all the pursuit aircraft being delivered, and by doing it, they also were facilitating the "rapid transitioning of male pilots to heavy cargo and bomber type planes"[9]—the Ferrying Division's other job.

It didn't matter. There were last-minute appeals to keep the women ferry pilots on duty. To no avail. An option was, male pilots graduating from pursuit school and headed for combat would be assigned, interim, to cover the loss of the WASP's service. The class size at pursuit school would have to be increased to make up the difference.

Gen. Robert E. Nowland, who had replaced Gen. William H. Tunner as head of the Ferrying Division in August 1944, wrote to General George, Air Transport Command, that the cost of training 117 pursuit pilots to replace the WASP pursuit pilots being deactivated would be a month's training at Brownsville (at that time the home of pursuit school) and a price to the taxpayers of $1,085,312.[10] There was Gill Robb Wilson's one-million-dollar price tag.

The WASP were deactivated December 20 as announced. All the women pilots—from the 18 original WAFS still actively flying to the 68 members of Class 44-10, the last to graduate (December 7, 1944)—were told their services were no longer needed.[11] The number of active WASP, on December 19, was 905.[12] They were dismissed and told to go home—on their own nickel. The Army did not pay their way, though many sympathetic base commanders saw to it that their WASP were flown home.

What about those 905 WASP?

After December 20, first came the dark days—wondering what to do with their lives now that they no longer were flying for the Army. Many WASP have said, of the unwelcome readjustment thrust on them, that it was like being thrown into a deep, dark hole. But life moved on.

Reactions ranged from the dark options—alcohol and even suicide—to bouts with depression, coping with a new emptiness. On the sunnier side, many congregated in WASP nests in warmer climates, six or eight living together while they tried to get jobs in aviation. Some enlisted in other services—many opted for the Red Cross. Those who had put off marrying until the war was over went ahead with plans. The women coped, some better than others.

The war moved on as well. Germany was crumbling. May 8, 1945, brought victory in Europe—VE Day. Then the US Army Air Forces dropped two atomic bombs on Japan in early August, and the Japanese surrendered on August 14, 1945, VJ Day. Time to return to peacetime and normality—whatever that was.

But as the years went by and the WASP matured and aged along with the rest of their generation—and they began to lose a few sisters, but then more in slowly increasing numbers—the women remembered their friends who hadn't survived the war. They remembered Dorothy Scott and thirty-seven others who didn't come home to marry, have children, build careers, live to middle age and beyond, and see the rebirth of the WASP as a factor in the history of World War II.

The quest for militarization was reborn.

It began on June 1973 when original WAFS Nancy Batson Crews, President of the Order of Fifinella—as the WASP organization was then known—sent the following letter to all WASP.[13]

Order of Fifinella
395 Timberidge Trail
Gates Mills, Ohio 44040
June 15, 1973

Memorandum to All Wasps[14]

The subject of WASP militarization is a matter of personal interest to all of us. It is of particular interest to those of us who joined the Reserves and would like military credit for WASP time; to those of us who are Federal civil servants and would benefit from receiving veteran's preference for job retention purposes; and to those of us who may have a need and could very well use veteran health benefits. While there have been several separate (and valiant) efforts made by individual WASPs to get Congressional approval for the item of specific application to them, I feel it is appropriate that one, coordinated and unified effort be made, under the aegis of the Order of Fifinella, with the aim of achieving veteran benefits for all.

I therefore established a WASP Militarization Committee in February of this year to take on this task. Colonel W. Bruce Arnold, USAF (Ret), whom you will remember was our special guest at the 30th Reunion, graciously consented to chair this committee. Serving with him are Faith B. Richards and Dorothy Deane Ferguson. Mary Jones, our Secretary-Treasurer, and I will serve as ex officio members of this committee.

I ask each of you to give your full and enthusiastic support to this committee by being responsive to any request you may receive from them. In addition, I would like to suggest that you pass on to Colonel Arnold, any information, suggestions and any special "influences" you may have that would help the committee. Please send your information directly to Colonel Arnold at the following address:

[Address given.]

On behalf of the Order of Fifinella, I would like to extend our thanks to the WASPs who made the initial efforts (and at their own expense) to achieve militarization/credit for military time. To those women go our sincerest thanks for breathing life into a subject most of us had all but abandoned.

Sincerely,
Nancy B. Crews
President
Order of Fifinella

Nancy served as president from 1972 to 1975, initiating the first steps toward militarization. Bee Haydu, WASP Class 44-7, followed Nancy as president and served 1975 to 1978. Bee led the fight for militarization, along with a team of WASP who lived in the Washington, DC, area. Among those East Coast WASP who volunteered were Lee Wheelwright, 43-6; Deane Ferguson, 44-9; Margaret Boylan, 43-2; Elaine Harmon, 44-9; Velta Benn, 44-7; Natalie Fahey, 43-4; Helen Snapp, 43-4; Lorraine Rodgers, 44-2; Toby Felker, 44-2; and Lucile Wise, 43-7.[15]

The WASP marshaled their forces and sought the help of their friends in high places, like Senator Barry Goldwater, who flew for the Air Transport Command and taught instrument flying to some of the women stationed at Wilmington, including WAFS Nancy Batson and Helen McGilvery. They also had the support of General Tunner, the retired commander of the women in the Ferrying Division who believed so strongly in Nancy Love and the women ferry pilots. Mrs. Tunner—the former Margaret Ann Hamilton, WASP Class 43-2—joined her husband in support of WASP militarization. All the women in Congress at that time gave bipartisan support to help the WASP gain their militarization: Representatives Lindy Boggs (D-LA), Elizabeth Holzman (D-NY), and Margaret Heckler (R-MA) and Senator Margaret Chase Smith (R-ME).[16]

After what seemed to the WASP like an endless struggle, the House approved HR 8701 on Thursday, November 3, 1977. The Senate followed suit on November 4. On Thanksgiving Day, November 23, 1977, President Jimmy Carter signed the bill giving veteran status to the WASP of World War II.[17]

Bee Haydu credits the efforts and support of Hap Arnold's son, Bruce Arnold, as the biggest reason they achieved their goal.[18]

Even then, their victory seemed a grudging one. Movement to complete the process was slow, and of course, they had missed the GI Bill by thirty years. None of this really fazed the WASP. They remained thankful. After all, they got to "fly those beautiful airplanes."

In the 1990s, as the celebrations of the fiftieth anniversary of World War II began, outside interest in the WASP soared and the women took on a new purpose, that of enhancing the WASP saga and sharing their personal stories.

At their own fiftieth reunion held in 1992 in San Antonio, the WASP officially chose the Woman's Collection at Texas Woman's University in Denton to be the repository of WASP stories, papers, photos, and memorabilia—that is, the WASP Archives. Soon it became obvious that the records of those who had died during the war, and where they were buried, were inadequate. In addition, contact with many of the deceased women's families had been lost.

Four WASP—Dawn Seymour (43-5), Jeanette J. Jenkins (44-1), and 44-2 classmates Clarice I. Bergemann and Mary Ellen Keil—took it upon themselves to correct that oversight. They opted to research, compile, and write the booklet *In Memoriam: Thirty-Eight American Women Pilots.* This book—small in size but historically significant—recognized the fallen among their sister WASP and made available for posterity a written record of whom they were. Appropriately, Texas Woman's University Press published the fifty-two-page booklet in 1996.[19]

Following is the booklet's Foreword—used with permission.

The story is told elsewhere about the long challenging days of World War II. Suddenly every able-bodied person was needed. Women had opportunities once found only in their dreams.

In 1942, H.H. "Hap" Arnold, Commanding General Army Air Forces, needed thousands of pilots. He was willing to recruit and train women. Jacqueline "Jackie" Cochran and Nancy Harkness Love were appointed leaders. American women pilots from every corner of the U.S.A. volunteered and answered this call.

They loved to fly.

They were willing to leave loved ones to learn, step by step, the knowledge, skill and art of flying military airplanes.

They were willing to risk everything so freedom would ring across the globe.

They served valiantly.

Thirty-eight American women pilots gave their lives during training or operational flying. It is to their memory that this book is dedicated.

The Addendum that concludes the body of the booklet's text gives an overview of the process of the WASP receiving their military status—thirty-three years after they were disbanded and sent home. (Used with permission)

The G.I. Improvement Act of 1977 and Public Law 95-202 authorized the Secretary of Defense to determine if certain types of civilian service in World War II could be classified as active duty. The bill was signed into law on November 23, 1977.

On March 8, 1979, it was announced that the service of the WASP had been determined by the Secretary to be active military service for the purpose of all laws administered by the Veterans Administration.

On May 21, 1979, the first Honorable Discharge from the Air Force was issued to a WASP.

The World War II Victory Medal and the American Campaign Medal were awarded to eligible WASP, May 1984.

On May 4, 2000, WASP friends and families of the thirty-eight were invited to the US Air Force Academy in Colorado Springs for the formal dedication of a bronze plaque "In Memoriam to the Women Airforce Service Pilots" who died in service during World War II. Dawn Seymour, Chair of WASP Memorials, then and now, and one of the authors of *In Memoriam*, chaired the WASP part of the ceremony and was present, as was then WASP World War II President Lucile Wise (Class 43-7).

Dorothy Scott's brother and sister-in-law, Ed and Ethel Scott; their older son, Tracy; and his younger son, Brian, were among the family members in attendance.

In the ensuing years, the WASP have lost many more of their number. As this book goes to press in the spring of 2016 there are just over 100 WASP still with us. The sacrifice of their thirty-eight sisters who died in service still haunts them, and they want to see those once almost forgotten thirty-eight recognized and honored.

WASP Florence "Shutsy" Reynolds of Class 44-5 began to rethink the sacrifice of the thirty-eight and decided to launch her own meaningful

Dorothy's bronze wings, made by Shutsy Reynolds, WASP Class 44-5. *Photo by the author.*

recognition of them. In the June 2007 issue of the *WASP News*, Shutsy—a talented artist and an accomplished silversmith—announced that she planned to donate a pair of bronze wings to the family of each of the thirty-eight. The bronze wings can be set into the WASP's headstone or cemetery marker, a Veterans Administration marker, a memorial plaque, or used in any way the family desires.[20] The bronze wings are identical to (though less costly than) the silver wings the majority of the WASP wore in service—and still wear proudly.

September 27–30, 2007, the Gathering of P-51 Mustangs and Legends was held at Rickenbacker International Airport in Columbus, Ohio, as part of the US Air Force's Heritage Weeks commemorating its sixtieth

Florence "Shutsy" Reynolds, WASP Class 44-5, is a silversmith and jewelry maker and for many years made wings and other jewelry for her WASP sisters and their families and friends. She made bronze grave marker wings for each of the thirty-eight WASP who lost their lives flying in World War II. *Courtesy Barbara Rey Photography.*

anniversary (1947–2007). One hundred thirty WASP pilots qualified to ferry the P-51 Mustang.[21] Because of that, the Air Force invited the WASP to participate and provided them with booth space and room for their exhibit. Many of the pursuit ferry pilots were gone by then, but four WASP P-51 pilots were in attendance: Betty Tackaberry Blake (43-1), Alice Jean May (A. J.) Starr and Virginia Lee Jowell Hagerstrom (both Class 43-4), and Vivian Cadman Eddy (43-5).

US Army Chaplain Capt. Jeffrey Clemens walked into the WASP exhibit at the gathering. There, he met the twenty WASP attending the event. He and Shutsy struck up a conversation. Captain Clemens "caught the WASP bug," took up the cause of WASP recognition alongside Shutsy, and agreed to help finance bronze flag holders for the graves of the thirty-eight—World War II veterans all. The mission was dubbed Operation Celestial Flight.

"Many of the thirty-eight gravesites have no military symbols or marking. On most, the American flag has never flown, nor were memorial services ever held," Reynolds wrote for the October 2008 *WASP News*. "Ignored by both the public and veteran organizations, these brave young women have been forgotten. Now, 65 years later, a U.S. Army Chaplain, intrigued by the history of the WASP, has embarked on a mission '. . . to honor the dead' and to ensure they are properly identified and honored."[22]

Shutsy had an ally. She also had a team: Sara Hayden and Scott Ferguson.

For years, Sara Payne Hayden, 44-10, the WASP in charge of Veteran's Affairs, has been working to obtain DD form 214s (honorable discharge) for the WASP. Requests for this document require that a family member file the application form. Contact with families of the thirty-eight was never maintained, so only a few were aware of this provision. Sara helped family members obtain their deceased WASP's DD-214.

Scott Ferguson, son of WASP Eileen Ferguson (44-7), working on his computer, researched records and found most of the thirty-eight's missing family members.

Reynolds says Clemens paid for the first ten bronze flag stands as well as the memorial service for missing WASP Gertrude Tompkins Silver (43-7).[23] Silver disappeared in her P-51 on October 26, 1944, and has never been found. Because there is no grave, Captain Clemens had a plaque designed for her instead of a flag stand. The service for Silver was held November 11, 2008, in Los Angeles. Photos and an article from that event were published in the March 2009 issue of the *WASP News*.[24]

Remaining funds needed for the flag holders were raised through several WASP efforts and donations.[25] To date, twenty-nine bronze flag stands have been mailed to the families or to friends and are in place at the various gravesites. The practice is that the family is asked to pay nothing.

Working with Shutsy Reynolds, Scott Ferguson, and Dorothy's nephew Tracy Scott led me to Dorothy Scott's gravesite in 2009. The bronze flag holder, as befitting a World War II veteran, now marks Dorothy's grave.

The team continues the effort to place the final eight bronze markers, but the gravesites of four WASP still are unknown. The others are in cemeteries that, for various reasons, will not allow the flag stands. The latest update (December 2015) from Shutsy is, "These are the names of the three whom we have been unable to locate: Peggy M. Martin (44-4), Marie Ethel Sharon (43-4), and Jane Delores Champlin (43-4, died in training). Current thinking is to place the markers in museums as close to their hometowns as possible."

For the names of the thirty-eight, please see Appendix 1.

Chapter Seventeen
Congressional Gold Medal

Washington: July 1, 2009—President [Barack] Obama today signed into law S. 614, a bill to award a Congressional Gold Medal to the Women Airforce Service Pilots (WASP). WASP was established during World War II with the primary mission of flying non-combat military missions in the United States thus freeing their male counterparts for combat missions. Its pilots were the first women ever to fly American military aircraft and flew almost every type of aircraft operated by the United States Army Air Forces during World War II on a wide range of missions.

"The Women Airforce Service Pilots courageously answered their country's call in a time of need while blazing a trail for the brave women who have given and continue to give so much in service to this nation since," said President Obama. "Every American should be grateful for their service, and I am honored to sign this bill to finally give them some of the hard-earned recognition they deserve."[1]

The bipartisan effort in Congress to recognize the contributions of the WASP was led by Senators Kay Bailey Hutchison (R-TX) and Barbara Mikulski (D-MD), and Representatives Ileana Ros-Lehtinen (R-FL) and Susan Davis (D-CA). At the July 1, 2009, signing, President Obama and Ros-Lehtinen were joined by three members of the WASP as well as five active-duty US Air Force pilots who have followed in their footsteps.

The WASP present were Bernice Falk Haydu (Class 44-7), who served as WASP president when the women received their militarization in 1977, and Washington, DC, area residents Elaine Danforth Harmon (Class 44-9) and Lorraine Zillner Rodgers (Class 44-2), both of whom also worked on the militarization effort. Also present was US Air Force Maj. Nicole Malachowski, who led the quest for the WASP to receive the Gold Medal. Major (now Colonel) Malachowski was the first woman to fly with the US Air Force Thunderbirds, the team that flies F-16s in precision flight at air shows around the country.

The signing of the Gold Medal legislation put the WASP front and center in the news, and articles began to appear in their hometown newspapers all around the country as reporters discovered the resident WASP in their backyards. One of the best-kept secrets of World War II, the WASP began receiving their due—at long last.

With the Gold Medal ceremony pending, the effort to locate missing WASP became a priority. Scott Ferguson's workload skyrocketed. By fall 2009, all the living WASP had been accounted for.

The stage was set.

Memorial Service, March 9, 2010

The two-day celebration was set in motion Tuesday, March 9, 2010, with a memorial service for the thirty-eight, held at the Air Force Memorial, followed by a blue-ribbon reception at the Women's Memorial (Women in Military Service to America, or WIMSA) located at the entrance to Arlington National Cemetery.

The Memorial Service began at 2 p.m. on a perfect day in the nation's capital. Vice Adm. Vivien Crea, US Coast Guard (Ret.), escorted WASP Memorials Chair Dawn Seymour (Class 43-5). Together, they placed the commemorative wreath: two women in different shades of military blue— arm in arm—both aviators, each a daughter of her time and her war.

Dawn is one of the few WASP who flew the B-17. She is a past president of the WASP. Vice Adm. Crea was the first woman promoted to flag rank in the US Coast Guard, the first woman USCG vice commandant, and the first woman in US history to serve as a vice chief (the Coast Guard's second in command). As a Coast Guard aviator, Vice Admiral Crea flew the C-130 Hercules turboprop, HH-65 Dolphin helicopter, and Gulfstream II jet.

Vice Adm. Vivien Crea, US Coast Guard (Ret.), and Dawn Seymour, Class 43-5, the WASP's Memorials chair, at the memorial service for the fallen thirty-eight, March 9, 2010, in Washington, DC. Together, they placed the memorial wreath (in the background right). *Photo by the author.*

"Flight is by nature hazardous, and accidents not uncommon, especially in the frenzy of America at war," Crea, the keynote speaker, told the nearly two hundred WASP and their family members and friends gathered in remembrance. "Mechanical failure, disorientation, mid-air collisions and training accidents took their toll. Sometimes you became the target. Thirty-eight of you died in the service to our nation.

"Those of us who have lost family, friends and crew-mates can identify so well with the sickening feeling of every tragic mishap. That terrible thud in your very gut when you first hear the news, that insatiable need, but the same time, dread to hear the cause of the accident, and that hollow emptiness that follows in its wake."[2]

Crea concluded by quoting Gen. Barton Yount, Army Air Forces

Training Command, who, on December 7, 1944, spoke to the last graduating class of WASP about their sisters killed while flying for their country: "Let us acknowledge the measure of their sacrifice. It is the heritage of faith in victory, and faith in the ultimate freedom of humanity."

Yours truly, author of this biography, had the privilege of representing Dorothy Scott and her family in Washington, DC, that day and placing Dorothy's red rose on the memorial stand—a moving experience that I will never forget.

Gold Medal Day, March 10, 2010

September 10, 1942, Secretary of War Henry Stimson announced that Nancy Harkness Love would lead a group of civilian women pilots who would ferry airplanes for the US Army. Gen. Harold L. George, commander of the Army's Air Transport Command (ATC), escorted his new squadron leader, Mrs. Love, to the secretary's office for this momentous announcement. It was a first. Women pilots were being employed by the ATC's Ferrying Division to ferry single-engine Army trainer airplanes from the factories to training fields.

Who could have foreseen the momentous occasion that, sixty-seven-and-a-half years later to the day, would celebrate the consequence of that simple announcement—and with such enthusiasm?

Seeing their faces Wednesday, March 10, at the US Capitol in Washington, DC, was worth it all. Each WASP had a uniformed military escort. Whether she walked in under her own power, used a walker, or arrived in a wheelchair, each WASP who gathered was an aviator—all of them women who still have their heads in the sky and their eyes on the stars.

They trace their lineage back to that September day in 1942 when Secretary Stimson and General George welcomed Mrs. Love and her first squadron of women pilots to the Army Air Forces and World War II service.

The road was a rocky one. Competing philosophies of how women pilots should be organized and utilized; male resistance to women being allowed into that special "brotherhood," sharing the mystique known only to pilots who fly those most powerful of airborne machines; jealousies over who did what first; gut-wrenching grief when girls barely out of their teens crashed and burned in training or on active duty; despondency at washing out of training; elation over earning one's wings; like Dorothy

Scott, joy at being sent to pursue school—the ultimate dream of most of the 1940s "fly girls."

So, when July 1, 2009, brought President Obama's signature to the Senate bill to honor them with the Congressional Gold Medal, these ladies took it to heart and, with the help of dedicated friends and families, planned to attend. Fewer than three hundred WASP remained alive when the Gold Medal became a reality. Still, nearly two-thirds of those surviving gathered in Washington for the big day. The youngest WASP attending were eighty-six years old.

The number of medals awarded totaled 1,114. Included in that number are Nancy Love's original 28, the 1,074 graduates of the flight-training school, and the 11 trainees who died before they had the opportunity to complete the training and receive their wings. Those numbers total 1,113. Medal number 1,114 went to Jacqueline Cochran. Nancy Love served actively as a WASP pilot during the war and is included in official WASP count. Cochran did not. But she was included in this remembrance.

Tears were shed, memories were shared, laughs were savored, as old and dear friends met once again. If they had doubts before, grown children, grandchildren, great-grandchildren, and friends of WASP got to see how much this unique experience meant to these pioneering women of the 1940s.

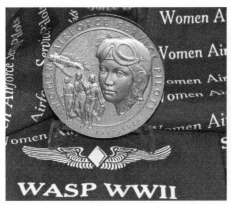

The WASP Gold Medal. Andy Hailey photographed both sides of his mother Lois's gold medal against her signature blue and white WASP scarf. Lois Brooks Hailey, WASP Class 43-3 (1915–2010). *Photos used with permission of Andy Hailey.*

Speaker of the House of Representatives Nancy Pelosi, the mistress of ceremonies—as the first woman speaker in US history, herself a pioneer—said it all. "Women Airforce Service Pilots, we are all your daughters. You taught us how to fly."

On that monumental day in our nation's capital, the living WASP—joined by their families and friends and by the families of their sister WASP who have flown west—took home the gold.

Five of Nancy Love's Originals were still living at the time of the awarding of the Gold Medal. Three made it to the event: Barbara "B. J." Erickson London, Gertrude Meserve Tubbs LeValley, and Barbara "Donnie" Donahue Ross. Unable to attend were Florene Miller Watson and Phyllis Burchfield Fulton; however, Phyllis's niece Lynne Shima attended to accept her medal.

A side note: B. J. Erickson London was flown to Washington by her corporate pilot granddaughter Kelly Rinehart in a corporate jet. Kelly's boss insisted she fly her grandmother to Washington in his aircraft. Flying with them were Kelly's mom and dad, Terry and Bob Rinehart, both retired airline pilots, and Kelly's twin sister, Lauren. Terry London Rinehart—following in her pioneering mother's footsteps—was one of the first women hired to fly commercial jets in the 1970s. May the circle be unbroken.

"Donnie" Ross was accompanied by several members of her family, and Charles Tubbs escorted his mother, Gertrude.

Sadly, since that Gold Medal Day, we have lost all five remaining original WAFS. The last survivor, Gertrude, took her final flight August 13, 2015. RIP, Gertrude, and your twenty-seven Original sisters.

Other WAFS family members attending to receive medals for those who are deceased included two of Nancy Love's daughters, Hannah Robinson and Allie Love; Honey Fulton Parker for her sister Dorothy Fulton Slinn; Dugie Fine Eyton-Hughes representing her mother, Kathryn "Sis" Bernheim Fine; and Sherrill Arnet and her daughter Julie Kelley, representing mother and grandmother Lenore McElroy.

Tracy Scott had asked me to pick up Dorothy's medal for their family. I also was privileged to pick up Nancy Batson Crews's medal for her three children and their families. Nancy, of course, was the one who made it possible for me to write the WAFS's story. And by March of 2010, I also had published her biography. Evelyn Sharp's biographer, Diane Bartels, picked up Evelyn's medal and laid her red rose at the memorial ceremony March 9.

A replica of Dorothy Scott's medal graces a memorial at the Dorothy Scott Memorial International Airport in Oroville, Washington. The Borderlands Historical Society of Dorothy's home Okanogan County headed up the effort.

Dorothy Scott in her WAFS uniform with the Air Transport Command wings worn by all the original WAFS. *Courtesy WASP Archive, Texas Woman's University, Denton.*

Epilogue

Before leaving Dorothy's story to posterity, a coda. A child of the era of the "winged gospel," she left us a glimpse into her personal "winged gospel," written in May 1940 when she was still dreaming of flying and trying to gain entry into the University of Washington's Civilian Pilot Training Program.

With sincerity of purpose, but with a hint of tongue in cheek lurking beneath, she deftly laid it all out in that junior-year essay. And the life she lived, to age twenty-three years, nine months, and seventeen days, shows the same idiosyncratic sense of life and humor. That is the window into her mind.

At twenty, Dorothy's ideal world—a fanciful future—sounded like this.[1]

Comp 6

May 29, 1940

A Private Utopia
"If wishes were horses, beggars would ride . . ."

But why stop there? If I could change the world to the way I wanted it, I would run all machinery with colored pushbuttons, have all corners rounded, and insist on getting more ice cream for a nickel.

Of course I would take care of the so-called "important" matters too. I would put people in big houses equipped with escalators, skylights, and automatic laundries. Each roof would be either a landing field or a parking lot. All walls would be soundproof and each individual would have at least one room to himself. The buildings could be built either out or up as desired. If people chose the "out" system and made land scarce, agriculture would be carried on by means of pills planted in basins of water. The "up" system would make aviation popular—and also slick banister slides.

The children would be "The Chosen People." All of them would be raised in the country, all learn to shoot, ride, and take care of pets. Their schooling would include more teachers, fewer exams, and better vocational guidance—and incidentally, longer vacations. They would be sorted according to ability, and competition made the incentive for work.

I had better state that this plan would include the entire world, of three United States: Europe, Asia, and the Americas. (Africa and Australia I'm stuck with.) There would be but one language (American, so as to utilize slang), one currency system, and one height for car bumpers. Wars would be settled by putting all politicians and munitions-makers into an arena and selling admission tickets to the citizens. There would be asylums for would-be dictators, ex-band leaders, and golf enthusiasts.

All highways would be four-lane and no speed limits, but only good drivers and cars allowed. I would approve the use of horns that said, "get the hell over," when necessity demanded, but soft chimes would be the rules in the cities. Aviation, however, would be the popular method of transportation and I would have to figure out some method of handling congested air traffic.

Religion would be a real problem. I'd turn that over to some subcommittee and popular vote. Perhaps standardization would be the answer.

Now for important matters: Informal gatherings would be encouraged and formal ones forbidden. Catty remarks and gossip would be taxed, but compliments subsidized. Bull sessions, kid circuses, and symphony orchestras would be encouraged but some Ladies Aid Societies, high-pressure salesmanship, and horror shows would be banned.

Dentists would be required to run Disney cartoons for their patients and all doctors would have the responsibility of keeping the people well instead of just getting them that way.

Men would have the right to wear as changeable clothes as women, but if women gave up those dangerous hats, the men would have to give up smoking cheap cigars and wearing squeaky shoes.

The whole system for "boy meeting girl" would be reorganized, and romance encouraged but cheap necking banned.

Just imagine the possibilities: Garbage pails of rubber so early-morning collections wouldn't disturb sleepers; fenders also of rubber—no traffic worries (or at least they would be lessened); wooden shoes would go back to Holland, stiff corsets to history, and stiff shirts to blazes. (Wow, is this a parallel!) A war to the finish would be declared on snakes, mosquitoes, flies, insurance salesmen and so-called "wits." The world would have free cake and coffee lines instead of bread and water ones. There would be no more *Amos and Andy*, eight o'clock classes, or after dinner speaking. Newspapers would have the comics on the front and politics hidden deep. The "Position Wanted" column would disappear along with the advertisements for Alka-Seltzer and Carter's Little Liver Pills. History books would carry brief accounts of the passing of billboards and woolen underwear.

And ME? Oh yes, I would be the greatest violin player, lead a symphony orchestra, be a stunt pilot, own five autos, have a private soda fountain, and live in the highest penthouse I could find. I would have one husband, four children, two Collies, and the biggest collection of medals in the world. Everyone would be my friend, but some would have to be strangers so I could meet them casually. Lastly, I would be extremely wise so that I could be illogical, inconsistent, and have a great many adventures and still not make too many errors.

"All This And Heaven Too"

The paper earned her a grade of A+.

Appendix 1

In Memoriam: The Thirty-Eight

The following are the thirty-eight young women who lost their lives flying for the WASP as part of the US Army Air Forces in World War II.[1]

Jane Delores Champlin, St. Louis, Missouri
Class 43-4—May 17, 1917–June 7, 1943

Susan Parker Clarke, Cooperstown, New York
Class 44-2—1918–July 4, 1944

Marjorie Laverne Davis, Hollywood, California
Class 44-9—died October 16, 1944

Katherine "Kay" Applegate Dussaq, Walla Walla, Washington
Class 44-1—died November 26, 1944

Marjorie Davis Edwards, Anaheim, California
Class 44-6—September 28, 1918–June 13, 1944

Jane Elizabeth Erickson, Preston, Washington
Class 44-6—April 24, 1921–April 16, 1944

Cornelia Fort, Nashville, Tennessee
WAFS—February 5, 1919–March 21, 1943

Frances Fortune Grimes, Morgantown, WV
Class 43-3—died March 27, 1944

Mary Hartson, Portland, Oregon
Class 43-5—January 11, 1917–August 14, 1944

Mary Holmes Howson, Wayne, Pennsylvania
Class 44-4—February 16, 1919–April 16, 1944

Edith "Edy" Clayton Keene, Pomona, California
    Class 44-1—died April 25, 1944

Kathryn Barbara Lawrence, Grand Forks, Nebraska
    Class 43-8—December 3, 1920–August 4, 1943

Hazel Ah Ying Lee, Portland, Oregon
    Class 43-4—1912–November 23, 1944

Paula Ruth Loop, Manchester, Oklahoma
    Class 43-2—August 25, 1916–July 7, 1944

Alice E. Lovejoy, Scarsdale, New York
    Class 43-5—1919–September 13, 1944

Lea Ola McDonald, Seagraves, Texas
    Class 44-3—October 12, 1921–June 21, 1944

Peggy Wilson Martin, Long Beach, California
    Class 44-4—February 8, 1912–October 3, 1944

Virginia C. Moffatt, Los Angeles, California
    Class 43-2—died October 5, 1943

Beverly Jean Moses, Des Moines, Iowa
    Class 44-5—December 21, 1923–July 18, 1944

Dorothy Mae "Dottie" Nichols, Van Nuys, California
    Class 43-2—died June 11, 1944

Jeanne Lewellen Norbeck, Columbus, Indiana
    Class 44-3—November 14, 1912–October 16, 1944

Margaret Sanford Oldenburg, Alameda, California
    Class 43-4—died March 7, 1943

Mabel Virginia Rawlinson, Kalamazoo, Michigan
    Class 43-3—March 19, 1917–August 23, 1943

Gleanna Roberts, Iowa City, Iowa
    Class 44-9—January 11, 1919–June 20, 1944

Marie Michell Robinson, Troy, Michigan
    Class 44-2—died October 2, 1944

Betty Mae Scott, Monrovia, California
    Class 44-3—July 26, 1921–July 8, 1944

Dorothy F. Scott, Oroville, Washington
    WAFS—February 16, 1920–December 3, 1943

Margaret "Peggy" Seip, Wauwatoosa, Wisconsin
Class 43-5—June 24, 1916–August 30, 1943

Helen Jo Anderson Severson, Brookings, South Dakota
Class 43-5—November 2, 1918–August 30, 1943

Marie Ethel Sharon, Portland, Oregon
Class 43-4—April 21, 1917–April 10, 1944

Evelyn Sharp, Ord, Nebraska
WAFS—October 20, 1919–April 3, 1944

Betty Pauline Stine, Santa Barbara, California
Class 44-2—died February 25, 1944

Marian Toevs, Aberdeen, Idaho
Class 43-8—died February 18, 1944

Gertrude Tompkins Silver, Jersey City, New Jersey
Class 43-7—October 16, 1912–October 26, 1944

Mary Elizabeth Trebing, Wilburton, Oklahoma
Class 43-4—died November 7, 1943

Mary Louise Webster, Ellensburg, Washington
Class 44-8—June 30, 1919–December 9, 1944

Bonnie Jean Alloway Welz, Inglewood, California
Class 43-6—June 22, 1918–June 29, 1944

Betty Taylor Wood, Auburn, California
Class 43-4—March 1921–September 23, 1943

Appendix 2

Army Aircraft Dorothy Flew and Associated Aviation Terminology

Dorothy flew the following aircraft, as listed in her official daily flight logs, Ferrying Division, Air Transport Command. Sources include Dorothy Scott's personal papers, the Scott family, and the author's personal collection. Descriptions of aircraft are from James C. Fahey, editor, *U.S. Army Aircraft (Heavier Than Air), 1908–1946* (New York: Ships and Aircraft, 1946), pages 20–37.

Single Engine
Liaison Aircraft

L-2B—Taylorcraft—Continental engine 65 hp; top speed 90 mph.

Primary Trainers

PT-17—Stearman—Continental engine 220 hp; bi-wing, open cockpit; top speed 124 mph.

The PT-17 Stearman is a biplane used as a military trainer aircraft. Stearman Aircraft became a subsidiary of Boeing Aircraft in 1934. The Stearman PT-17, sometimes called the Kaydet, served as a primary trainer for the USAAF, the USN (as the NS & N2S), and with the RCAF as the Kaydet throughout World War II. . . . There were 3,519 PT-17s with Continental R-670-5 engines delivered. Many are still flying today.

PT-18A—Stearman—Jacobs engine 225 hp—fitted for blind flying.

PT-19A—Fairchild—Ranger engine 175 hp (later version 200 hp); low wing, open cockpit; top speed 132 mph.

This is the trainer the original WAFS ferried from the Fairchild factory in Hagerstown, Maryland, near their base, New Castle Army Air Base, Wilmington, Delaware. The PT-19 was the trainer brought to Avenger Field, Sweetwater, fall of 1943 to help the WASP trainees better learn to handle landings in a narrow-geared airplane prone to ground loops.

Basic Trainers

BT-13A—Vultee—Pratt & Whitney engine 450 hp; top speed 156 mph.

BTs had fixed landing gear, a radio, and trim tabs, and cruised at about 140 miles per hour. Dorothy described them as "low wing jobs with greenhouse hatch covers."

BT-15—Vultee—Wright engine 450 hp (otherwise the same).

Advanced Trainers

AT-6C (and D)—North American—Pratt & Whitney engine 600 hp; top speed 208 mph.

AT-6—The North American T-6 Texan two-place advanced trainer was the classroom for most of the Allied pilots who flew in World War II. Called the SNJ by the Navy and the Harvard by the British Royal Air Force, the AT-6 (advanced trainer) was designed as a transition trainer between basic trainers and first-line tactical aircraft. It was redesignated T-6 in 1948 . . . and trained several hundred thousand pilots in thirty-four different countries over a period of twenty-five years. A total of 15,495 of the planes were made. Though most famous as a trainer, the T-6 Texan also won honors in World War II and in the early days of the Korean War.

The Texan was an evolution of the company's BC-1 basic combat trainer, which was first produced for the US Army Air Corps with fixed landing gear in 1937 under a contract that called for 174 planes. North American Aviation designed the NA-49 prototype as a low-cost trainer with all the characteristics of a high-speed fighter.

Although not as fast as a fighter, it was easy to maintain and repair, had more maneuverability, and was easier to handle. A pilot's airplane, it could roll, Immelmann, loop, spin, snap, and vertical roll. It was designed to give the best possible training in all types of tactics, from ground strafing to bombardment and aerial dogfighting. It contained such versatile equipment as bomb racks, blind flying instrumentation, gun and standard cameras, fixed and flexible guns, and just about every other device that military pilots had to operate. Source: http://www.theharvard.co.za/a-brief-history-of-the-north-american-harvard (accessed 11-27-2015), originally found at www.boeing.com/history/bna/t6.htm.

BC-1A—North American—Pratt & Whitney engine—600 hp.

Similar to the AT-6. This is the aircraft Dorothy was flying when she crashed and was killed.

Attack/Light Bombardment Aircraft

A-24B-DT—Douglas—Wright engine—1,200 hp; top speed 254 mph.

The A-24B (SBD-5) was produced, beginning in 1942, by the Douglas plant in Tulsa, Oklahoma. Six hundred fifteen were built. Dorothy ferried several of these. The Douglas Dauntless was primarily a naval scout plane and dive-bomber, but the US Army had its own version of the SBD that lacked the tail hook used for carrier landings and a pneumatic tire replaced the solid tail wheel.

RA-24B—Douglas—Wright engine—1200 hp, R stands for redesignation as "restricted" from combat.

A-25—Curtiss—Wright engine—1700 hp; top speed 275 mph.

These three types of aircraft were also used as high-horsepower single-engine trainers for those going to pursuit school.

Twin Engine

AT-7C—Beech—Pratt & Whitney engines—450 hp; top speed 224 mph. Used to train navigators.

AT-9A—Curtiss—Lycoming engines—295 hp; top speed 197 mph. Twin-engine transition.

AT-11—Beech—Pratt & Whitney engines—450 hp; top speed 215 mph. Used to train bombardiers.

AT-17B—Cessna—Jacobs engines—245 hp each; top speed 170 mph. Same as the UC-78 and known as the "Bobcat" or "Bamboo Bomber."

C-47A—Douglas—Pratt & Whitney engines—1,200 hp each; top speed 220 mph.

The Douglas C-47 Skytrain or Dakota is a military transport aircraft that was developed from the Douglas DC-3 airliner. C-47s that had been DC-3 airliners were the backbone of the Air Transport Command's "airline" (SNAFU) that, from late 1943 on, picked up ferry pilots at their delivery point and flew them back to base so that they could ferry yet another aircraft. It was used extensively by the Allies during World War II. On D-Day, the C-47 was used to tow gliders and drop paratroops. In the Pacific, C-47s were used to ferry soldiers serving in the Pacific theater back to the United States.

C-60A—Lockheed—Wright engines—1200 hp each; top speed 257 mph.

Appendix 3

Description of the Accident

Brief narrative of accident:

Include statement of responsibility and recommendations for action to prevent repetition.

Both aircraft involved in this accident were on routine training flights. The BC-1, with instructor Lt. Robert M. Snyder in the rear seat and WASP Dorothy F. Scott, student, in the front seat, having made several landings, was on final approach and had established a normal gliding attitude. When P-39 number 42-19531, pilot Lt. Wilson A. Young, turned into final approach from a shorter base leg it collided with the other aircraft, in such a manner that the tail section of the BC-1 was severed. Both ships crashed into the ground a short distance from each other with the BC-1 bursting into flames upon impact.

It is believed this accident was caused by the inability of Lt. Young, the pilot of the P-39, when turning on to the final approach, to see the B-1, which was already on final approach, because of the position of the sun and the banking attitude of the P-39. It is also believed that the operation of camouflaged aircraft in this area (Palm Springs area) is a contributing factor to the accident.

It is recommended that:

a. All aircraft used in pursuit transition be painted yellow.

b. Instructions in BC-1 and AT-7 [This is a typo, it should be AT-6] type aircraft be conducted elsewhere than Army Air Field Palm Springs California, when pursuit-type aircraft are in the traffic pattern.

c. It be ascertained before the departure of any aircraft from this field that the radio is in proper working condition and, if not, the Tower will so notify the Operations Officer and not allow the aircraft to depart until this situation is remedied.

d. If pursuit transition is to be continued at this airfield for a protracted period, consideration be given to the construction of parallel runways.[1]

Appendix 4

WAFS Roster

Below is a list of the original WAFS in the order they joined:[1]

1942

1. Nancy Harkness Love
2. Betty Huyler Gillies
3. Cornelia Fort
4. Aline "Pat" Rhonie
5. Helen Mary Clark
6. Adela "Del" Riek Scharr
7. Esther Gebbert Nelson (Carpenter)
8. Teresa James (Martin)
9. Barbara Poole (Shoemaker)
10. Helen Richards (Prosser)
11. Barbara Towne (Dickson, Faskin)
12. Gertrude Meserve (Tubbs, LeValley)
13. Florene Miller (Watson)
14. Barbara Jane "B. J." Erickson (London)
15. Delphine Bohn
16. Barbara "Donnie" Donahue (Ross)
17. Evelyn Sharp
18. Phyllis Burchfield (Fulton)
19. Esther Manning (Rathfelder, Shively, Westervelt)
20. Nancy Batson (Crews)
21. Katherine "Kay" Rawls Thompson

22. Dorothy Fulton (Slinn)
23. Opal "Betsy" Hulet Ferguson (Woodward)
24. Bernice Batten
25. Dorothy Scott

1943

26. Helen "Little Mac" Schmidt McGilvery
27. Kathryn "Sis" Strouse Bernheim (Fine)
28. Lenore "Mac" McElroy

Notes

Preface

1. William K. Kershner, *The Student Pilots Flight Manual,* Seventh Edition (Ames: Iowa State University Press, 1993), 6–7. Horsepower is the most common measurement for power. One horsepower is equal to a power of 550 foot-pounds per second or 33,000 foot-pounds per minute. The airplane engine develops horsepower within its cylinders and, by rotating a propeller, exerts thrust. Thrust moves the aircraft through the air.

2. Sarah Byrn Rickman, "WASP Pilots and 'the 5th'—Dallas Love Field," *Legacies, A History Journal for Dallas and North Central Texas* (Spring 2008), 48.

Introduction

1. Charles E. Planck, *Women with Wings* (New York: Harper & Brothers, 1942), 16–17.

2. http://en.wikipedia.org/wiki/Blanche_Stuart_Scott; http://www.ctie.monash.edu.au/hargrave/scott.html.

3. http://www.women-in-aviation.com.

4. http://earlyaviators.com/eblanche.htm.

5. http://www.women-in-aviation.com.

6. https://en.wikipedia.org/wiki/Early_Birds_of_Aviation (accessed 11-21-2015).

7. Henry M. Holden, "Bessica Raiche," © 1991 Black Hawk Publishing, http://www.women-in-aviation.com, accessed 11-21-2015.

8. Féderátion Aéronautique Internationale (FAI) is a nongovernmental and nonprofit international organization that encourages and oversees the conduct of sporting aviation events throughout the world and certifies aviation world

records. The FAI was founded by representatives from Belgium, France, Germany, Great Britain, Italy, Spain, Switzerland, and the United States, meeting in Paris on Oct. 14, 1905. In 1999 the FAI headquarters moved from Paris to Lausanne, Switzerland. http://www.britannica.com/EBchecked/topic/203551/Federation-Aeronautique-Internationale-FAI (accessed 3-12-2014).

9. Sources: http://womenshistory.about.com/od/aviationpilots/p/harriet_quimby.htm; http://www.ctie.monash.edu.au/hargrave/moisant_m.html; http://www.collectair.com/moisantindex.html; and http://en.wikipedia.org/wiki/Julia_Clark (all links accessed 3-2-2014). Planck, *Women with Wings,* 18; Debra L. Winegarten, *Katherine Stinson: The Flying Schoolgirl* (Austin, TX: Eakin Press, 2000), 15.

10. http://en.wikipedia.org/wiki/Ruth_Bancroft_Law.

11. Planck, *Women with Wings,* 27–35.

12. http://www.hill.af.mil/library/factsheets/factsheet.asp?id=5877 (accessed 3-2-2014). When the United States entered World War I in 1917, Ruth Law volunteered to fly for the Army but was turned down. Even though their offers were dismissed by the secretary of war with the statement, "We don't want women in the Army," many women aviators wanted to contribute to the war effort. Law and other female American pilots were only allowed to fly in bond drives and recruiting tours, while women in various other countries flew in military roles.

13. Neta Snook Southern, *I Taught Amelia to Fly* (New York: Vantage Press, 1974), 80–89.

14. Patti Marshall, "Neta Snook," *Aviation History* 17, no. 3 (January 2007).

15. Southern, *I Taught Amelia,* 2–3.

16. Southern, *I Taught Amelia,* 102–103.

17. http://en.wikipedia.org/wiki/Amelia_Earhart. Including citation to Aerospace: Amelia Earhart 1897–1937, http://www.u-s-history.com/pages/h1658.html (accessed 6-3-2012).

18. Amelia Earhart, *20 Hrs., 40 Min.—Our Flight in the Friendship* (Washington, DC: National Geographic Society, 2003). Rerelease of this title, © 1928, originally published by George P. Putnam & Sons. Her story of the flight.

19. Kathleen Winters, *Amelia Earhart: The Turbulent Life of an American Icon* (New York: Palgrave MacMillan, 2010), 73. See footnote 1 on page 222: Colonel Hilton H. Railey, introduction to Briand Jr., *Daughter of the Sky,* xvi.

20. Gene Nora Jessen, *The Powder Puff Derby of 1929: The True Story of the First Women's Cross-Country Air Race* (Napierville, IL: Sourcebooks, 2002), 177.

21. Jessen, *Powder Puff Derby,* 67, 197, 202.

22. Jessen, *Powder Puff Derby*, 117.

23. Jessen, *Powder Puff Derby*, 240.

24. Lu Hollander, Gene Nora Jessen, Verna West, Ninety-Nines History Book Committee, *The Ninety-Nines Yesterday, Today, Tomorrow* (Paducah, KY: Turner Publishing Company, 1996), 11–12.

25. Jessen, *Powder Puff Derby*, 211, 240–243.

26. Jessen, *Powder Puff Derby*, 241.

27. Joseph J. Corn, *The Winged Gospel: America's Romance with Aviation* (New York: Oxford University Press, 1983; paperback edition published 2002, Johns Hopkins University Press), 76.

28. Corn, *Winged Gospel*, 77.

29. Louise Thaden, *High, Wide, and Frightened* (New York: Air Facts Press, 1973) 201–202.

30. Sarah Byrn Rickman, *Nancy Love and the WASP Ferry Pilots of World War II* (Denton: University of North Texas Press, 2008), 28.

31. Deborah G. Douglas, "WASPs of War," *Aviation Heritage* (January 1999), 48.

32. Planck, *Women with Wings*, 52–53.

33. http://www.ctie.monash.edu.au/hargrave/woods.html (accessed 3-12-2014). Recommended: Ann Cooper, *On the Wing: Jessie Woods and the Flying Aces Air Circus* (Mt. Freedom, NJ: Black Hawk Publishing, July 1993).

34. Glenn Kerfoot, *Propeller Annie: The Story of Helen Richey* (Lexington: Kentucky Aviation History Roundtable, 1988), 43–51. Also Corn, *Winged Gospel*, 80; and Susan Ware, *Still Missing: Amelia Earhart and the Search for Modern Feminism* (New York: W. W. Norton, 1993), 76–77.

35. http://www.ctie.monash.edu.au/hargrave/omlie.html (accessed 3-12-2014).

36. Louise Thaden, "Five Women Tackle the Nation," *NAA* (National Aeronautic Association magazine), August 1936, clipping found at the International Women's Air and Space Museum, Cleveland, Ohio.

37. http://www.militarymuseum.org/Barnes.html (accessed 3-20-2014).

38. Janann Sherman, *Walking on Air: The Aerial Adventures of Phoebe Omlie* (Jackson: University Press of Mississippi), 88–90.

39. Letter from Amelia Earhart to Eugene Vidal, date November 17, 1935, written on Purdue University letterhead. From the George Palmer Putnam Collection of Amelia Earhart Papers, Purdue University Libraries, Archives and Special Collections. "Earhart, who was a Purdue career counselor and adviser to the Department of Aeronautics from 1935–1937, was recruited by then-President Edward Elliott, who was impressed by her spirit of adventure and her message to women. . . . In April of 1936 an Amelia Earhart Fund for

Aeronautical Research was created with the Purdue Research Foundation. The fund purchased the $80,000 Lockheed Electra that became known as Earhart's flying laboratory." See https://news.uns.purdue.edu/x/2009b/091019CordovaEarhart.html (accessed 3-22-2014).

40. Rickman, *Nancy Love*, 35–36. Also Thaden, *High, Wide and Frightened*, 163–170.

41. https://airandspace.si.edu/explore-and-learn/topics/women-in-aviation/ Noyes.cfm.

42. Rickman, *Nancy Love*, 11–13.

43. Doris L. Rich, *Jackie Cochran, Pilot in the Fastest Lane* (Gainesville: University Press of Florida, 2007), 28–29.

44. Diane Ruth Armour Bartels, *Sharpie: The Life Story of Evelyn Sharp, Nebraska's Aviatrix* (Lincoln, NE: Dageforde Publishing, 1996), 40, 47, 58.

45. Rob Simbeck, *Daughter of the Air: The Brief Soaring Life of Cornelia Fort* (New York: Atlantic Monthly Press, 1999), 62–69.

46. The Bureau of Air Commerce Aeronautics Branch was established in the Department of Commerce May 20, 1926, and renamed Bureau of Air Commerce July 1, 1934. Personnel and property were transferred to the Civil Aeronautics Authority August 22, 1938. http://www.libraries.psu.edu/psul/socialsciences/ docdigiproj/aircommerce.html (accessed 3-14-2014).

47. Dominick A. Pisano, *To Fill the Skies with Pilots: The Civilian Pilot Training Program, 1939–1946* (Champaign: University of Illinois Press, 1993; Smithsonian Institution reprint, 2001), 3–4.

48. Pisano, *To Fill the Skies*, 4–5.

49. Pisano, *To Fill the Skies*, 45.

50. http://www.hill.af.mil/library/factsheets/factsheet.asp?id=5815 (accessed 3-11-2014).

51. The Tuskegee Airmen were the first African American military aviators in the US Armed Forces. They formed the 332nd Fighter Group and the 477th Bombardment Group of the US Army Air Forces, serving as fighter and bomber pilots in World War II. http://en.wikipedia.org/wiki/African_ American (accessed 1-27-2015).

52. Pisano, *To Fill the Skies*, 55–56.

53. Pisano, *To Fill the Skies*, 58, 60.

54. Pisano, *To Fill the Skies*, 44.

55. Planck, *Women with Wings*, 142–146.

56. Patricia Strickland, *The Putt-Putt Air Force: The Story of the Civilian Pilot Training Program and the War Training Service (1939–1944)* (Washington,

DC: Department of Transportation, Federal Aviation Administration, Aviation Education Staff, GA-20-84), 55.

57. Pisano, *To Fill the Skies,* 77–78.

58. Planck, *Women with Wings,* 148.

59. Strickland, *Putt-Putt Air Force,* 55.

60. Strickland, *Putt-Putt Air Force,* 56.

61. Strickland, *Putt-Putt Air Force,* 56.

62. Strickland, *Putt-Putt Air Force,* 56.

63. Planck, *Women with Wings,* 148.

64. Pisano, *To Fill the Skies,* 76–77.

Chapter One

1. *Post-Intelligencer,* Seattle, March 18, 1941, "Dorothy Scott, University Senior, Flies Before Her Father."

2. *Post-Intelligencer,* March 18, 1941.

3. *Post-Intelligencer,* March 18, 1941.

4. Edward A. Scott wrote a four-page memoir of what he knew of his father's (G. M. Scott's) life. It is the basis for much of this chapter, along with other noted sources. The piece is not dated. Edward's son, Tracy, found it among his papers.

5. Photocopy of article.

6. From Tracy Scott in a March 2010 conversation with Jim and Ellen Zosel of Oroville. Jim was Dorothy's classmate in school.

7. Letter dated June 26, 1996, from Edward A. Scott to Clarice I. Bergemann (WASP Class 44-2). Clarice, in cooperation with Dawn Seymour (43-5), Jeanette J. Jenkins (44-1), and Mary Ellen Keil (44-2), researched and wrote the booklet *In Memoriam: Thirty-Eight American Women Pilots* (Denton: Texas Woman's University Press, 1996), telling the stories of the thirty-eight WASP who were killed in training or in service during World War II.

8. Email from John Townsley to the author dated October 2, 2005.

9. Email from John Townsley to the author dated October 12, 2005.

10. *Okanogan Valley Gazette-Tribune,* Oroville, Washington, June 10, 1993.

11. This information is found in Dorothy's letters written home to her father during the war. It is an ongoing discussion between them. Dorothy was planning to take a couple of courses by mail, while serving in the WAFS, to complete her requirements for her degree.

12. Woodbury University—"a Southern California Tradition Since 1884"—was Woodbury College when Dorothy attended classes there. The school cele-

brated 125 years in 2009 and has grown as Los Angeles—with a population of seven thousand in 1884—has grown. To quote the website: "Business leaders recognized that future growth was dependent upon education, and entrepreneur F. C. Woodbury established this institution to meet community needs. Moving beyond those highly pragmatic beginnings, Woodbury has made a difference for generations by shaping the economic, social, and cultural landscape of Southern California and beyond." Websites as of 12-12-2009: http://www.woodbury125th.org/ and http://www.woodbury.edu/s/131/index.aspx.

13. Letter from G. M. to Dorothy dated April 27, 1942.

14. William H. Tunner and Booton Herndon, *Over the Hump* (New York: Duell, Sloan and Pearce, 1964), 25.

Chapter Two

1. Barbara Erickson's letter to Dorothy, dated October 20, 1942. Dorothy Scott Collection, TWU, WASP Archive.

2. "Women Pilots in the AAF, 1941–1944." Army Air Forces Historical Studies: No. 55. Military Affairs/Aerospace Historian, Eisenhower Hall, Kansas State University, Manhattan, KS 66506. ISBN 0-89126-138-9. General Arnold to Commanding General AAF Training Command, November 3, 1942, 25. Copies at the WASP Archive, TWU; the Dwight D. Eisenhower Library; and in author's hands. Referred to hereafter as #55.

3. Letter to Edward Scott dated October 29, 1942.

4. WACO (pronounced wah-ko) airplanes: the Weaver Aircraft Company (known by its acronym WACO) founded 1920, Loraine, Ohio. Moved to Troy, Ohio, in 1923. WACO ceased producing aircraft in 1946, but the brand still enjoys enormous popularity among aviation enthusiasts. Many WACOs remain flying today, their style and mystique evoking images of aviation's "golden age." From the following website—last accessed 1-7-2010: http://www.pilotfriend.com/aircraft%20performance/Waco/waco_page.htm. See also http://www.wacoairmuseum.org/. For information on WACO Air Museum, Historic WACO Field, and the WACO Aviation Learning Center, see http://en.wikipedia.org/wiki/Waco_Aircraft_Company.

5. From the complete text of a report by Jacqueline Cochran to General H. H. Arnold, together with a summary of the report—both for release to the press August 8, 1944. Copy held by WASP Archive, TWU, in the Jernigan/Archambault collection, and elsewhere. In the document under "E—How Trained WASPs Are Serving"—first subsection #1. Under #4, Cochran also states regarding target towing work done by the WASP: "Target towing is work that

most male pilots dislike and, consequently, they take little interest in doing a good job. Further, such flying affords little opportunity for experience [that] would be of value as pre-combat training."

6. Mary Catharine "Jary" Johnson McKay, WASP Class of 43-W-2, an Oral History. Interviewed by Dawn Letson, October 14, 1994, Washington, DC. Held in the WASP Archive, TWU.

7. Letter from Edward Scott to Donald Scott dated April 27, 1976.

8. *Oroville Gazette,* December 1942, "Scott Returns From 7,000 Mile Trip to the East."

9. The Link Trainer is a flight simulator used for instrument flight training during World War II. The original Link Trainer was created to satisfy the need for a safe way to teach new pilots how to fly by instruments. "The little blue box" was its nickname. It was produced between the early 1930s and early 1950s by Link Aviation Devices, Inc., founded and headed by Ed Link, based on technology he pioneered in 1929 at his family's business in Binghamton, New York. These simulators became famous during World War II, when they were used as a key pilot training aid by almost every combatant nation. http:// en.wikipedia.org/wiki/Link_Trainer (accessed 1-27-2015).

10. In her October 4, 1943, letter home, Dorothy writes: "[Nancy Love] knew I could fly but didn't think much of my leadership qualities—not after the boner I pulled letting Don ride with me back in Delaware last December."

11. Love Field is named for 1st Lt. Moss L. Love, of Wright County, South Carolina, the tenth Army officer to lose his life in an airplane accident—September 4, 1913. From WASP Archive.

12. Rickman, *Legacies,* "WASP Pilots and 'the 5th,'" 51.

Chapter Three

1. Sarah Byrn Rickman, "Born to Fly," *Kansas Heritage* 14, no. 4 (Winter 2006), 16–22. Information from author's interview with Betsy Ferguson's niece Jeannette Duncan Currier, November 2005.

2. George W. Cearley, Jr., *Dallas Love Field: A Pictorial History of Airline Service* (Self-published, 1989), 5.

3. Dallas Love Field Home Page: Love Notes, Chronology of Events and Love Field Facts: www.dallas-lovefield.com/lovenotes/lovechrono.html.

4. http://www.flightmuseum.com/about.htm.

5. http://www.flightmuseum.com/about.htm.

6. Marion Stegman Hodgson, *Winning My Wings* (Albany, TX: Bright Sky Press, 2004—text originally published 1996), 147.

7. Delphine Bohn, "Catch a Shooting Star," an unpublished memoir, Chapter 9, pages 11–12. Copies at TWU library and in the author's possession.

8. Bernice "Bee" Falk Haydu, *Letters Home 1944–1945: Women Airforce Service Pilots* (Riviera Beach, FL: Self-published, printed by Topline Printing and Graphics, 2003), 53.

9. Rickman, *Nancy Love*, 109.

10. *Look* magazine, February 9, 1943, 17–21.

11. *Oroville Gazette,* January 29, 1943, "Dorothy Scott Picture in Feb. 9 *Look* Magazine."

Chapter Four

1. Sarah Byrn Rickman, "They Also Served," *Aviation History* (July 2011), 54–59. Article about Helen Richards. Original source, interview with Don Prosser, Helen Richards's husband, March 17, 2004, held in the WASP Archive, TWU.

2. RON means to remain overnight. That is the term the Ferrying Division used to refer to their pilots' overnight stops when en route to deliver an airplane.

3. Information from wedding photos in the possession of Dorothy's nephew Tracy Scott.

4. Simbeck, *Daughter of the Air*, 226–230.

5. Report of Aircraft Accident, US Army Air Forces, 6th Ferrying Group, Long Beach, California, March 21, 1943. US Air Force Academy Archives, Academy Library. Copy also held at TWU.

6. Cornelia Fort, "At Twilight's Last Gleaming," *Woman's Home Companion,* June 1943.

7. Letter from B. J. Erickson (London) to her parents dated March 27, 1943— From B. J. London's private collection. Copy in author's hands.

8. Simbeck, *Daughter of the Air*, 234.

9. Rickman, *Nancy Love*, 120.

10. #55, "Women Pilots AAF," 37–38.

11. www.pbs.org/wgbh/amex/flygirls/peopleevents/pandeAMEX03.html. People & Events, Nancy Harkness Love (1914–1976), The American Experience. *Fly Girls,* a documentary film written, produced and directed by Laurel Ladevich, 2000, PBS, WGBH Educational Foundation.

12. #55, "Women Pilots AAF," 40.

13. Lt. Col. Oliver LaFarge, for the Historical Branch, Intelligence and Security Division, Headquarters, Air Transport Command, "Women Pilots in the Air Transport Command," prepared in accordance with ATC Regulation 20-20, AAF Regulation 20-8, and AR 345-105, as amended 1946, p. 85. Copies in

author's possession and at TWU.

14. #55, "Women Pilots AAF," 40–41.

15. #55, "Women Pilots AAF," 41.

16. Capt. Walter J. Marx, "Women Pilots in the Ferrying Division, Air Transport Command," written in accordance with AAF Regulation No. 20-8 and AA Letter 40-34. In the author's hands, 114–115.

17. LaFarge, "Women Pilots," 83; also Marx, "Women Pilots," 111.

18. Tunner letter of April 26, 1943—Nancy Harkness Love Private Collection, held by her daughters, Margaret and Alice Love.

Chapter Five

1. Email to the author from Iris Cummings Critchell, 1-29-2015.

2. AT-6—The North American T-6 Texan two-place advanced trainer was the classroom for most of the Allied pilots who flew in World War II. See Appendix 2, Aircraft Dorothy Flew.

3. PT-17, the Stearman (Boeing) Model 75 is a biplane used as a military trainer aircraft. See Appendix 2, Aircraft Dorothy Flew.

4. Ceiling and visibility unlimited (CAVU): the ideal flying conditions in which there are neither large clouds nor haze. CAVU is an acronym that is used on Teletype weather. http://www.answers.com/topic/cavu-aerospace-engineering #ixzz2IfySjUsH (accessed 1-21-2013).

5. *Oroville Gazette,* July 9, 1943, "Scott Family Holds Reunion In Texas."

Chapter Six

1. Letter from Zimmy Sluder to G. M. Scott, March 20, 1944.

2. Dorothy got the idea of handwritten carbon copies from her brother Donald.

3. The two who flew with Dorothy were Byrd Granger, Class 43-1, and Helen Ricketts, Class 43-2. They are pictured with Dorothy in Birmingham, Alabama, where they were weathered in. In the photo with the three of them is an RAF officer. Ricketts is shown in the cockpit and the other three are standing on the wing of an AT-6.

4. World War II cargo ships: http://en.wikipedia.org/wiki/Liberty_ship.

5. Author interview with Jeannette Duncan Currier, Betsy's niece, the daughter of Betsy's sister Sally Hulet Duncan Strempel, in Scottsdale, Arizona, November 2005.

6. Short Snorter Project Home Page: http://www.shortsnorter.org/index.html (accessed 2-28-2013).

7. This website carries a photo of Eleanor Roosevelt signing short snorters for

some very young soldiers on March 27, 1944, during her visit to the Panama Canal Zone: http://www.shortsnorter.org/index.html.

Chapter Seven

1. Rough draft of a letter from Jacqueline Cochran to General Arnold, Cochran/ Eisenhower. Reference also found in Byrd Howell Granger, *On Final Approach: The Women Airforce Service Pilots of W.W.II* (Scottsdale, AZ: Falconer Publishing Company, 1991), 119 (Granger places the date of the letter as May 3, 1943); and Rich, who alludes to the letter in *Jackie Cochran*, 127–128.
2. AAF Memorandum No. 20-4. LaFarge, "Women Pilots," Appendix II, 69–70.
3. Memorandum from General Tunner to Commanding Officers all Ferrying Groups Subject: Duties of Executive for WAFS. LaFarge, "Women Pilots," Appendix II, 71–72.
4. Betty Gillies, a speech, "The WAFS: Women's Auxiliary Ferrying Squadron," presented at the Ninety-Nines Inc. International Convention Banquet, Baltimore, Maryland, July 27, 1985, and to the Southern California WASP, Laguna Hills, California, June 14, 1987. From Betty Gillies Collection, International Women's Air and Space Museum, Cleveland, Ohio.
5. An oleo strut is a hydraulic device used as a shock absorber in the landing gear of aircraft. It consists of an oil-filled cylinder fitted with a hollow, perforated piston into which oil is slowly forced when a compressive force is applied to the landing gear—as in landing. http://www.hangar9aeroworks .com/Aeroncastrut/Aeroncastrut.html (accessed 12-16-09).
6. The Douglas SBD Dauntless was a naval scout plane and dive-bomber that was manufactured by Douglas Aircraft from 1940 through 1944. See Appendix 2, Aircraft Dorothy Flew.
7. Granger, *On Final Approach,* 173.
8. Rickman, *Nancy Love,* Chapter 12, "A B-17 Bound for England," 134–146.
9. Nancy Love's logbook, August 24, 1943. Copy in the author's hands.
10. Tunner and Herndon, *Over the Hump,* 37–38.
11. Telex dated September 4, 1943, from Gen. C. R. Smith to Gen. Paul Burrows and Maj. Roy Atwood—TWU.
12. Cable from General Arnold in London to Presque Isle Air Base, September 5, 1943—TWU.
13. Rickman, *Nancy Love,* 144–145.

Chapter Eight

1. The beam was a Morse Code radio signal you listened through your earphones. "The beam—a radio signal—is a hum and you listened through your

earphones. If you got off to one side you heard a 'dit dah.' If you got off to the other side, you heard a 'dah dit.' It told you if you were to the right or the left of the directional beam." The dit dah/dah dit is Morse code (A and N) being broadcast by the radio range and beeps in the pilot's earphones. From Nancy Batson Crews, quoted in Rickman, *Nancy Batson Crews*, 52.

2. *The Flying V*, 5th Ferrying Group . . . ATC, September 24, 1943, Love Field, Dallas, Texas, vol. 1, no. 46. Published weekly by the Post Exchange. Copies in Tracy Scott's possession.

3. TARFU, SNAFU, and FUBAR were the nicknames for the Air Transport Command's airline that transported ferry pilots to or from home base as needed for deliveries.

Chapter Nine

1. LaFarge, "Women Pilots," 126.

2. Letter from Tunner to Commanding General ATC, September 14, 1943. BHG F3 #2 (1269–70), Archambault/Jernigan collection, Bolling AFB, Washington, DC. Copies held at TWU.

3. Memo dated September 18, 1943, from C. R. Smith, deputy commander, ATC, to Asst. Chief Air Staff, Training, Subject: Lack of Flight Qualifications, WASP. BHG F3 #2 (1268), Archambault/Jernigan collection, TWU.

4. Telegram to Jacqueline Cochran from Class W-4, September 22, 1943. BHG F3 #1 (310), Archambault/Jernigan collection, Bolling AFB, Washington DC, TWU. Also, Granger, *On Final Approach*, 182.

5. Letter from Jacqueline Cochran to Air Inspector, dated September 29, 1943. Subject: Lack of Flight Qualifications, WASP. BHG F3 #2 (1264–65), TWU.

6. LaFarge, "Women Pilots," 127–128.

7. Letter from Tunner to Commanding General ATC, September 14, 1943. BHG F3 #2 (1269), Archambault/Jernigan collection.

8. LaFarge, "Women Pilots," 127.

9. Rickman, *Nancy Love,* 82–84.

10. Marx, "Women Pilots," 61.

11. Gen. C. R. Smith to Tunner, March 19, 1943, by command of General George (ATC) following a directive received from General Stratemeyer. Subject: Women Pilots. LaFarge, "Women Pilots," Appendix II, 63.

12. Letter from Tunner to Commanding General ATC, September 14, 1943. BHG F3 #2 (1269), Archambault/Jernigan collection.

13. Cochran to AC/AS, Operations, Commitments & Requirements: Subject, WASP Eliminations. October 5, 1943. BHG F3 #2 (1262), Archambault/ Jernigan collection, TWU.

14. WASP Elimination Utilization of Women Pilot Graduates Resume of Report: Dudley N. Outcalt, Lt. Colonel, A.C., Investigating Officer. BHG F3 #2 (1271-1295).

15. Author's phone conversations and email exchange with Iris Cummings Critchell, March 1–9, 2015.

16. LaFarge, "Women Pilots," 134.

Chapter Ten

1. Granger, *On Final Approach,* 61.

2. Granger, *On Final Approach,* 191.

3. Email from Catherine Vail "Cappy" Bridge to the author, April 10, 2013.

4. Bernice Batten, barely five feet tall, was the twenty-fourth woman to join the WAFS. A Kansas native born in 1913, she earned her private license and her limited commercial in 1934 and her transport license in 1936. She was sent to Long Beach to the 6th Ferrying Group in February 1943 and to Dallas in the fall of 1943 for instrument training. She remained there ferrying AT-6s and AT-24s. She had to bail out of a stricken A-24 in western Pennsylvania, landed in a tree, wriggled out of her harness, and shinnied down the trunk. She started walking downhill and was eventually met by her rescuers—farmers, state forestry personnel, and inhabitants of a nearby religious sect. She is the only member of the original WAFS to join the Caterpillar Club. Members are pilots who bail out of a disabled airplane. They wear a membership pin in the form of a caterpillar—shaped like the ring that the pilot pulls to activate the parachute. Rickman, *Originals,* 244–246 and 349.

5. #55, "Women Pilots in the AAF," 59.

6. Iris Cummings Critchell (WASP Class 43-2), phone conversation with author May 27, 2007.

7. Granger, *On Final Approach,* 325.

8. Letter from General Tunner to the ATC following an October 6, 1943, conference—Subject: WASP. In this letter, General Tunner spells out a new program for the women in training at Sweetwater. He also recommends and names fifty-six women for pursuit school and recommends and names seventeen women to be returned to Sweetwater for additional training. Jernigan/Archambault collection BGH F 3 #1, held at TWU.

9. Kay Gott, *Women in Pursuit: Flying Fighters for the Air Transport Command Ferrying Division during World War II* (McKinleyville, CA: Self-published, 1993), 76–78, 96, 140, 168.

10. Iris Critchell, May 27, 2007, phone conversation with the author.

Chapter Eleven

1. Granger, *On Final Approach*, A-62/B.
2. The Douglas C-47 was the Army Air Forces' workhorse aircraft throughout World War II. See Appendix 2, Aircraft Dorothy Flew.
3. The Waco CG-4A was a glider designed for World War II. The Waco CG-4A glider was designed by the Waco Aircraft Company, flight testing began in May 1942, and eventually more than 13,900 CG-4As were delivered. http://en.wikipedia.org/wiki/Waco_CG-4 (accessed 2-14-2013).
4. Betty Stagg Turner, *Out of the Blue and into History* (Arlington Heights, IL: Aviatrix Publishing, 2001). This is a book of compiled WASP minibiographies. Ann Karlson (Kenney), 169.
5. Letter from WAFS Dorothy Scott to Nancy Love dated November 26, 1943. From the Nancy Love collection of private papers, in the hands of her daughters Margaret and Allie Love.
6. Nancy Love's logbook, November 29–30, December 1, 1943. Copy in the author's possession.

Chapter Twelve

1. Accident report.
2. Nancy Love's logbook, December 3, 1943.
3. Author's conversation with Florene Miller Watson at the WASP 64th Reunion, Portland, Oregon, September 6, 2006.
4. Photocopy of the Scott aircraft accident and description of accident, TWU.
5. Aircraft accident report.
6. Statement of Witness, Robert A. Nichol, 1st Lieutenant, aircraft accident report.
7. Taped interview by author with Florene Miller Watson, June 1999, Odenville, Alabama. She relates the story of her P-47 flight.
8. http://en.wikipedia.org/wiki/Valhalla_Memorial_Park_Cemetery.

Chapter Thirteen

1. "WASP Leader KO's Love Field Lights, Lands Big Fighter by Emergency Beams," *Dallas Morning News*, November 29, 1943, clipping found at TWU.
2. Gott, *Women in Pursuit*, 172–173.
3. Author's videotaped interview with Florene Miller Watson.
4. LaFarge, "Women Pilots," 140–141. The Air Inspector's report came out in late November, and AAF Headquarters sent a memo containing the report to the Air Transport Command. It was entitled "WASP Eliminations—Utilizations of Women Pilot Graduates."

5. Marx, "Women Pilots," 235. Also LaFarge, "Women Pilots," 141, though the quotes are taken from Marx.

6. Marx, "Women Pilots," 236.

7. LaFarge, "Women Pilots," 141; Marx, "Women Pilots," 235–236.

8. Marx, "Women Pilots," 235.

9. Granger, *On Final Approach*, 270.

10. Iris Critchell, Class 43-2, phone conversation with the author, February 13, 2015.

11. Marx, "Women Pilots," 236–237.

12. Marx, "Women Pilots," 236–237.

13. Marx, "Women Pilots," 236.

14. Marx, "Women Pilots," 237.

15. Marx, "Women Pilots," 238.

16. Granger, *On Final Approach*, A-106/R—A-107/R.

17. LaFarge, "Women Pilots," 134.

18. Ruth Adams, Class 44-2, and Maurine Miller, Class 44-4. Miller had been an instructor before becoming a WASP. Adams had experience prior to entering WASP flight training and established an extraordinary record in training. Source for Miller, Kay Gott, *Women in Pursuit*, 130. Source for Adams, a 1989 oral history on file at TWU.

19. Fahey, *U.S. Aircraft 1908–1946*, 33–34.

20. Bartels, *Sharpie*, 5–10.

21. Cornelia Fort Airpark (FAA LID: M88) was a privately owned, public-use airport located five nautical miles (9 km) northeast of the central business district of Nashville, Tennessee. The airport was established in 1944 by the Colemill Flying Service and was named for World War II aviator Cornelia Fort. Cornelia Fort Airpark, elevation 418 feet above mean sea level, had one runway designated 4/22 with an asphalt surface measuring 3,500 by 50 feet. In 2010, the airpark was inundated by floodwaters from the Cumberland River. http://en.wikipedia.org/wiki/Cornelia_Fort_Airpark. In 2011, the 130+ acres of Cornelia Fort Airpark was the first acquisition under the Nashville Open Space Plan. It is now part of Shelby Bottoms Greenway and Nature Park. http://www.nashville.gov/Parks-and-Recreation/Nature-Centers-and-Natural-Areas/Shelby-Bottoms-Nature-Center/Shelby-Bottoms-Park .aspx (accessed 2-5-2015).

Chapter Fourteen

1. Two articles, *Oroville Gazette*, dated February 15 and February 22, 1946.

2. The original WAFS uniform was gray-green worsted wool trousers or a skirt

worn with fitted, belted jacket. The new WASP uniform that Helen speaks of is a dark blue—better known as Santiago Blue—wool waist-length jacket with matching slacks or skirt. The latter became the recognized WASP uniform.

3. Interview with Donald N. Prosser, husband of original WAFS Helen Richards, March 15, 2004, in Clearlake, California. This oral history is on file in the Woman's Collection, Texas Woman's University library, WASP Archive.

4. Photocopy of the Resolution, Town of Oroville, in the possession of Tracy Scott, Dorothy's nephew.

Chapter Fifteen

1. Corn, *Winged Gospel*, xiii.

2. Corn, *Winged Gospel*, xiii.

3. Corn, *Winged Gospel*, 136–37.

4. Corn, *Winged Gospel*, 137.

5. Marx, "Women Pilots," 114–115; #55, Women Pilots AAF, 41–42.

6. Corn, *Winged Gospel*, 137.

7. Gillies, "The WAFS."

8. Ploesti was a vast complex of oil refinery facilities located some 30 miles north of Bucharest, Romania. It supplied an estimated 60 percent of the refined oil necessary to keep the German war machine running. http://www.eyewitness tohistory.com/ploesti.htm (accessed 2-5-2015).

9. Barrett Tillman, *Forgotten Fifteenth* (Washington, DC: Regnery, 2014), 56–57.

10. Gill Robb Wilson, *New York Herald Tribune*, December 13, 1944. Aviation editor of the *New York Herald Tribune,* aviation enthusiast, writer, founder of the Aircraft Owners and Pilots Association (AOPA), and founder of the Civil Air Patrol (CAP). Served as editor and publisher of *Flying* magazine, 1952–1962. Author, *The Airman's World,* 1957.

11. Nicole Malachowski (Colonel, USAF) was the first female pilot selected to fly as part of USAF aerobatic team, the Thunderbirds. Emily Howell Warner was the first woman captain of a scheduled US airline—Frontier—in 1976. She has since been inducted into the National Aviation Hall of Fame. Eileen Collins (Colonel USAF, retired, and NASA astronaut, retired) was the first woman to pilot the Space Shuttle. She went on to serve as the first female Space Shuttle commander. She, too, has been inducted into the National Aviation Hall of Fame.

Chapter Sixteen

1. Dawn Seymour, Clarice J. Bergemann, Jeanette J. Jenkins, and Mary Ellen Keil,

In Memoriam: Thirty-Eight American Women Pilots (Denton: Texas Woman's University Press, 1996).

2. Rickman, *Originals,* 251.

3. Merryman, *Clipped Wings: The Rise and Fall of the Women Airforce Service Pilots (WASP) of World War II* (New York and London: New York University Press, 1998), 44.

4. Merryman, *Clipped Wings,* 63.

5. Keil, *Those Wonderful Women in Their Flying Machines* (New York: Four Directions Press, 1979, 1990).

6. Granger, *On Final Approach,* 334; also Keil, *Those Wonderful Women,* 302.

7. #55, "Women Pilots with the AAF," 101.

8. Wilson, *New York Herald Tribune,* December 13, 1944.

9. Marx, "Women Pilots," 341.

10. Marx, "Women Pilots," 358–359.

11. The last WASP class, 44-10, graduated from the Sweetwater training facility at Avenger Field on December 7, 1944. The sixty-eight graduates were sent to duty stations to serve the few remaining days until December 20, the date of the official deactivation of the WASP program. General Arnold and Jacqueline Cochran were present, as were many other dignitaries. General Arnold was the graduation speaker.

12. Keil, *Those Wonderful Women;* Jackie Cochran's Final Report, 381. Later it was discovered that Cochran inadvertently had included 11 of the women who died in service in the 916. The count was actually 905.

13. Letter from WAFS Nancy Batson Crews collection, TWU. Summer intern David Lopez found it in the collection when the author was writing Nancy's biography in 2008. The author retains a copy of the letter.

14. Memorandum to all WASP signed by Nancy Batson Crews, President of the Order of Fifinella, dated June 15, 1973. TWU WASP Archives. Author has copy. Reprinted in the *WASP News,* October 2009, Volume 47, no. 2. The Gates Mills, Ohio, address belonged to Order of Fifinella secretary Mary Regalbuto Jones (44-9), who processed the letter. Crews credits Jones with the outstanding work in the reorganization of the Order of Fifinella that took place within the same time frame.

15. Lucile Wise, "Report of WASP Militarization Campaign," *WASP News* 47, no. 1 (March 2009), 10.

16. Keil, *Those Wonderful Women,* 340–341.

17. Keil, *Those Wonderful Women,* 348.

18. Bee Haydu, "Bruce Arnold—Credit Where Credit Is Due," *WASP News* 47, no. 1, (March 2009), 11.

19. Seymour et al., *In Memoriam.*

20. *WASP News*, Volume 45, no. 1, published in Denton, Texas, June 2007; page 13.

21. Gott, *Women in Pursuit.* The number 130 was arrived at by counting the names of the women listed in each of the five Ferrying Groups as listed in the book. These women either graduated from Pursuit School or received transition at their home bases.

22. *WASP News,* Volume 47, no. 2, published in Denton, Texas, October 2009; 16.

23. Marianne Verges, *On Silver Wings* (New York: Ballantine Books, 1991), 212–214. The information from two of these pages was told to author Verges by a friend of Gertrude Silver during an interview. It is the story of her disappearance. Unfortunately, the final sentence (on page 214) states that Gertrude Silver's body was found in 1985. The search continues today [2015]. That piece of information turned out to be erroneous. (See the next two endnotes.) Turner, *Out of the Blue.* This is a book of compiled WASP minibiographies. A note in Gertrude's biography states the following: "Rumors reported that her [Silver's] body had been found, but according to HQ Air Force Safety Agency reports of June 8, 1994, no wreckage of this mishap has been located" (p. 226).

24. *WASP News*, Volume 47, no. 1, published in Denton, Texas, March 2009; 8, 22.

25. Funds for bronze flag holders have been raised through the sale of WASP (44-7) Bee Haydu's book *Letters Home;* through the sale of John Marsh's WASP ball caps; Shutsy Reynolds's silverwork and inventory; and other donations. Marsh is the son of WASP Marie Barrett Marsh (Class 43-7) now deceased. John has remained active with the WASP Kids' organization.

Chapter Seventeen

1. Official press release, carried in the *WASP News* 47, no. 2 (October 2009).

2. Quotes from Vice Adm. Vivien Crea (US Coast Guard Retired) given March 9, 2010, at the WASP Memorial Ceremony, US Air Force Memorial—used with her permission.

Epilogue

1. Dorothy Scott, "A Private Utopia," Comp 6, May 29, 1940, University of Washington.

Appendix 1
1. Seymour et al., *In Memoriam.*

Appendix 3
1. Official Report.

Appendix 4
1. Rickman, *Originals,* 89–91.

Bibliography

Archives and Unpublished Sources

Bohn, Delphine. "Catch a Shooting Star," an unpublished memoir, circa 1980s.

LaFarge, Lt. Col. Oliver. "Women Pilots in the Air Transport Command"—for the Historical Branch, Intelligence and Security Division, Headquarters, Air Transport Command, prepared in accordance with ATC Regulation 20-20, AAF Regulation 20-8, and AR 345-105, as amended 1946. Also, LaFarge, Appendix II for "Women Pilots in the Air Transport Command."

Marx, Capt. Walter J. "Women Pilots in the Ferrying Division, Air Transport Command," written in accordance with AAF Regulation No. 20-8 and AA Letter 40-34.

Scott, Dorothy. Collected letters. WASP Archive, The Woman's Collection, Texas Woman's University, Denton.

"Women Pilots in the AAF, 1941–1944."Army Air Forces Historical Studies: No. 55. Military Affairs/Aerospace Historian, Eisenhower Hall, Kansas State University, Manhattan. ISBN 0-89126-138-9.

Articles

Douglas, Deborah G. "WASPs of War." *Aviation Heritage* (January 1999).

Flying V, The. "5th Ferrying Group . . . ATC," September 24, 1943, Love Field, Dallas, Texas, Vol. 1, No. 46. Published weekly by the Post Exchange.

Fort, Cornelia. "At Twilight's Last Gleaming." *Woman's Home Companion* (June 1943).

Marshall, Patti. "Neta Snook." *Aviation History* (January 2007).

Okanogan Valley Gazette-Tribune. (Oroville, Washington, June 10, 1993).

Oroville Gazette, several articles dating from 1920 to 1946. Articles contained in bound volumes.

Rickman, Sarah Byrn. "They Also Served." *Aviation History* (July 2011). Article about Helen Richards.

Rickman, Sarah Byrn. "Born to Fly." *Kansas Heritage* (Winter 2006). Article about Betsy Ferguson.

Rickman, Sarah Byrn. "WASP Pilots and 'the 5th'—Dallas Love Field." *Legacies, A History Journal for Dallas and North Central Texas* (Spring 2008).

Thaden, Louise. "Five Women Tackle the Nation." *NAA* (National Aeronautic Association) Magazine (August 1936).

Wilson, Gill Robb. Column. *New York Herald Tribune* (December 13, 1944).

WASP News. Volume XLV No. 1 (June 2007). Volume XLVII No. 1 (March 2009). Volume XLVII No. 2 (October 2009). Published in Denton by Texas Woman's University, the Woman's Collection, WASP Archive.

Books

Bartels, Diane Ruth Armour. *Sharpie: The Life Story of Evelyn Sharp.* Lincoln, Nebraska: Dageforde Publishing, 1996.

Cearley, George W., Jr. *Dallas Love Field: A Pictorial History of Airline Service.* Self-published, 1989.

Cooper, Ann. *On the Wing: Jessie Woods and the Flying Aces Air Circus.* Black Hawk Publishing Company, 1993.

Corn, Joseph J. *The Winged Gospel: America's Romance with Aviation.* Baltimore, MD: Johns Hopkins University Press, 2002. A paperback edition of the book by that name was originally published in New York by Oxford University Press, Inc., 1983.

Earhart, Amelia. *20 Hrs., 40 Min.: Our Flight in the Friendship.* Washington, DC: National Geographic Society, 2003. Rerelease of this title, © 1928, originally published by George P. Putnam & Sons. Her story of the flight.

Fahey, James C., ed. *U.S. Army Aircraft 1908–1946.* New York: Ships and Aircraft, 1946.

Gott, Kay. *Women in Pursuit: Flying Fighters for the Air Transport Command Ferrying Division during World War II.* McKinleyville, CA: Self-published, 1993.

Granger, Byrd Howell. *On Final Approach: The Women Airforce Service Pilots of W.W.II.* Scottsdale, AZ: Falconer Publishing Company, 1991.

Haydu, Bernice "Bee" Falk. *Letters Home 1944–1945: Women Airforce Service Pilots.* Riviera Beach, Florida: Self-published, 2003.

Hodgson, Marion Stegman. *Winning My Wings.* Albany, Texas: Bright Sky Press, 2004.

Holden, Henry M., and Captain Lori Griffith. "Bessica Raiche." In Ladybirds: The Untold Story of Women Pilots in America. Mt. Freedom, NJ: Blackhawk Publishing, 1991.

Hollander, Lu, Gene Nora Jessen, Verna West, The Ninety-Nines History Book Committee. *The Ninety-Nines Yesterday, Today, Tomorrow.* Paducah, KY: Turner Publishing Company, 1996.

Keil, Sally VanWagenen. *Those Wonderful Women In Their Flying Machines.* New York: Four Directions Press, 1979, 1990.

Kerfoot, Glenn. *Propeller Annie, the Story of Helen Richey.* Lexington, KY: The Kentucky Aviation History Roundtable, 1988.

Kerschner, William K. *The Student Pilots Flight Manual.* 7th ed. Ames: Iowa State University Press, 1993.

Jessen, Gene Nora. *The Powder Puff Derby of 1929: The True Story of the First Women's Cross-Country Air Race.* Napierville, IL: Sourcebooks, Inc., 2002.

Lubben, Kristen, and Erin Barnett, editors. *Amelia Earhart, Image and Icon.* Göttingen, Germany: International Center of Photography, 2008.

Merryman, Molly. *Clipped Wings: The Rise and Fall of the Women Airforce Service Pilots (WASP) of World War II.* New York and London: New York University Press, 1998.

Pisano, Dominick A. *To Fill the Skies with Pilots: The Civilian Pilot Training Program, 1939–1946.* Champaign: University of Illinois Press, 1993; Smithsonian Institution reprint, 2001.

Planck, Charles E. *Women with Wings.* New York: Harper & Brothers, 1942.

Rich, Doris L. *Jackie Cochran, Pilot in the Fastest Lane.* Gainesville: The University Press of Florida, 2007.

Rickman, Sarah Byrn. *Nancy Batson Crews, Alabama's First Lady of Flight.* Tuscaloosa: University of Alabama Press, 2009.

Rickman, Sarah Byrn. *Nancy Love and the WASP Ferry Pilots of World War II.* Denton: University of North Texas Press, 2008.

Rickman, Sarah Byrn. *The Originals: The Women's Auxiliary Ferrying Squadron of World War II.* Sarasota, Florida: Disc-Us Books, Inc., 2001.

Seymour, Dawn, Clarice J. Bergemann, Jeanette J. Jenkins, and Mary Ellen Keil. *In Memoriam: Thirty-Eight American Women Pilots.* Denton: Texas Woman's University Press, 1996.

Sherman, Janann. *Walking on Air: The Aerial Adventures of Phoebe Omlie.* Jackson: University Press of Mississippi, 2011.

Simbeck, Rob. *Daughter of the Air: The Brief Soaring Life of Cornelia Fort.* New York: Atlantic Monthly Press, 1999.

Southern, Neta Snook. *I Taught Amelia to Fly.* New York: Vantage Press, 1974.

Strickland, Patricia. *The Putt-Putt Air Force: The Story of The Civilian Pilot Training Program and The War Training Service (1939–1944).* Department of Transportation. Federal Aviation Administration, Aviation Education Staff, GA-20–84, ca. 1970.

Thaden, Louise. *High, Wide, and Frightened.* New York: Air Facts Press, 1973.

Tillman, Barrett. *Forgotten Fifteenth: The Daring Airmen Who Crippled Hitler's War Machine.* Washington, DC: Regnery, 2014.

Tunner, William H., and Booton Herndon. *Over the Hump.* New York: Duell, Sloan and Pearce, 1964.

Turner, Betty Stagg. *Out of the Blue and into History.* Arlington Heights, IL: Aviatrix Publishing, 2001.

Verges, Marianne. *On Silver Wings.* New York: Ballantine Books, 1991.

Ware, Susan. *Still Missing: Amelia Earhart and the Search for Modern Feminism.* New York: W. W. Norton, 1993.

Winegarten, Debra L. *Katherine Stinson: The Flying Schoolgirl.* Austin, TX: Eakin Press, 2000.

Winters, Kathleen. *Amelia Earhart, The Turbulent Life of an American Icon.* New York: Palgrave MacMillan, 2010.

Index

About the Author

Sarah Byrn Rickman is editor of the official WASP of World War II newsletter, the author of five previous books about the WASP, and an amateur pilot.